Doing Business in the New Latin America

Doing Business in the New Latin America

A Guide to Cultures, Practices, and Opportunities

Thomas H. Becker

Westport, Connecticut
London

Library of Congress Cataloging-in-Publication Data

Becker, Thomas H.

Doing business in the new Latin America : a guide to cultures, practices, and opportunities / Thomas H. Becker.

p. cm.

Includes bibliographical references and index.

ISBN 0–275–98132–0 (alk. paper)

1. Business enterprises—Latin America. 2. Corporations, American—Latin America. 3. Investments, American—Latin America. 4. Business etiquette—Latin America. 5. Corporate culture—Latin America. 6. Latin America—Commerce. 7. Latin America—Commercial policy. I. Title.

HF3230.5.Z5.B43 2004

330.98—dc22 2004054667

British Library Cataloguing in Publication Data is available.

Library of Congress Catalog Card Number: 2004054667
ISBN: 0–275–98132–0

First published in 2004

Praeger Publishers, 88 Post Road West, Westport, CT 06881
An imprint of Greenwood Publishing Group, Inc.
www.praeger.com

Printed in the United States of America

The paper used in this book complies with the Permanent Paper Standard issued by the National Information Standards Organization (Z39.48–1984).

10 9 8 7 6 5 4 3

To

Diane, My finest companion and steadiest compass point in life's astonishing excursions.

Colleen, Mary Ellen, and Tom, Like the different republics of the Americas in which each was born, you build the future not by repeating history, but by reaching beyond history's grip.

Contents

Illustrations

Figures

Tables

Part I

PEOPLE, PLACES, AND POSSIBILITIES

Only a comparatively few U.S. executives have had extensive first-hand experience doing business in Latin America. Fewer still can point to an unbroken record of success in doing business in one or more of the twenty Spanish- and Portuguese-speaking countries with which the United States shares the Western Hemisphere. Yet, the epic changes now taking place in that vast region are creating unprecedented opportunities for U.S. companies. The economic and social transformations occurring in Latin America are tailor-made to respond to the competencies at which U.S. small- and medium-sized enterprises (SMEs) excel. When conditions are shifting rapidly, the SME's ability to turn on a dime gives it an edge in spotting, shooting at, and taking home moving targets of opportunity. It is that strength that has made the SME the powerful growth engine of the U.S. economy during the last quarter century. That same strength is now positioning the SME to become the pivot point of business growth between the United States and Latin America during the next quarter century.

This book describes business as it is practiced and lived in Latin America today. It is written especially for forward-looking executives of U.S. SMEs who are prepared to apply to Latin America the successful lessons they have learned in the North American market. These executives are in a position to use much of their U.S. experience to cash in on business opportunities now surfacing in Latin American markets. Many of today's market opportunities were either nonexistent or were closed to smaller players as little as five years ago. Under today's new rules of the game, smaller domestic players are able to compete successfully internationally. Whether they are exporters seeking new customers, distributors looking for new suppliers, owners of know-how who seek to license their technology, or manufacturers looking for low-cost suppliers or strategic alliance partners, many smaller companies are learning that new and powerful forces are at work, reshaping the way business is done in the Western Hemisphere. These firms recognize that, like life itself, economies do not stand still. As history always has shown, when economies are rapidly transforming, deep-seated forces open windows of opportunity that were formerly closed. To exploit those momentary windows of opportunity, SMEs need practical knowledge about how to break into the new Latin American marketplace, converting its untapped profit potential into a cash-flow reality. This book satisfies that need, explaining the widespread changes that are taking place and relating them to the special competencies of smaller firms.

The two chapters in Part I of this book describe what Latin America is and why it will pay for you to learn about its business potential. Chapter 1 introduces you to the lands of Latin America from a business perspective, sketching the varied panorama of its vast territory and profiling the region's national markets. Chapter 2 acquaints you with the size, shape, and flavor of Latin America's windows of opportunity at both regional and country levels.

Chapter 1

Where and What Is Latin America?

What is your mind's-eye image of Latin America? Is it . . .

- the land of Chiquita Banana? Or Juán Valdez?
- the legend of Simón Bolívar? Or Pancho Villa? Or Ché Guevara?
- the aroma of a street vendor's tacos cooking on a wood stove?
- easy memories of noontime sand, sun, and Tecate beer, followed by a late-afternoon bullfight?
- marimba notes floating across a plaza on soft tropical evenings as children play and lovers kiss?
- a village priest ministering to the sick child of a destitute mother?
- a tattered Indian praying to a Sun God carving in a ruin hidden by jungle overgrowth?
- a bull crocodile roaring its challenge to the Amazon night?
- a lazily gliding condor framed against a snow-capped Andean peak?

Because Latin America is a world where magic is real, all of those images are as real as today. If some of them are already yours by virtue of personal experience, I applaud your sense of adventure and romance. And I assure you that reading this book will not diminish their vibrancy. But as you turn the pages that follow, you will find another image unfolding to add to those already present in your mind. This new image reveals Latin America as an emerging powerhouse in today's world economy, a new market frontier, beyond which profitable business opportunities are coming to life.

To find those opportunities, use this book as your chart while you travel along the sometimes twisting road leading to that new frontier. To help guide you in that journey, you will find it useful to recognize some of the landmark features that define that vast and diverse realm we call Latin America.

AMERICAS AND AMERICANS

Will the Real American Please Stand?

Many otherwise savvy marketers would be surprised to learn that the American marketplace contains about three times as many consumers as are found in the United States. Their surprise, of course, stems from the implied but mistaken assumption that the only one of the thirty-five countries of the Western Hemisphere qualified to be called America is the United States of America. A trait shown by many residents of the United States is to appropriate for their own exclusive use the nationhood label "American." Albeit unintended, the assumption underlying that self-description is understandably offensive to the half-billion souls residing in the other thirty-four nations of the two continents of the hemisphere of the Americas.

As residents of the United States of America, we have grown accustomed to the geographically ambitious habit of calling ourselves Americans. How, when we label ourselves Americans, can we avoid offending millions of Argentines, Brazilians, Colombians, Mexicans, and nationals of all the other countries who also reside in the Western Hemisphere is a question that has not yet been satisfactorily answered. Perhaps the most commonly practiced solution is to call ourselves *Norteamericanos* (North Americans) when in the company of Latin Americans. Still, to identify ourselves as *Norteamericanos* is to stake out as our own exclusive national property a piece of real estate that is as territorially overstated as it is geographically mistaken. This huge error occurs because the geographic boundaries of North America take in all of the Western Hemisphere lying north of the equator. In addition to the United States, these "North American" boundaries would encompass portions of the South American countries of Venezuela, Colombia, Ecuador, and Brazil; the entire territorial extension of Central America and the Caribbean; Mexico; and Canada. Compounding the unintended misperceptions spawned by the popular use of North American as a geographic descriptor is the relatively recent use of the term North American as an economic descriptor.

This additional layer of confusion stems from the 1994 inaugural of NAFTA (North American Free Trade Agreement), a pact in which Canada, Mexico, and the United States have formally ratified themselves as North American trade partners. To its credit, using the term North American to describe residents of the United States only offends about half as many Latin Americans as when we call ourselves Americans, thus making claim to the entire Western Hemisphere. For that reason, if you identify yourself as *Norteamericano* instead of as *Americano* you chance offending the national pride of fewer Latin Americans. If you wish to be even more precise and ingratiating, thus exposing yourself to even less possibility of being rude, you may (if your Spanish is up to it) describe yourself as *Estadounidense* (literally, Unitedstatesian). Whichever you choose, *Estadounidense* or *Norteamericano*, you will lower the risk of offending the justifiably strong territorial sensitivities of Latin Americans, a few of whom may still harbor dark suspicions that you or your firm serves as a conspiratorial tentacle of U.S. economic and cultural imperialism.

As a general rule, you will find the self-describing terms mentioned above to be useful defenses in helping you avoid being perceived as culturally myopic, geographically unsophisticated, or historically uninformed when dealing with Latin Americans. But, for the important purpose of enabling you to read these pages in a natural, smooth-flowing manner, this book violates that general rule. In the interest of convenience, Anglo American and Anglo are used interchangeably from this point forward as shorthand references to persons raised in the Northern Europe-oriented cultural mainstream of the United States. This sacrifice of historic and ethnic accuracy is a compromise, an offering at the altar of reading simplicity.

Scope and Size

The territories of the New World that were colonized by Spain and Portugal are uniquely marked by what an anthropologist would call a "similar character structure."[1] Yet, in spite of unmistakable similarities in their historic and cultural connections, the territories make up a geographic region of such diversity that it eludes easy labeling. The noun component of Latin America is accurate because it conveys the common location of those erstwhile colonies in the Americas. However, when the adjective Latin is used to designate only the Spanish- and Portuguese-speaking peoples of the Americas, it fails to acknowledge the presence of the hemisphere's Francophone populations, peoples whose language was also derived from the Latin spoken by the Roman legions that once occupied

Europe. While the cultural richness possessed by France's present and former New World colonies cannot be denied, the dim growth prospects for such economies as Haiti and French Guiana explain their exclusion from a book written to identify promising business opportunities. Nor does the term Latin America represent either the cultural legacy of the tens of millions of indigenous peoples who inhabited the Americas ages before the arrival of their Iberian conquerors, or that of the masses of Negroes who were introduced soon thereafter. While the umbrella descriptors Hispanic America and Ibero America at least perfunctorily imply the cultural heritage of the African slaves held in preconquest Spain and Portugal, they ignore the influence of the Inca, Aztec, Maya, Chibcha, and the scores of other pre-Columbian societies that have made essential contributions to the region's culture. Equally exclusionary is the term Indo America, which leaves out both the Iberians and the Negroes. While the label Indo-Afro-Ibero-America[2] qualifies as a comprehensive descriptor, it fails the test of sliding easily off the tongue. Despite its many limitations, "Latin America" will be the default term used in this book to describe those Spanish- and Portuguese-speaking societies that share the Western Hemisphere with the United States. By derivation, "Latin" and "Latins" will often be used as shorthand terms to describe peoples and persons of Latin American cultural origins.

Because it includes only the Spanish- and Portuguese-speaking territories of the Western Hemisphere's two continents, Latin America is not a contiguous geographical entity. It embraces Middle America, which includes Mexico, Central America (except Belize), and the Caribbean states of Cuba, the Dominican Republic, and Puerto Rico (see Figure 1.1) and South America, excluding Guyana, Surinam, and French Guiana (see Figure 1.2). Covering more than 8 million square miles, it has a land area almost three times that of the contiguous United States and a population that surpasses it by 70 percent.

A BIRD'S-EYE VIEW OF LATIN AMERICA

Poring over a decent atlas is a good first step toward understanding Latin America. The region's varied topography and climate underscore its immense diversity. Yet, the ways in which geography has been intertwined with history to weave the tapestry of human behavior lie beyond the ability of a mere map to convey. To bring life to a flat map, let us adapt a venerable historian's device to our purpose: Imagine you are an economic anthropologist, and are observing Latin America as an air traveler.[3]

Figure 1.1
Middle America

Mexico and Central America

Your 15,000-mile swing around the continents of North and South America begins over the scorched desert of the U.S.–Mexico borderland. It is a no-man's-land that uncounted thousands of refugees, fleeing from hopeless poverty further south, have risked death crossing to find work in the fields, factories, kitchens, and construction sites of the United States. Their readiness to work under trying conditions and for low pay makes it possible for innumerable smaller U.S. businesses not only to survive, but to provide good jobs for U.S. citizens.

Placing the unbroken ridgeline of the western Sierra Madre on your left and the glittering Pacific beach sands on your right, you soar over a panorama of modern commerce ranging from automobile assembly plants, winter-vegetable farming, and tourism spas to marijuana farming, cocaine trafficking, and prostitution—all driven by the U.S. market. As you approach the one and one-half-mile high Valley of Mexico, your thoughts slip back to 1521. As the modern skyscrapers of Mexico City fade away, you see the gleaming temples of Tenochtitlán, the heart of the Aztec empire. Seeing Cortés offer gifts to the Aztec chief, you imagine the Spanish conquistador barely able to conceal his glee as the interpreter conveys the welcome extended by Moctezuma: "*Mi casa es su casa*" (My home is

Figure 1.2
South America

your home). Of the two leaders, only Cortés can come close to imagining the extent to which that hospitable greeting was to foreshadow the most massive transfer of wealth the world has ever known.

Continuing southward, you are struck by a curious change that has occurred in the world below you: Altitude has replaced latitude as the primary determinant of climate. Whereas one travels north or south to experience climate change in temperate zones, in tropical latitudes one goes higher or lower to experience changes in climate-driven economic and cultural behavior. A half mile of vertical separation in the tropics can make more difference than thousands of miles of north-south distance in the ways that people dress, eat, build shelters, and earn a living. The economies and lifestyles of residents in the cities and rural areas of the highlands of Mexico, Central America, and South America have more in common with each other than between these peoples and their neighbors who reside in nearby lowland coastal plains or rainforests.

As you fly further south, you observe more and more poverty. And as you watch, Mexico's southern states and Central America's republics are becoming linked together in an emerging initiative labeled the Plan Puebla-Panamá. Designed to counter the specter of hunger that forces people in meso-America to move north to find jobs in Mexico's over-crowded cities and in the United States, the Plan Puebla-Panama aims to move the jobs south to the people. As the more than $3 billion plan unfolds, it will kindle the area's economic potential by knitting together and upgrading its fragmented and underdeveloped highways, telecommunications, and energy systems into an integrated, competitively viable economic structure. It holds the promise of putting both food on the tables of idle workers in the south and sales on the order books of idle companies in the north.

The flight over southern Mexico and Central America takes you along the Ruta del Maya (Route of the Maya), 1,400 miles dotted with ruins of more than 200 Mayan complexes, where, over a thousand years, this extraordinary civilization mapped the heavens, developed writing, and devised the ancient world's most sophisticated system of mathematics. Along the way, you are introduced to the broad variety of its cities: shining, Indian-faced Guatemala City; business-friendly San Pedro Sula in the north, and bureaucratic Tegucigalpa in the south of Honduras; dynamic, democratic, and dollarized San Salvador; Managua, the economic victim of political paralysis; friendly San José with a healthy, diversified economy anchored by tourism and Intel's half-billion dollar chip factory; and Panama where European, Asian, and African blood mix to form a world-class financial and distribution center.

South America

Central America's crowded puzzle board of small neighbors contrasts with the vastness of South America, a landmass stretching 4,500 miles from north to south and 3,200 miles from east to west. Leaving the low-lying green ribbon of Panama behind, you pass over the Spanish Main of

Cartagena, yesterday's gateway to colonial riches, today's sanctuary of security in Colombia's bloody struggle against heavily armed, well-financed alliances between drug traffickers and rebel forces. The steep-sloped Magdalena River valley cleaves its way inward and upward to the elbow of the Andean cordillera. Below you sprawl the plains of Bogotá, where this massive range turns south after running west from Venezuela, and continues to the tip of Chile.

The 5,000-mile stretch of the Andes is an unbroken two- to four-mile-high barrier that, paralleling the ocean, bars access to the broad remainder of the continent from its narrow coastal strip. With perpetual snow at the top and suffocating heat at the base, the Andean geography has historically promoted a pattern of local trade and cultural links within a succession of naturally bountiful microclimate valleys that permitted small populations to survive in relative isolation. At the same time, its frigid north-south ridgeline and deep east-west cuts have blocked the wider economic ties that could have knitted the continent into the kind of regionally integrated economic and political systems that developed in the United States.

Just after crossing the equator, you pass over picture-perfect Quito. Nestled on a 9,300-foot plain between the snow-capped Andes ranges, Ecuador's political capital enjoys three seasons on most days: spring mornings, summer afternoons, and fall evenings. Down below, on the coastal horizon, is steamy Guayaquil, ambitiously dubbed the Pearl of the Pacific. As Ecuador's bustling commercial capital, its port is ringed by a chain of freighters bringing in consumer and capital goods, and carrying off bananas, oil, frozen shrimp, sugar, coffee, and cocoa.

Continuing southward into Peru, your gaze is drawn to mysterious and stunning Machu Picchu. Clinging to a cloudy peak high above the white-waters of the Urubamba River, the concavely cut and seamlessly fitted multi-ton stones of the Lost City of the Incas give long-silent testimony to the sophisticated economic organization and technical prowess of the Inca civilization. Not far away, the Tiahuanaco civilization, precursors of the Inca, had built the largest city in the world in the tenth century. Its ruins hold the secret to the mystery of how they transported, without wheels, and are fitted with hair-width precision, massive megaliths from quarries at least twenty-five miles away.

Dropping down the mountain ledge toward the Pacific, you notice a sharp transition in the coastal environment: Ecuador's drenched coastal zone has given way to Peru's bone-dry dunes and scorched sands that stretch from the coast to the Andes foothills. You have entered the Atacama Desert, 2,000 miles of tinder-dry biosystem, squeezed between the mighty Andes and the Pacific. Almost nothing survives in these windblown tracts, broken only intermittently by oases where crops of long-staple cotton, sugarcane, alfalfa, dates, mangos, rice, and asparagus thrive. The largest of these refuges is Lima and its port, Callao. Studded with magnificent parks and flower-lined avenues of posh colonial-era neighborhoods in its center, and ringed by wretchedly poor *pueblos jóvenes* (young towns), the City of Kings mirrors the social tension that plagues Latin America. Turning away from the Pacific coast, you cross the barren coastal desert and climb toward the towering Andes. The chain of white-capped jagged crests stretches as far as you can see, with little sign of human activity, save occasional pack mule or llama trails that wind through icy, narrow passes at 14,000–16,000 feet. In this severe setting, your attention is captured by Lake Titicaca, through which the Peru-Bolivia border passes, and, at 12,500 feet, is the world's highest navigable body of water. Almost within sight of urban La Paz, the scene on this lake is surreal: The high altitude makes colors appear deeper and more intense; the colors seem most vivid on the eons-old body dress of the Uro and Aymará natives who inhabit the lake's floating reed islands—man-made structures that will make you feel you are walking on a mammoth water bed. It is interesting to note that the black bowler hats you see worn by virtually all Aymará women trace their origin to the 1880s, when an enterprising British hat salesman, anxious to dispose of a factory overrun, convinced indigenous leaders that the hats were the rage in Europe. As European fashion was considered the ultimate word in civilized standards, the hats (and, incidentally, those ubiquitous billowy hoop skirts) became—and remain—the style norm for indigenous women in the Peruvian and Bolivian Andes.

Proceeding southward from the starkness of 13,000-foot La Paz, you soon find yourself over the long, narrow strip of northern Chile's section of the Atacama Desert. A wasteland today, this zone's huge deposits of bird guano brought nitrate wealth to Chile from the 1880s to 1920. As you approach Santiago in mid-Chile, the scene below transforms from empty desert to fruited groves. Thanks to the protective wall of the Andes, these fertile vineyards were spared destruction by the filoxera insect plague that devastated grape producers throughout the world during the late-1800s.[4] Since the late 1900s, enterprising Chileans export from those same vineyards to fill U.S. demand for high-quality table grapes during the off-season months for northern-hemisphere California growers. As if living in the shadow of the Andes were good for business in general, Chileans (although typically modest) could justifiably boast of having some of the most forward-looking economic policies and management practices—as well as democratic political processes—you will find in Latin America.

Turning east from Santiago, you cross the Andes and enter the rich grasslands of Argentina's vast pampas, finally arriving at Buenos Aires on the banks of the Río de la Plata. Its residents, who are seldom criticized for being too unassuming, may be right in claiming that the broad boulevards, tree-lined avenues, belle époque theaters, majestic mansions, upscale restaurants, sidewalk cafés, and late-night bookstores of their city make it the most cultured and cosmopolitan metropolis of the Americas.

Heading north from the birthplace of the soulful tango, you cross tiny Uruguay, created as a buffer between its two giant neighbors, Argentina and Brazil. Soon, you reach aggressive, fast-paced São Paulo, the Chicago of South America and the center of Brazil's industrial production. For a slower-paced experience, you fly on to Rio de Janeiro. The shining beaches of Ipanema and Copacabana and massive granite blocks thrusting up abruptly from the heart of the city, and its island-studded harbor and jagged backdrop of Mount Tijuca may make Rio the hemisphere's most stunning city.

After departing Rio, you seem to be flying endlessly over the Amazon basin, an area about as large as the contiguous forty-eight states of the United States. The Amazon River itself stretches further than the distance between New York and London, discharging into the Atlantic a volume of fresh water four times that of the Mississippi River and greater than that of any river in the world. For years it was hoped that agriculture would transform the water-wealthy Amazon rainforest into the bread-basket of the world. Regrettably, the basin's rains are so heavy that they leach its thin soils of soluble nutrients. Soil fertility is further inhibited by high temperatures that restrain the growth of fungi and the formation of humus. An unmistakable sign of the Amazon's demise is the horizon-to-horizon smoke you see as the virgin forest is burned to clear its canopy, providing secondary growth for cattle to graze on, thus dooming the unprotected, leafless topsoil to be washed away by drenching rains. That topsoil, together with great trees and shrubs, can be seen as a muddy runoff extending some 200 miles into the Atlantic Ocean from the Amazon Delta. To promote nonagricultural job growth, Brazil offers generous tax incentives to attract industry to Manaus, 1,000 miles upstream from (and only 100 feet above) the river's mouth. Some smallish Original Equipment Manufacturers (OEMs) and second-tier suppliers to the country's twenty-two automobile producers have responded by building assembly and light-production facilities.

As you fly over Venezuela's great llanos (plains), the Amazon basin falls behind you, and the land below begins to rise. Soon you rejoin the Andes at its most easterly spur, where the plateau upon which Caracas was built is located. Once agriculturally self-sufficient, Venezuela's economy became hostage to its petroleum sector some fifty years ago. While agriculture was allowed to languish, oil revenues were channeled into the hands of a fortunate few, and to rebuilding the urban centers where they resided. The effects of those policies endure today: The impressive—if not pretentious—downtown center and the wide, curving boulevards of Caracas are ringed by slums of cardboard and tar paper shacks, monuments to the misery that attest to one of the world's records for unequal income distribution and breeding grounds of social and political ferment. Venezuela now has to import most of its food supplies (its black beans, the diet staple of the poor, are grown in Colorado), as well as most of its continuously large demand for capital equipment and intermediate goods. Except for oil and secondary petroleum products, it is not internationally competitive in any major industry.

The Caribbean

Leaving Venezuela at the port of La Guaira (a short journey down the mountain slope from Caracas), you follow the ring of the Lesser Antilles toward Puerto Rico. Topped by afternoon clouds, the northern slope of its mountainous interior opens to meet San Juan's modern port, the logistics center of the Caribbean. No longer the mecca for investment incentives once favored under Section 936 of the U.S. tax code, the island struggles to regain forward momentum as a competitive supplier to the United States and other markets.

A ten-minute flight over waters covering the two and one-half mile deep Mona Trench brings you to the eastern tip of the Dominican Republic's Samaná Peninsula. After another twenty minutes of flight, with the clear waters of the Caribbean lapping against palm-fringed, gleaming-white beaches below and the green mountains of the Cibao interior off the right wing, you arrive over colonial Santo Domingo, the first permanent European settlement in the New World. While it shares two-thirds of the island of Hispaniola with Haiti, the half-as-numerous Dominican population has fared better. Rooted in a productive agricultural sector, the Dominican economy has shown remarkable growth for most of the last two decades, from tourism, to cutting and sewing of garments, and assembly of consumer electronics and toys.

Some thirty minutes after flying over the appalling spectacle of Port-au-Prince's poverty, the eastern shore of Cuba comes into view. If you choose to land at Havana's José Martí international airport, you may wonder what the U.S. trade embargo against Cuba really has accomplished, as a recent-model Ford F-250 pickup pulls up to position the passenger staircase for your plane. Soon after becoming accustomed to time-warp-like scenes of 1956 Chevrolet Bel Airs rolling past sixteenth-century colonial buildings, your reconnaissance of this anachronistic economy leads you to make a tentative conjecture: When relations between the United States and Cuba become normal, the entry of Cuba as a low-cost competitor will trigger large disruptions in today's patterns of international trade in tourism, winter fruit and vegetable production, and low labor-cost assembly operations. To gear up for expanded trade in those sectors, of course, Cuba would require sizable imports of capital goods, supplies, and services—for most of which, nearby U.S. vendors will be the lowest-cost source.

Although you have put the Caribbean's balmy beaches behind you (and you have survived the stern-faced U.S. immigration officer's interrogation about your visit to Cuba), your tour is not complete. Your return to the United States occasions an opportunity to survey at close range the swiftest growing of all Latin American markets.

The U.S. Republic of Latino

This consumer segment does not profile one of the twenty country markets shown on a map of Latin America, delineated in its own color and lying somewhere south of the United States. Rather, it describes a market that is so close at hand that, like the air you breathe, you tend to ignore it. In a few brief decades, this market has gone far beyond our doorstep, having become a permanent part of our national home. It can no longer be ignored. Not only has it become the most rapidly growing of all Latin markets, but it is more easily accessible than any of them. You will not need a passport to visit customers in this nearby Latin market. They may be found in your own home, living next door, or working in the adjacent office. To make doing business with these customers even easier, you will not have to pay any import taxes when you deliver your product, accept any pesos when you take payment, or settle any business disputes outside of a U.S. jurisdiction.

If you think Canada is a large market for U.S. products, you would certainly be correct. Indeed, Canada is the number one trading partner of the United States. But here is a curious fact: There are more Hispanics in the

United States than there are Canadians in Canada. If they were formed into a single separate nation, the 38 million Hispanics residing in the United States would constitute the third-largest Spanish-speaking population in the world and the third-largest economy in Latin America (placing behind only Mexico and Brazil). Its growth has outstripped that of any other segment of the U.S. population. By 2002, Hispanics had surpassed African Americans as the largest U.S. minority group.[5] By 2020, the U.S. population of Latin American or Iberian cultural origin will be almost 60 million, and is forecast to exceed 73 million by 2030, accounting for some 20 percent of the U.S. population (one and one-half times its 2004 share of 13.5 percent).[6]

U.S. history is no longer being written in black and white. The greatest multicultural show in history is now playing in the United States. Unlike the cast of black and white actors who starred in the ethnic drama of the twentieth century, the current performers are following a script written as a bridge for people to cross through cooperation, not as a great divide that keeps people separate through confrontation. As Generation Ñ takes center stage and matures, its economic power, political clout, and pivotal influence on the shape of U.S. lifestyles has become a potent reality.

An early indicator of the potency with which Latin culture was to permeate U.S. daily life and markets came into view in the 1970s with the explosion of national chains of so-called Mexican restaurants and fast-food chains. Just as U.S. consumers were quick to discover that Taco Bell was not a Mexican telephone company, so was their growing awareness of Latin cuisine, which was soon to affect supermarket buying habits. As the consumer palate began to acquire a taste for south-of-the-border flavors, food- and beverage-shopping patterns shifted correspondingly. Chili consumption doubled between 1980 and 2000, red peppers tripled in the same period; between 1990 and 2000, imported beer, led by Mexican brands, doubled its U.S. market share.[7] By the year 2000, tequila consumption in the United States had surpassed that in Mexico.[8] In 1991, salsa sales had overtaken ketchup in U.S. supermarkets, and continues to outsell ketchup today.[9] U.S. Latinos are responsible for reviving Mott's Clamato juice brand, boosting sales of the formerly torpid product by 20 percent between 1999 and 2002. Learning that many Latinos enthusiastically consider Clamato's pinch of clam juice to be an aphrodisiac, Mott's focused its entire marketing budget on the Latino segment of the U.S. market.[10] Piercing through the tortilla curtain in the opposite direction was Mexico's Bimbo brand (ranked the number three baker worldwide) that gained access to the U.S. market for tortillas, breads, and snacks after having invested almost $1 billion in acquiring U.S. companies between 1998 and 2002.[11]

The influence of *Hispanidad* on U.S. lifestyles and markets extends well beyond ethnic gastronomy. During the 1990s, a strong rise in the average household income of Hispanics to $40,500 has put them in marketing's mainstream.[12] New automobiles and light truck registrations by Hispanics have grown by more than 20 percent annually, twice the rate of the overall vehicle market.[13] Sales of Latin music soared 25 percent in 2000, a year in which the music industry saw its total revenues fall by 3 percent. Not wanting to miss the Hispanic bandwagon, Liz Claiborne Cosmetics jumped on board in 2001 with a $200 million campaign to promote Mambo, its first "Latin-influenced fragrance for both men and women."[14] Whether fashionable or faddish, favorite attractions like Jennifer López, Emilio and Gloria Estefan, Antonio Banderas, Shakira, Cheech Marín, Salma Hayek, Ricky Martin and *Livin' La Vida Loca*, José Feliciano, *La Bamba*, and *La Macarena* attest to the growing impact of the Hispanic presence on U.S. popular culture and entertainment.

In sports, it is hard to overstate how truly American baseball has become. It is rare today to watch a baseball game without the presence of champion pitchers and hitters hailing from the Dominican Republic, Mexico, Cuba, and other nations of the Americas. If your child plays soccer and you did not, that generation gap testifies to the swift increase in popularity that Latin America's favorite sport has had in U.S. athletics.

Their social stereotype is another feature of the U.S. Hispanic presence that has undergone an image remake. No longer predominantly seen as lazy and slow-witted laborers, rebellious Cholos, Chicano low-riders, or violence-prone drug dealers, mainstream Hispanics are increasingly recognized as an entrepreneurial and upwardly mobile social force, conservative and more likely than blacks to own their own businesses and homes, and less likely than blacks to be attached to the public sector or to collect social benefits.[15, 16] The Hispanic presence extends to the Internet, its users spending 16 percent more time online than the overall U.S. population. U.S. Hispanics reflect the general population in its propensity to buy concert, event, or movie tickets and CDs or DVDs online, and are more likely buyers of consumer electronic goods and home-delivered groceries.[17]

In the political sphere, it is notable that for the first time, during the 2000 U.S. presidential election campaign, the candidate of each major party was compelled to appeal to U.S. voters in both English and Spanish. It is also notable that, in that year's cliffhanger election aftermath, it was Florida—a state defined by its politically powerful Latino population—that held the key to the presidency. Recognizing the newly pivotal importance of Latinos, both President George W. Bush and Congressional Democrats began, in 2001, to record their weekly radio addresses in English and Spanish. Using Spanish to court Hispanics is politically astute because it is language, more than place of origin, culture, or skin color, that unites this large electorate. Mexico's Independence Day, Cinco de Mayo, was celebrated in the White House for the first time in 2001. President Bush's effort to stay ahead of the Latin curve came as no surprise to those who had heard the president welcome Mexico's President Vicente Fox, saying, "Mexico is the first country I visited as President. Today it is my privilege to welcome President Fox for the first state visit of my administration. This is a recognition that the United States has no more important relationship in the world than the one we have with Mexico."[18]

It is a matter of historic record that for the greater part of the fifthteenth through seventeenth centuries, Spanish was the dominant European voice that was heard throughout the lands that were to become the United States. Is it merely a curious accident of history that, in the twenty-first century, the voice of the U.S. marketplace, entertainment industry, sports, and political stage is acquiring an unmistakable Spanish accent?

Given the wildly diverse ingredients of the cultural salad formed by minorities in the United States, it is a challenge for members of any ethnic group to sustain a strong sense of their national heritage. A deep sense of cultural identity explains why so many immigrants from Latin America and their descendants cling to tradition as a way of honoring their homelands and remembering their past. For a product to gain acceptance in the patchwork quilt of U.S. Latin markets, it is essential to create an emotional link with the homegrown customs specific to each national community. Some ethnic groups can be reached through tying in with their country's independence tradition, such as Mexico's Cinco de Mayo celebration. However, the nationalistic fervor many immigrants once felt for political symbols has weakened as the distances imposed by geography and time take their toll. More commonly recognized, and more warmly received by those many immigrant families whose once-passionate political attachment to their homeland has cooled, are promotional appeals tied to the religious traditions and celebrations of each country, as noted below in Quick Notes: Country Visit.

A NAME, A PLACE, A SECRET, AND A PROMISE

There is no one-size-fits-all description of Latin America. Each country has its own striking idiosyncrasies. Nonetheless, there are strong threads of commonality woven throughout the length and breadth of the region. As connecting fibers of a single, coherent historical and cultural tapestry, these tightly intertwined strands hold Latin America together as a shared human experience. The chapters that follow emphasize key traits that lend a remarkable measure of uniformity to this astoundingly diverse region. As common denominators, these traits are essential knowledge for doing business anywhere in Latin America.

Latin America Close-Up

As business in the region takes you from one country to another, you will need more information about the peculiarities of specific locales. While lacking the fine granularity of an encyclopedic presentation, the country snapshots shown in the tables of this chapter and Chapter 2 show a wide-angle view of country particulars without burdening you with details of places you may not visit. As you narrow your target-market focus, it will pay to add flesh to the bare-bones information summarized in these tables. The descriptions in this chapter show at a glance features of interest to casual visitors; those in Chapter 2 contain information of interest to more earnest business visitors. Arranged in a standardized format of six categories, the Quick Notes: Country Visit are a first step to help you choose and plan a visit to any of the region's twenty countries.

The country descriptions in the following Quick Notes listing are formatted to show:

1. **Country area.**[19] Latin American countries vary enormously in size. Knowing that large countries tend to have more diverse and distinct submarkets can help you in arranging an itinerary to fit your time schedule.
2. **Population.**[20] As one key indicator of market size, the number of potential consumers can point both to markets that are large enough to be of interest and to those that are small enough to be overlooked by large multinational competitors.
3. **Average income.**[21,22] Per capita income, adjusted for purchasing power, is a shorthand measure of the level of economic development and affordability of your product by the broad market.
4. **Climate.**[23,24] Knowing what weather to anticipate will help you pack for and schedule your visit.

5. **Holidays.**[25, 26, 27] Religious, national, and local holidays control the pace of business in Latin America and, hence, the availability of people you will want to meet. As most Latin American countries observe 1 January as New Year's Day, 1 May as Labor Day, 12 October as Columbus Day, 8 December as the Immaculate Conception, and 25 December as Christmas, these dates are not included in the country listings. *Note 1*: Be cautious about scheduling any meetings on the Monday preceding a Tuesday holiday or the Friday following a Thursday holiday. Latins often use those days as *puentes* (bridges) for a long weekend break. Be equally careful about scheduling meetings between mid-December and mid-January, as business engagements occupy an especially low priority during year-end festivities. *Note 2*: In the interest of realistic scheduling, remember that airline arrival times in Latin America tend to be early in the morning. This means that while you can begin doing business early on your first day, you may feel good about not having scheduled an event for that evening, after having been without a good rest for the previous twenty-four hours or more. *Note 3*: Dates are written in the day-month-year order used in Latin America, rather than in the customary U.S. order of month-day-year.
6. **Quick Tips.**[28] Odds and ends that you may find useful as you go through the day.

QUICK NOTES: COUNTRY VISIT

ARGENTINA **Sq. mi.:** 1.1 million. **Pop.:** 38 million. **Avg. income:** $11,500. **Climate:** (Remember, seasons are reversed in South America.) Mostly temperate, arid in the southeast, subantarctic in the southwest, subtropical in the northeast, hot in the north. **Holidays:** 25 May, anniversary of the Revolution (1825); 8 June, Malvinas Islands memorial; 22 June, Flag Day; 9 July, Independence Day; 17 August, anniversary of the death of General San Martín. **Quick Tips:** (1) Argentines are justifiably proud of the tango (the now-world-famous dance originated in the bordellos of Buenos Aires in the late-nineteenth-century), their red wines (while not marketed heavily in the United States, they are of exceptional quality) and free-range beef (they consume a world-record average of 132 lbs. per capita that is more flavorful than U.S. grain-fed beef and contains less cholesterol), and Jorge Luís Borges, a prolific twentieth-century writer whose works include *Ficciones*, a literary classic. (2) Both La Recoleta, Buenos Aires's chic shopping district, and its ornate and historically intriguing cemetery are worth a visit. (3) Electricity is 220 volts, 50 hz.

BOLIVIA **Sq. mi.:** 424,052. **Pop.:** 8.6 million. **Avg. income:** $2,600. **Climate:** Varying with altitude, it can be humid and tropical in Santa Cruz to semiarid in 12,000-foot La Paz where it can freeze during the November–April rainy season. **Holidays:** 6 August, Independence Day (1825); 24 September, Santa Cruz Day; 1 November, All Saints Day. **Quick Tips:** (1) Bolivia has had seventeen constitutions and more presidents than years of independence. (2) La Paz is the world's highest capital above sea level, and visitors may avoid *soroche* (altitude sickness) by resting, not using alcohol, and drinking *mate de coca* (coca-leaf tea).

BRAZIL **Sq. mi.:** 3,285,615. **Pop.:** 180 million. **Avg. income:** $6,600. **Climate:** Mostly tropical, but temperate in the south. **Holidays:** 22 April, Discovery Day (1500); 7 September, Independence Day (1822); 15 November, Proclamation of the Republic. **Quick Tips:** (1) Brazil is the most populous and most industrialized country in Latin America; it is also the largest Portuguese-speaking country in the world. (2) Fleeing just ahead of Napoleon's advancing armies, the royal family of Portugal took up residency in Brazil, thus establishing that country as an independent monarchy in 1822. Shortly thereafter, the United States became the first country to recognize Brazil's independence. (3) Cachaça, a potent sugar cane liquor used in the caipirinha cocktail, is the national drink of Brazil (by presidential decree). (4) Electricity is 220 volts in Brasilia and the northeast, 110 volts elsewhere. (5) Be wary of crime in São Paulo and Rio, especially at night, and never venture into the *favelas* (shantytowns).

CHILE **Sq. mi.:** 292,183. **Pop.:** 15.5 million. **Avg. income:** $10,000. **Climate:** Temperate; Mediterranean in the central region; cool and damp in the south; Atacama Desert in the north is one of the world's driest regions. **Holidays:** 21 May, Battle of Iquique; 6 September, National Unity Day; 18 September, Independence Day (1810). **Quick Tips:** (1) In many of the communities settled by northern European immigrants in Chile's rugged south during the nineteenth century, it is not unusual to hear residents speak German more often than Spanish. While there, wear sunblock, sunglasses, and a hat—the combination of altitude and proximity to the hole in the Antarctic ozone layer may leave your skin vulnerable to sun damage. (2) While you are sampling some of the world's finest wines, try *curanto*, a regional dish of shellfish, fish, beef, lamb, pork, potatoes, and local spices prepared as a stew. (3) Electricity is 220 volts, 50 Hz.

COLOMBIA **Sq. mi.:** 439,619. **Pop.:** 40 million. **Avg. income:** $6,500. **Climate:** Tropical along the coast and eastern plains; cooler in the highlands. **Holidays:** 20 July, Independence Day (1810); 7 August, Battle of Boyacá; 16 November, independence of Cartagena. **Quick Tips:** (1) Media coverage focuses on the negative, creating an impression of endemic chaos and violence. In reality, the vast majority of terrorist kidnappings and murders are committed against the poor in rural areas, not against foreigners or city dwellers. Major cities like Bogotá have lower urban crime rates than many other world capitals. Reporters rarely write about the day-to-day lives of 40 million Colombian citizens going about their normal lives, largely untouched by the narcotics-financed misdeeds of fewer than forty thousand armed rebels. (2) While *la violencia* is discussed among themselves, Colombians prefer to engage outsiders in a discussion of the arts, perhaps about Gabriel García Márquez, Nobel Prize-winning author of works such as *One Hundred Years of Solitude* and *Love in the Time of Cholera*. (3) Day and evening dress is formal. (4) Bogotá's *Museo de Oro* (Gold Museum) houses a spectacular collection of some 33,000 pre-Columbian gold relics.

COSTA RICA **Sq. mi.:** 12,750. **Pop.:** 4 million. **Avg. income:** $9,500. **Climate:** December–April is dry, May–November is rainy; San José has year-round spring. **Holidays:** 15 September (1821), Independence Day; 11 April, Battle of Rivas; 25 July, annexation of Guanacaste Province; 2 August, Our Lady of Angels; 15 August, Mother's Day; 15 October, Cultures Day. **Quick Tips:** (1) Costa Rica is known as nature's vacation paradise and for its democracy, literacy, and pro-U.S. attitudes. Since abolishing their standing army in 1949, *Ticos* (an affectionate nickname for Costa Ricans) have enjoyed a longer period of stability and prosperity than any society in Latin America, earning their country its reputation as the Switzerland of Central America. (2) While you can walk to many appointments in downtown San José, finding where they are located can be confusing because landmarks (e.g., thirty *varas* east of the old fire station), not street numbers, are used for addresses. (3) English is widely understood and there is a large colony of (primarily U.S.) expatriates.

CUBA **Sq. mi.:** 42,792. **Pop.:** 11.5 million. **Avg. income:** $2,300. **Climate:** Tropical, moderated by trade winds; dry season, November–April; rainy season, May–October. **Holidays:** Independence days: 10 December (1898) is the date of independence from Spain; 20 May (1902) is the date of independence from U.S. control. **Quick Tips:** (1) Cuba has been officially an atheist state for most of the Castro era. In 1962, Castro shut down some 400 Catholic schools, charging they were seditious. But in 1992, the constitution was amended to make the state secular instead of atheist. While Catholicism is the largest religion, Afro-Cuban spiritualism is widely practiced. (2) Cubans are philosophical about their situation. A story heard on the island shows their ability to use humor as a foil to adversity: Visitor—"What is most difficult about life under communism?" Cuban—"The first one hundred years." Avoid talking politics with Cubans, whether of the Miami or Havana variety.

DOMINICAN REPUBLIC **Sq. mi.:** 18,810. **Pop.:** 8.8 million. **Avg. income:** $5,800. **Climate:** Tropical maritime; little seasonal variation in temperature; afternoon showers are common in the late spring and again in the fall; serious hurricane threats are June–October. **Holidays:** 21 January, Feast of Our Lady of Altagracia; 26 January, Duarte Day; 27 February, Independence Day (1844); 29 April, Dominican Labor Day (instead of 1 May); 16 July, founding of Sociedad La Trinitaria; 16 August, restoration of the Republic; 24 September, Feast of Our Lady of Mercy. **Quick Tip:** The island of Hispaniola, of which Dominicans occupy the eastern two-thirds and Haitians the rest, was occupied by Taino Indians when Columbus established the first European settlement in the Americas in 1492. The combination of Spanish brutality and disease reduced the formerly thriving Taino population from 1 million to 500 in 50 years. To replace Taino labor on plantations and in the mines, the Spanish brought African slaves to the island. Today, the Dominican Republic is predominantly Negro with virtually no sign of its original indigenous inhabitants.

ECUADOR **Sq. mi.:** 106,454. **Pop.:** 12.5 million. **Avg. income:** $3,100. **Climate:** Tropical along the coast, becoming cooler inland at higher elevations; tropical in the Amazonian jungle. Guayaquil and other coastal cities are hot and rainy January–April. Quito and the cities of the sierra enjoy springtime climates. **Holidays:** 24 May, Battle of Pichincha; 24 July, birthday of Simón Bolívar; 10 August, Independence Day (Quito, 1822); 9 October, Independence Day (Guayaquil, 1820); 3 November, Independence Day (Cuenca, 1822); 6 December, founding of Quito. **Quick Tips:** (1) Ecuador is one of Latin America's best travel bargains. (2) Old Town Quito preserves much of its early sixteenth-century colonial flavor, having been declared a World Cultural Heritage site by UNESCO. (3) Although Ecuador is the world's largest exporter of bananas and Latin America's fourth largest oil exporter, a fringe group of die-hard fortune hunters aspire to discover much greater riches, Atahualpa's Lost Horde. Their quest is fueled by persistent legends alluding to the gold and silver treasures that were hidden from the advancing conquistadores by Inca priests in the gloomy, mostly uncharted high rain forest region of the Llangañate.

EL SALVADOR **Sq. mi.:** 8,122. **Pop.:** 6.4 million. **Avg. income:** $4,400. **Climate:** Tropical; rainy season, May–October; dry season, November–April; tropical on the coast; temperate in the uplands. **Holidays:** First Sunday and Monday in August, Feast of San Salvador; 15 September, Independence Day (1821); 5 November, First Cry of Independence. **Quick Tips:** (1) The *pupusa* (poo-*poo*-sah—don't be put off by the pronunciation) is the national snack, if not the national passion. Vaguely reminiscent of tamales, *pupusas* are sold from ever-present street stands and neighborhood *pupuserías*, or prepared at home from secret recipes passed from mother to daughter over generations, and are the theme of songs and poems. Evincing an interest in the institution of the *pupusa* will endear you to Salvadoreans. (2) Animosities and easily available weapons still remain from the brutal, decade-long civil war in which over 70,000 perished and almost one million people were forced to flee the country.

GUATEMALA **Sq. mi.:** 42,032. **Pop.:** 13 million. **Avg. income:** $3,700. **Climate:** Tropical; hot and humid in the lowlands, cooler in the highlands. Guatemala City lows average 55°F, highs 77°F. **Holidays:** 30 June, Army Day; 15 September, Independence Day (1821); 2 October, anniversary of the 1944 Revolution; 20 October, anniversary of the 1944 revolution. **Quick Tips:** (1) A visit to Antigua is worthwhile. It was founded in 1543 after Guatemala's first capital was leveled by an earthquake and was itself destroyed by the same fate in 1773, after which Guatemala City became the capital. Preserved remnants of its colonial origins make Antigua a favorite of vacationers and Spanish-language students. (2) Latin American and U.S. leftists still recall the 1954 CIA-backed toppling of the popularly elected Árbenz regime as evidence of ongoing U.S. meddling in Latin America. The United States also comes under criticism for not having been more vigorous in opposing the brutal 1960–1996 civil war in which entire indigenous villages were massacred by the military.

HONDURAS **Sq. mi.:** 43,267. **Pop.:** 6.7 million. **Avg. income:** $2,650. **Climate:** Tegucigalpa is noticeably cooler than the city of San Pedro Sula. April is the warmest month, with average highs of 86°F. January and February lows average 57°F; rainfall is heaviest in May and June, December–April is dry. **Holidays:** 15 September, Independence Day (1821); 21

October, Armed Forces Day. **Quick Tips:** (1) Hondurans are nicknamed *Catrachos* by their Central American neighbors. (2) Honduras was the archetype of the Banana Republic until well into the twentieth century when U.S. agribusiness firms controlled the country's economic and political life from their plantations along the north coast. Nonetheless, Hondurans are pro-United States. (3) The country still feels the effects (including the poverty-driven rise in crime) of Hurricane Mitch, which left 5,000 dead and $3 billion in damage in 1998.

MEXICO **Sq. mi.:** 761,404. **Pop.:** 104 million. **Avg. income:** $9,100. **Climate:** Mexico City, Guadalajara, and Puebla have springlike temperatures, with highs averaging 80°F–85°F in April, and lows of 43°F–48°F in January and February. Mexico City's pollution can irritate allergy sufferers and wearers of contact lenses. **Holidays:** 5 February, Constitution Day; 21 March, birthday of Benito Juárez; 5 May (Cinco de Mayo), Battle of Puebla; 16 September, Independence Day; 2 November, All Souls' Day (commonly called *Día de Los Difuntos*, Day of the Dead); 20 November, anniversary of the Revolution; 12 December, Our Lady of Guadalupe Day. **Quick Tips:** (1) Mexico City's hurried (by Latin American standards) and sometimes discourteous residents are known as *Chilangos* in the rest of the country. With more affection, residents of Mexico's second-largest city, Guadalajara, are known as *Tapatios*. (2) Mexico has the largest Spanish-speaking population in the world, and is Latin America's second-most populous. The country has become heavily urban, as many flee hopeless unemployment in the rural areas of the south to find work in its major cities and along the U.S. border. Mexico City is not only the world's most populous metropolitan area, it is also among its most polluted and crime ridden. Beware using taxis at night that are not associated with a hotel or designated taxi site. (3) *The Labyrinth of Solitude*, by Nobel Prize-winner Octavio Paz, offers a wealth of insights into the character of Mexico and how it differs from that of the United States.

NICARAGUA **Sq. mi.:** 49,985. **Pop.:** 5.2 million. **Avg. income:** $2,400. **Climate:** Warm, tropical; rainy season is May–October. **Holidays:** 20 July, Liberation Day; 10 August, Managua Day; 14 September, Battle of San Jacinto; 15 September, Independence Day; 7 December, Feast of *La Purísima*. **Quick Tips:** (1) From the time of their establishment in the early sixteenth century, León and Granada were Nicaragua's major urban centers. Their bitter political and commercial rivalry caused Managua to be created midway between them to defuse the conflict. (2) Nicaraguans maintain they have the world's highest number of poets, a claim surely made more plausible by the fact that Rubén Darío, perhaps Latin America's most revered poet, was born, died, and buried there.

PANAMA **Sq. mi.:** 30,185. **Pop.:** 3.1 million. **Avg. income:** $5,500. **Climate:** Temperatures in the 70s and 80s year-round, the rainy season is May–December. The short-sleeved, pleated Panama shirt, or *guayabera,* is appropriate (and comfortable) nonformal business dress. **Holidays:** The last week in February, Carnival; 15 August, founding of Old Panama; 11 October, Revolution Day; 1 November, Day of the National Anthem; 3 November, independence (from Colombia) Day; 4 November, flag day; 10 November, day of first call for independence; 28 November, Independence (from Spain) Day. **Quick Tips:** (1) Panamanians are no strangers to U.S. ways: With U.S. backing, the country seceded from Colombia in 1903. In 1904, the U.S. dollar was adopted as the official currency, and construction began on the Panama Canal on a strip of land ceded to U.S. control; the canal was completed in 1914, and control was returned to Panama in 1999. English is widely understood. (2) Perhaps more than anywhere in Latin America, Panama is obsessed by boxing. Among its top boxers, the best known is Roberto Durán.

PARAGUAY **Sq. mi.:** 157,006. **Pop.:** 5.9 million. **Avg. income:** $4,500. **Climate:** Summers are hot, with January and February highs around 95°F, falling to the low 70s F during July and August; there are no prominent dry or wet seasons, but significant rainfall in the east, transitions to semiarid conditions in the west. **Holidays:** 3 February, San Blás Day; 1 March, Heroes Day; 14–15 May, Independence days; 12 June, end of Chaco war; 15 August, founding of Asunción; 25 August, Constitution Day; 29 September, Battle of Boquerón. **Quick Tips:** (1) A society in no hurry to catch up with the rest of the world, but of charming contrasts, Paraguay contains solitary, German-speaking colonies founded in the nineteenth and twentieth centuries, proud and independent Guaraní Indians, a military reminiscent of the Napoleonic era, and a sense of isolation from the modern mainstream. (2) Electricity is 220 volts, 50 Hz.

PERU **Sq. mi.:** 496,095. **Pop.:** 28 million. **Avg. income:** $4,600. **Climate:** The climate varies from tropical rainforests in the east to dry deserts in the west, and from temperate to frigid in the Andes. Lima's January–

March temperatures can reach into the mid-90s, falling to the mid-40s in June–September. Although rain is scarce, the *garúa* (light drizzle) is a frequent and uncomfortable feature of the coastal climate. **Holidays:** 28 and 29 July, Independence days; 30 August, St. Rose of Lima; 12 October, Battle of Angamos. **Quick Tips:** (1) Peru's rich Spanish and indigenous heritage shape its social, artistic, and cultural faces. Do not miss an opportunity to visit its wealth of museums, Inca and pre-Inca ruins, and colonial towns. (2) Day and evening dress is formal. (3) Electricity is 220 volts, 60 Hz.

PUERTO RICO **Sq. mi.:** 68,021. **Pop.:** 4 million. **Avg. income:** $12,000. **Climate:** Similar to that of the Dominican Republic, the coastal area is comfortable and warm throughout the year; hurricanes threaten during June–October. **Holidays:** 11 January, birthday of Eugenio María de Hostos; 22 March, emancipation of slaves; 16 April, birthday of José de Diego; 4 July, U.S. Independence Day; 17 July, birthday of Luís Muñoz Rivera; 27 July, constitution day; 19 November, discovery of Puerto Rico. **Quick Tips:** (1) Like Cuba, Puerto Rico's status changed from being a Spanish colony to being a U.S. possession as a result of the 1898 Spanish-American War. Unlike Cuba, Puerto Ricans were extended most of the benefits of U.S. citizenship in 1917 with one exception: Puerto Ricans have no voting representation in the U.S. Congress. (2) Puerto Rico legitimately qualifies to be included in this listing because of the many cultural, linguistic, economic, social, and historical similarities it has in common with other Latin American societies.

URUGUAY **Sq. mi.:** 176,125. **Pop.:** 3.5 million. **Avg. income:** $9,300. **Climate:** Winter (May–August) temperatures rarely reach freezing, Montevideo's summer (November–February) temperatures can soar into the 90s. **Holidays:** 19 April, landing of the thirty-three patriots; 18 May, Battle of Las Piedras; 19 June, birthday of General Artigas; 18 July, constitution day. **Quick Tips:** (1) Traditionally one of the region's most statist economies and socialist societies, highly literate, middle-class, and democratic Uruguay is evolving toward a market and capitalist orientation as a member of MERCOSUR (Common Market of the South). Like the United States, Western Europe, and Japan, it is also becoming an elderly society because of its low birthrate, high life expectancy, and high rate of emigration of younger people. (2) Other South Americans sometimes refer to their Uruguayan neighbors as "Argentines Lite," a gentle reference to the ways in which Uruguayan speech, dress, and behavior are perceived to be similar to Argentine patterns. (3) Fashionable sportswear can substitute for formal business attire. (4) Electricity is 220 volts, 50 Hz.

VENEZUELA **Sq. mi.:** 352,051. **Pop.:** 24.5 million. **Avg. income:** $6,200. **Climate:** Average temperatures in Caracas are in the low 70s; the rainy season is June–October. Maracaibo averages in the mid-80s with frequent rain. **Holidays:** 19 April, Declaration of Independence; 24 June, Battle of Carabobo; 5 July, Independence Day; 24 July, birthday of Simón Bolívar; 4 September, Civil Servants' Day. **Quick Tips:** (1) Easygoing Venezuelans are both geographically and culturally the most Caribbean society in South America. (2) A long history of unequal income and weakly managed, corrupt government has made Venezuela a tinderbox for social unrest. (3) Formal dress is standard for business. Be alert to street crime in Caracas.

HOW THIS BOOK WILL HELP YOU

You have finished your surface reconnaissance of Latin America. You are now prepared to learn how to do business profitably in its markets. The new markets of Latin America are wide open for business to anyone desiring to become a part of this rapidly unfolding twenty-first-century frontier. History tells us that whenever fresh economic frontiers are opening, those who are most able to stay ahead of the pack and gain control of the competitive high ground are those who will be best positioned to sense, select, and seize the top opportunities from among the explosion of newly born possibilities. Use the next five chapters to stay ahead of the pack by learning the five key lessons they teach for business success in Latin America:

Chapter 2: Learn where to find the most promising opportunities for your small- or medium-sized business.

Chapters 3 and 4: Learn the historic and cultural reasons underlying why and how your Latin American customers do business differently.

Chapter 5: Learn how to negotiate with and sell to those customers.

Chapter 6: Learn how to keep the good deal you have made from falling apart.

Notes

1. Frank Tannenbaum (1964), *Ten Keys to Latin America*. New York: Alfred A. Knopf, p. 5.

2. Hubert Herring (1968), *A History of Latin America.* New York: Alfred A. Knopf, p. 3.

3. Hubert Herring (1968).

4. Harvey O. Beltrán (2000), "El Aroma del Buen Vino Chileno," *American Airlines Nexos,* April/June.

5. Lynette Clemetson (2003), "Hispanics Now Largest Minority, Census Shows," *New York Times,* January 22.

6. "Past, Present, and Future." (2004), *Hispanic Business,* June, pp. 26–35.

7. Doreen Hemlock (2001), "Savoring Success," *Sun-Sentinel* (Fort Lauderdale), pp. 14–15, April 2.

8. "Viva Margarita." (2001), *American Way,* September 1.

9. Barbara D. Phillips (2000), "TV: The Latino Wave Hits the Small Screen," *Wall Street Journal,* June 26, p. A44.

10. Gabriel Sama (2003), "La 'pasión latina' revive bebida olvidada en EE.UU," *Wall Street Journal* in *El Comercio* (Quito), p. B3, October 21.

11. Geri Smith (2002), "Can Bimbo Cook in the U.S.?," *BusinessWeek Online,* March 4. Retrieved June 28, 2004, from http://www.businessweek.com/@@*ctwolUQmG4luxYA/magazine/content/02=09/b3772148.htm.

12. Eduardo Porter and Emily Nelson (2000), "P&G Reaches Out to Hispanics," *Wall Street Journal,* October 13, p. B1.

13. Eduardo Porter (2000), "Ford, Other Auto Makers Target Hispanic Community," *Wall Street Journal,* November 9, p. 5.

14. Rod Stafford Hagwood (2001), "Next," *Sun-Sentinel* (Fort Lauderdale), May 31, p. 10E.

15. "Latino Power at the Polls." (2000), *The Economist,* December 8, pp. 30–31.

16. "Yo Te Quiero Mucho." (2000), *The Economist,* September 30, pp. 30–33.

17. Juán Carlos Perez (2003), "Study: US Hispanics' Net Use Grows," *IDG News Service/Latin American Bureau,* January 27.

18. "Mexico." (2001), *Business Traveler,* November–December, p. 60.

19. "Country Profiles." (2002), *CIA World Factbook 2002,* Washington, DC: Central Intelligence Agency (conversion to square miles by author).

20. "Country Profiles." (2002).

21. *Country Commercial Guides* (various; 2002 and 2003), International Trade Administration, Washington, DC: U.S. Department of Commerce.

22. "Country Profiles." (2002).

23. *Country Background Notes* (various; 2000, 2001, 2002, 2003), International Trade Administration, Washington, DC: U.S. Department of Commerce.

24. "Country Profiles." (2002).

25. *Country Commercial Guides* (various; 2002, 2003).

26. *Country Background Notes* (various; 2000, 2001, 2002, 2003).

27. "Corporate Travel Guide to Latin America." (2004). *Latin Finance*, pp. 9, 15–23, 25–29, 31–32.

28. Author's experience and other sources (as noted).

Chapter 2

Latin America Means Business

For some forty years, I have had the benefit of doing business and having as friends a large and varied assemblage of executives who understand Latin America. While the majority of these executives were Latin Americans, a few were Anglo Americans, and a handful were nationals of countries located outside of the Americas. Over the years, I was privileged to be able to learn from this multinational assortment of business veterans how they had earned their spurs in the rough-and-tumble business arenas of Latin America. The similarities I observed among their diverse and lively accounts of triumph and defeat began to take on the shape of recognizable and predictable patterns. These patterns form the bedrock on which rest the foundations for success and failure that appear in these pages. Without weakening the muscle behind these executives' real-life lessons, I have organized the body of their experiences around a skeleton formed by my own years of doing business research in the region.

The guidelines resulting from that amalgam of practical experience and academic research are what make this book different. It contains concepts that clients and colleagues have put into practice to increase profits, decrease hassles, and reduce risks related to their Latin American dealings. I shall be delighted to learn from you, the reader, how this book has helped to sharpen your own competitive edge. I invite you to send me your comments via e-mail to: DrBeckerIs@yahoo.com.

The typical business scenario of the first thirty years of my own experience in Latin America is markedly different from that which I have been pleased to see evolve during the last ten years. While the past never dies in Latin America, a different future is being born there as today's less corrupt, more democratic leadership has reduced transportation and tariff rates, has promoted wider access to world-class know-how, and is thus unchaining the region's economic potential. This process is revolutionizing the way business is done in the mega-market of the Americas. As the fear of being left behind overcomes the fear of change, yesterday's cliché of the global village is becoming today's reality for 800 million consumers who inhabit the Americas hemisphere.

You will not find in this book one single key to doing business in Latin America. Success is tied to a whole key ring. The keys that will unlock profits for the medium-size exporter of consumer goods are not the same ones that will open the door for the firm aiming to set up master franchisees for industrial security systems. And the distributor of specialty furnishings will require yet a different set of keys to find a reliable supplier of custom chairs and tables fashioned by hand from tropical hardwoods. Nonetheless, among the many keys described in this book, there is a set that can open the doors you will need to make doing business in the new Latin America a productive and satisfying venture. The strongest foundation on which to ground that venture is to understand (a) the region's business possibilities and (b) the ways in which smaller businesses can exploit them.

HOW DOES LATIN AMERICA MEASURE UP IN THE WORLD? SPEEDING LOCOMOTIVE OR SLOW-MOVING TRAIN WRECK?

When exporters scan the globe for promising market targets, they may use GDP (Gross Domestic Product) share to indicate how a particular economy is performing in relation to the rest of the world. Like market share, GDP share is a shorthand measure to gauge if an economy is gaining, falling behind, or just holding its own in the world.

Figure 2.1 tracks the total economic output (measured by GDP) of Latin America as a proportion of the total economic output of the world. We see Latin America gaining share in the late 1970s. This was near the end of the region's period of Import Substitution Industrialization (ISI), when international bankers were tripping over themselves in a rush to make loans, as the mounting prices of Latin America's commodities propelled its regional GDP skyward. The commodity bubble burst in 1981, precipitating Latin America's Lost Decade as plunging raw material prices, exacerbated by the competitive paralysis imposed by years of protectionist policies, choked economic output. Following the end of the Lost Decade, Latin America gained GDP share. This was a period in which the

Figure 2.1
Latin America: Share of World Economic Output

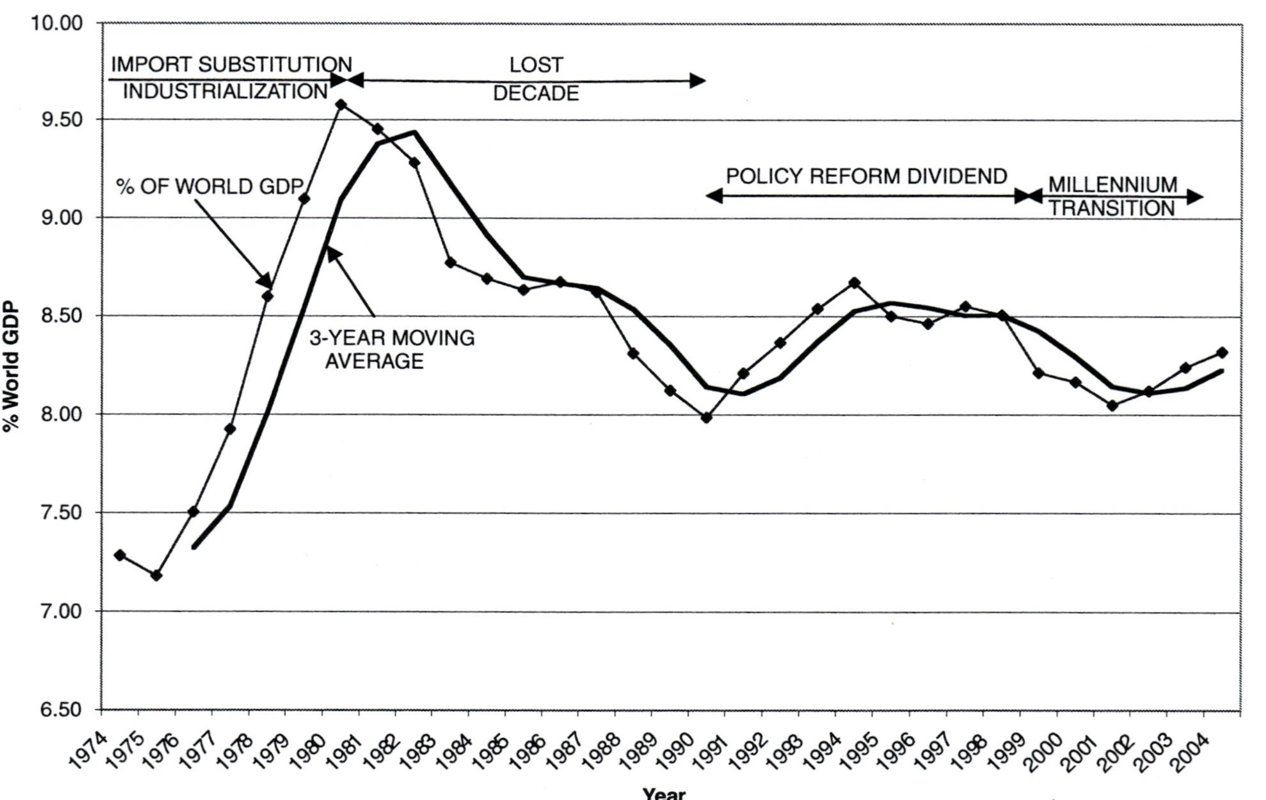

Sources: http://www.imf.org/external/pubs/ft/weo/2002/02/data/index.htm, author's calculations.

region's economies cashed in on open-market reform policies, and grew at annual average rates of about 5½ percent, one and one-half times faster than the United States. As Latin America moved from one century to the next, its GDP share fell off, largely in response to slumps in Argentina and Venezuela. Although the story is still being written, by 2004 both the annual and moving average measures suggest that Latin America may be poised to regain its previous status of the early 1990s as a rising star on the world's economic stage.

Make Time Your Ally, Not Your Enemy

The graph in Figure 2.1 makes it obvious that recessions do not last forever and that, just as day follows night, upturns follow downturns. What the graph does not show is that the present early-stage recovery from the decline of recent years is marked by more accountability from public officials and a Darwinian purge of weakly run companies and banks. Political, business, and banking leaders who have lived through hyperinflation, plunging currencies, crushing debt, falling commodity prices, mass unemployment, and civil unrest know the potholes to avoid on the road toward survival in a competitive global economy. Moreover, those leaders now have a more informed and involved public looking over their shoulders, one that is not willing to endure further loss. Since suffering its Lost Decade of the 1980s and more recent body blows from the Lost Half-Decade of the late 1990s and early 2000s, Latin America has moved ahead on the learning and accountability curves. While it will always undergo economic cycles, changes in some key measures[1] suggest that its newfound sense of direction and self-confidence will make the business swings that lie ahead less volatile than in the past:

- Inflation that averaged 500 percent in 1990 was down to 7 percent by 2001.
- Real GDP grew at an annual average rate of 3.4 percent in the 1990s, almost three times greater than the 1.2 percent rate of the 1980s.
- Real per capita income rose at an annual average rate of 1.5 percent in the 1990s, far superior to the decline of nearly 1 percent suffered in the 1980s.
- Annual growth in exports jumped from 5 percent in the 1980s to 10 percent in the 1990s.
- Poverty fell from 41 percent to 35 percent during the 1990s.

It is human nature to move with the herd, and avoid taking a chance on uncertain markets. But if the real internal reforms that Latin America has adopted coincide with economic recovery in the United States, the region may be poised to resume a course of high growth. Only time will tell when that rebound will happen and whether the 2003 and 2004 upturns are the leading edge of an economic turnaround or a hiccup. But time waits for no man. So moving ahead of the herd could be a smart bet for those U.S. firms that act now, before the region's recovery gains momentum and competitors move to occupy its fresh pastures.

Confidence that Latin America is entering a new growth stage is evidenced in the region's financial markets. While the S&P rose 26 percent in 2003, stock markets in Brazil, Argentina, Chile, and Mexico easily topped that healthy U.S. gain by climbing, respectively, 142, 134, 77, and 33 percent in dollar terms.[2] For the region as a whole, private investment flows were estimated at $35.5 billion in 2003, a gain of some 40 percent over investment inflows for 2002.[3] By 2004, the signs were unmistakable that Latin America had regained favor with investors:

- The Carlyle Group, the world's largest private capital firm, was opening its first international office in Mexico City and was bringing on board Thomas McLarty, former chief of staff in the Clinton administration.
- J.P. Morgan Partners had $500 million available to invest in Brazil.
- Discovery Capital Management had raised $50 million for new investment in the region.
- Baring Latin American Partners was raising $200 million to invest in medium-size Mexican companies.[4]
- Boston Advent International had acquired Argentina's largest private mail service, OCA, SA, a firm that had been sold in 1997 for $605 million.[5]
- The region's bond spreads in 2003 were one half those of 2002, the lowest since the Russian default of 1998.[6]
- Issuance of Latin American bonds in 2003 reached its highest level since 1997.[7]

Be Prepared for Doing Business in the Largest Market on the Planet

Size matters

At least it does when countries compete in global markets. It is the reason why countries join together to form market juggernauts like the European Union. By integrating their own markets with those of their neighbors, smaller countries acting collectively can acquire the economic power and political clout needed to prosper and have influence in global affairs. In the process of gaining sway externally, members of regionally integrated markets also gain strength internally. Thus, it is little surprise that a kaleidoscopic array of regional and bilateral market pacts have been signed in Latin America. Among these, NAFTA, MERCOSUR, and FTAA (Free Trade Area of the Americas) stand out as having the greatest potential to raise the profit pulse of U.S. businesses.

NAFTA

The leading example in Latin America of the effect of size on the economic health of a country is Mexico's involvement in the North American Free Trade Agreement. NAFTA has been in effect since 1994 and is now responsible for 20 percent of Mexico's economic output,[8] creating many more jobs than it has lost, while simultaneously lowering the cost of living for countless Mexican households.[9] By fusing the economies of the U.S., Canada, and Mexico into a mega-market of 420 million consumers, NAFTA changed the business face of Mexico almost overnight, propelling its economy into a world-class manufacturing and assembly powerhouse.

NAFTA drove Mexico to displace Japan as the number two trading partner of the United States by 1998. Between 1994 and 2002, U.S.–Mexico trade had almost tripled, and had made both countries more competitive internationally.[10] The incoming tide of export and import deals made the possibility of trading with Mexico loom large on the radar screens of U.S. firms that had never before considered doing business in Latin America. Meanwhile, those same screens were blipping another regional-market trade target further to the south.

MERCOSUR

After NAFTA, the largest (227 million consumers) and most dynamic integrated market in the Western Hemisphere is MERCOSUR (Common

Market of the South, called MERCOSUL in Brazil), made up of Argentina, Brazil, Paraguay, and Uruguay, with Bolivia and Chile as associate members. Unlike the free trade agreement model on which NAFTA is based, MERCOSUR is a customs union, a market-integration model in which members charge commonly agreed tariffs to outsiders. Those tariffs are relatively high, making some see MERCOSUR, which began in 1991, as a mechanism to perpetuate the protectionism that sheltered Latin American economies from international competition until the 1980s.

Larger firms can circumvent MERCOSUR's taxes on imports by going behind its tariff wall to set up local manufacturing, instead of supplying the market through exports. Few SMEs can follow that strategy, as they are unable to finance the investment needed to produce products or services within MERCOSUR. Hence, as they are shut out of the market for export sales, most U.S. SMEs must use licensing or contract manufacturing in order to tap into MERCOSUR's revenues.

FTAA

The Free Trade Area of the Americas would unite all of the North American, Central American, South American, and Caribbean economies, except Cuba, into a single massive trading bloc that, with a combined GDP of some $12 trillion, would eclipse both Europe and Asia as the planet's largest-ever, integrated-regional market. While receiving its initial stimulus from President Reagan in 1986, movement toward the FTAA was jump-started in 1994, the same year in which NAFTA went into effect, as the leaders of the thirty-four Western Hemisphere democracies pledged to create a seamless market of 800 million consumers by 2005. Progress on the agreement was restrained but steady until 2002, when the U.S. Congress finally granted fast-track or trade promotion authority, permitting the president to expedite negotiations for the historic pact. The prospects for hoisting FTAA's flag over the hemisphere on 1 January 2006, are favorable, even if that flag represents "FTAA Lite"—a watered-down startup version of the pact visualized in 1994. U.S. business and agricultural interests are backing the accord, and the view of the Bush administration is that "Latin America is not our back yard, but our front yard."[11]

What will be the shape of the FTAA? The answer will be found between two competing approaches that negotiators will use to frame the pact: NAFTA and MERCOSUR. The main contenders are the United States, which views the FTAA as the instantaneous southward extension of NAFTA free trading, and Brazil, which, in its role as the tacit leader of

MERCOSUR, would like to eventually see that model used as the template for the FTAA. Free trade à la NAFTA gets few votes from powerful Brazilian industry groups that, challenged to compete without protection, have relied on MERCOSUR's high-tariff wall to shelter them from lower-cost competitors. Indeed, Brazil's competitive advantage rests on exporting bulk agricultural commodities like beef, soybeans, orange juice, cotton, and sugar. Brazilians fear that as MERCOSUR's tariff wall comes down, there will be no incentive for U.S. firms to build factories in Brazil, preferring to export duty-free to Brazil from assembly or manufacturing facilities already established in Mexico. While open markets under the FTAA would favor Brazilian farmers in theory, the political reality is that their low-cost products will be shut out of the pact's richest market by U.S. trade barriers and farming subsidies. Brazil is ready for fierce negotiations as it sees its top twenty exports to the United States being charged average tariffs of 39 percent, whereas it imposes duties averaging only 12.9 percent on its top imports from the United States.[12] To add to its negotiating firepower at the talks, Brazil is attempting to expand MERCOSUR into a trade alliance covering all of South America.[13] But complicating Brazilian negotiators' efforts to reconcile United States–Brazil differences is the possibility that the political will for the FTAA may soften if a weak recovery of Latin America's economy spurs a backlash against market reforms.

Regardless of whether the final form of the FTAA follows a procompetitive, NAFTA-style model or a more protectionist MERCOSUR model, several existing subregional agreements in the hemisphere will likely be subsumed by the FTAA. In the process, much of the untapped trade potential among members of those often weakly administered agreements could bear fruit under a well-managed FTAA regime. For example, Italian tile imports stocked in El Salvador were charged a 20 percent duty under the tariff code of the Central American Common Market. Exporting the tile to a buyer in Nicaragua, also a member of the Central American Common Market, triggered another 20 percent tariff charge, but Salvadoran customs authorities refused to refund the initial tariff paid by the distributor. Similarly discouraging are problems arising from nonuniform product standards: Guatemala requires all commercially traded sugar to contain vitamin A. Even though sugar sold in the Dominican Republic at international prices could undercut price-controlled domestic sugar in Guatemala, the Dominican sugar cannot be imported because it lacks vitamin A.[14] Costly bureaucratic wrinkles like these would be ironed out under the FTAA.

Fortress America?

The rise of regionalism in the Western Hemisphere adds to the forces propelling the world toward a triad of powerful economic zones. It is too early to say whether the trade coalitions created in Asia, Europe, and the Americas are steps toward a single integrated global market or the division of the world into three economic fortresses. One factor boosting the fortress argument is the threat to Latin American industry from Asian exports. For example, between 2000 and 2002, Mexico lost 500 manufacturing plants and 250,000 jobs to China, where hourly wages for factory workers are $0.47, less than one-third of Mexico's $1.47 per hour.[15] The growing assault of low-cost Chinese and ASEAN (the Association of Southeast Asian Nations, which competes directly with Latin American exports)[16] producers on United States and other markets could sway some FTAA negotiators toward protectionism and the MERCOSUR model of setting high barriers against outsiders.

U.S. negotiators could also find some incentive to be amenable to a fortress Americas approach for reasons having less to do with preferential market access than with national security. One fear following in the wake of the September 11 terrorist attacks is the possibility that bacterial, chemical, explosive, or nuclear weapons could be introduced into the United States in shipping containers. Guarding against such threats would entail placing inspection delays on containers inbound from regions and shippers considered most susceptible to terrorist access. Under such a scenario, shipments originating from Latin America could be less subject to profit-stripping administrative holdups, thus providing CTPAT (Certified Trade Partner in Anti-Terrorism) intra-FTAA shippers with a competitive advantage over extra-FTAA shippers, especially those originating in the Middle East.[17]

Proximity's Benefits

The partnerships among North American firms that were spawned by NAFTA made U.S. firms more able to compete against rivals in Asia and Europe. Under FTAA, the same production-cost benefits made possible by those NAFTA partnerships would be expanded geographically and magnified by savings in logistics and control functions. Shorter intra-FTAA distances mean lower transportation, inventory, storage, and insurance costs than if trading partners were located in Asia. Intra-FTAA business also means lower communication and travel costs, and fewer control problems for firms than if their trade partners were a dozen time zones away. Another FTAA advantage is that Asian producers tend to use

Asia-origin inputs, whereas Latin American finished-goods assemblers use more U.S.-origin components. Moreover, there is a greater tendency in Asia, especially in China, for a supplier to export under its own brand, and compete directly with its erstwhile U.S. buyer. Finally (as discussed in Chapter 3), if progress continues in Latin America to adopt the U.S. dollar as a national currency, it will have the same trade-stimulating effect of eliminating traders' currency risks and foreign exchange commissions costs in the FTAA as the euro has had in the European Union.

These factors may foreshadow a shift in sourcing from Asia to Latin America by many U.S. manufacturers and resellers, if and when the FTAA goes into effect. As that shift occurs, it would be accompanied by a growing need for components to be exported from the U.S. to Latin America for assembly into finished products. It is a scenario that bodes well for all U.S. suppliers, but especially for SMEs.

A Shift in the Trade Winds?

Telling indicators of Latin America's potential to ring export cash-register bells are the gaps between the region's share of world trade and its share of world economic output and population. Although the region accounts for 7 percent of the world's economic output and 8 percent of the world's population, its trade volume (exports plus imports) is only 5 percent of the world's total. To equate Latin America's trading activity with its share of world economic output, the region would have to boost its exports and imports by 40 percent. To make its share of world trade proportionate to its share of the world's population, Latin America would have to increase its exports and imports by 60 percent. In the language of any exporter, importer, licensor, banker, freight carrier, or underwriter, the prospect of a 40 to 60 percent jump in revenue translates to business opportunities.

To lend perspective to the significance that Latin America's potential for economic growth could have on the sales of U.S. vendors, consider that a 1 percent increase in Japan's GDP would bring about an increase of $1 billion in U.S. exports. But a 1 percent increase in Latin America's economy would translate into a $5 billion jump in U.S. exports.

Latin America's Welcome Mat Is Out for Smaller Businesses

Charles Darwin taught the world that it was not the strongest or the most intelligent species that survived, but the ones most responsive to change. What Darwin knew about species applies equally to business. There are periods in history when great changes occur, and responsiveness to those changes controls whether a business survives or becomes extinct. Latin America is in one of those periods. The changes occurring in the region are tipping the scales of survival in favor of swift-to-adapt, small- and medium-size enterprises (SMEs). As globalization is the major force driving new opportunities, trade-oriented SMEs are strategically well positioned to profit from them.[18] To appreciate how SMEs in both of the Americas can benefit from globalization, consider how globalization is reshaping Latin America's social order and integrating its markets.

The Social Order: Why Democracy Matters to SMEs

The last two decades have been a defining period for Latin America. While many ills of the past have not yet been laid to rest, a crucial line was crossed that has altered the old social order. Crossing that line meant rejecting dictatorships and crony capitalism, and embracing political and economic self-determination as cornerstones of a new social order. Having hardwired self-determination into their mind-set, Latin Americans now look to the democratic principle of freedom to reform political practice and inform economic policy. The ascendancy of political and economic freedom parallels embracing the gospel of entrepreneurship, the strongest tenet of winning SMEs. The process of taking a giant step away from rule by the few and toward rule by the many has altered the old requirements for success in Latin American markets and tips the scales in favor of the entrepreneurial strengths in which SMEs routinely excel. As a result, smaller U.S. and Latin firms are better positioned to compete in Latin American markets today than at any time in the past. The advantages of being small are especially pronounced in Latin America where, in 2002, SMEs recorded sales and profit gains of 27 percent and 1,000 percent, respectively, while the corresponding growth rates for big business were 15 percent and 388 percent.[19] Table 2.1 summarizes how the forces of political and economic freedom benefit SMEs.

Best Beats Big in the Information Age

Theory says that the main reason large companies exist is to lower their transaction costs. By doing business on a large scale when they bought and sold, large firms could capture economies of scale that small-fry buyers and sellers could not achieve. As technology, deregulation, and the Internet reduced transaction costs, the optimal size for firms was similarly re-

Table 2.1
Democracy's Dividends to SMEs

These Trends Toward Political Freedom	Make Smaller Business More Competitive By
Rule by men to rule by law	Minimizing economic or political clout as factor in settling disputes
Shadowy to transparent decision making	Reducing uncertainty of business environment
Less tolerance for corruption	Not having to pay bribes to win business
Greater availability of information	Having affordable access to marketing and production data
The state: from planner and creator of growth to facilitator of growth	Having access to SME-suitable infrastructure and services and opportunities to compete fairly
Less government patronage	Dealing with rational bureaucracy (e.g., *ventanilla única*)
These Trends Toward Economic Freedom	**Make Smaller Business More Competitive By**
Power shifts from producer to consumer	Applying its customer service advantage
Lower international communication cost	Gaining knowledge of international markets, customers, and technology
Lower international transportation cost	Lowering cost of access to international markets and inputs
Lower international tariffs	Quoting lower export prices
Lower domestic tariffs	Lowering cost of inputs
Greater availability of small credits	Financing working capital needs with debt
Easing foreign investment rules	Financing investment capital needs with equity
Stable exchange rates	Lowering cost and risk of doing business internationally

duced. When David-sized SMEs can buy and sell as cheaply as Fortune 500 Goliaths, size is no longer an insurmountable barrier to doing business across borders.

The SME-Customer Connection

As buyers of both consumer and industrial products, Latin Americans have become demanding and informed customers. This new buyer mentality is tailor-made for the customer-focused approach and nimble response to market changes that are the hallmarks of SMEs. Future stories about business successes within Latin America, and between Latin America and the United States, will likely be dominated by SMEs launching new customer-centered ventures. In the 1990s, the production-oriented firms that dominated Latin American business for centuries found it difficult to adapt as the pendulum of market power began to swing toward the consumer. For example, food giants Molinos Río de la Plata (Argentina, $1.4 billion in sales) and Santista Alimentos (Brazil, $2 billion in sales) suffered costly consequences for being slow to adapt to consumer marketing. Molinos's net profit margins were only 43 percent of Latin America's food industry average, while Santista's capitalized market value was less than half its book value.[20] Firms that fail to adapt to the new customer-dictated market rules are learning the hard way that if they continue to do business as they have in the past, they will become business history.

NARROWING THE SEARCH FOR BUSINESS OPPORTUNITY

We will tighten the focus of our SME-exporter telescope at this juncture, and concentrate our survey on specific features of Latin American markets, thus bringing into sharper focus some of the current and future export sales possibilities of this opportunity-rich region.

Four Steps to Cash Flow

In business—as in sports, comedy, and romance—timing is everything. A window of opportunity has been opened by the power of self-determination that has gripped Latin America during the last two decades and is now reshaping the region's social order. That power acts through the economic and political realms to create a potential for SMEs to compete more advantageously for the reasons shown in Table 2.1. The trick is to transform that potential from a strategic concept to a cash flow reality. It entails narrowing the range of choices, a process that will be different for every business. But, the process for all businesses is an identical four-step procedure:

1. Understand the underlying forces that are propelling new business opportunities in Latin America. Those forces are creating prime platforms of opportunity, two examples of which are outlined below.
2. Identify which of your company's strengths are in alignment with those forces. Though this step means the difference between success and failure, too many U.S. executives treat it as a Ouija board exercise in decision making. Use this book to help you estimate to what degree your company's strengths in people skills, product offerings, finances, and organizational culture will enable you to use the new platforms of opportunity as competitive springboards.
3. Search for those countries whose economies and industries seem good matches for that alignment. Take advantage of the Quick Notes in Chapter 1 and in this chapter to screen for potential matches.
4. Prepare to develop the business, close the deal, fill the order, and sustain the cash flow. The information found in Chapters 3 to 6 will help you make cash flow happen in Latin America.

Two Platforms of Opportunity

Two of the most durable and broad platforms of opportunity for SMEs in Latin America are defined by the imperatives of infrastructure and electronic commerce (e-commerce). They are the springboards from which many of the foremost Best Prospects for U.S. Exports (mentioned in Quick Notes: Business Visitor) arise. These two platforms are durable because they represent factors that are essential to a process that drives an economy from closed and protectionist to open and competitive. That process defines the race for survival in today's global economy. As the race begins as a sprint to catch up and continues as a marathon to keep up, it creates ongoing needs that translate into business opportunities that will not soon disappear. These two platforms are broad because the scope of change they represent cuts a wide swath across virtually all sectors of Latin America's rapidly modernizing economies.

Infrastructure Needs

Many U.S. executives would be appalled to see how run-down and inadequate are the roads, telephones, electricity and water systems, schools, hospitals, and port services in Latin America. Yet, it is precisely the decrepit condition of the region's infrastructure that is now creating major business opportunities for U.S. firms. As the forces of globalization force Latin American economies to compete in world markets, a colossal obstacle to success is the inability of run-down infrastructures to support modern production and distribution systems. Indeed, an unanswered question is how Latin America has been able to sustain moderately high economic growth rates for most of the last fifty years with an infrastructure that is less than 15 percent of the Western Hemisphere's total,[21] representing only:

- 3 percent of the paved roads (less than in California)
- 5 percent of the electrical generation capacity (about the same amount as in Texas)
- 5 percent of the telecommunications equipment (there are more telephone lines in New York City than in all of Latin America)

As providers of state-of-the-art infrastructure services, U.S. vendors hold a key competitive advantage when selling to Latin America. The telecommunications, manufacturing, transportation, health, mining, and energy sectors face heavy global competitive pressures. They have no other alternative than to leapfrog over the outmoded existing installations and facilities that date from a much earlier era. To a surprising degree, therefore, Latin Americans have been quick to adopt the Internet, cellular phone systems, air and seaport facilities, electrical generating plants, and a variety of other infrastructure upgrades that, in a growing number of cases, contain more advanced technology than systems commonly found in the United States or Europe. As a result, the definition of the region's preference for appropriate technology is undergoing rapid change. Whereas in the past, appropriate technology signified a design scenario of equipment and processes that were intensive in low-skilled labor, the term is now coming to signify those technologies that will permit the economies of the region to produce at the world-class standards required to sell in global markets.

The magnitude of energy requirements in Central America alone provides a microcosmic snapshot of the business opportunities available to meet the infrastructure expansion needs of the entire region. In that narrow isthmus stretching from Mexico to Colombia, the demand for reliable energy is increasing at more than twice the rate of population growth. Among the many infrastructure needs foreseen by Central American planners is a project to interconnect the national power grids of six countries through a 1,100-mile, 230-kilovolt transmission system.

The range of business opportunities is not limited to the vast and growing potential to help modernize the region's obsolete infrastructure. There also are attractive possibilities to acquire high-quality assets and operating concessions in oil and gas, telecommunications, air and rail transportation, pharmaceuticals, mining, manufacturing, and electricity sectors under favorable prices and terms. Moreover, instead of facing yesterday's skeptical, and sometimes hostile, nationalistic governments, foreign investors find welcome mats extended by today's helpful public- and private-sector executives, eager to make every reasonable effort to compete for U.S. capital, technology, management ability, and market access.

E-Commerce

¿Habla Ud. E-Com? The Internet has speeded up the world and torn secrecy down. These changes have freed people from the tyranny of place and set in rapid motion a fundamental transformation in the way business is done in Latin America. Representing only 1 percent of world trade in 2001, the Internet is projected to grow to nine times that proportion in 2005.[22] As a direct result of the emergence of this powerful marketing hub, the conventional model governing buyer-to-seller relationships is being redefined everywhere.

Nowhere is the Internet growing more rapidly than in Latin America. The pace of growth of Internet usage in Latin America is four times the world's average. Business-to-business (B2B) sales on the Net in Latin America probably surpassed $5 billion in 2003. Forecasters project that by 2005 more than 27 million Latins will have access to the wireless Internet.[23] Tiny Costa Rica may be a leading indicator of the power of e-commerce to reach broad segments of the Latin American market. Every citizen in Costa Rica can have a free e-mail address provided by the government. Any Tico (a nickname for Costa Ricans) can walk into a post office anywhere in the country, log on to one of the PC terminals made available for the purpose, and immediately become connected to the outside world. Examples like this make it clear that companies that have not yet climbed on board the e-commerce bandwagon may not be around to compete in tomorrow's markets without having to play an increasingly expensive game of catch-up.

Small business Internet success rule: Best beats big. Today's Internet allows smaller sellers to reach global audiences once reserved for large multinational corporations. The investment barriers in telecommunications, staff, and facilities that previously made it tough for smaller firms to compete in international markets lose their sway in niche-dominated marketplaces. By making their catalogues available on the Internet, SMEs not only save on printing costs, but can also immediately correct errors and make updates.

Size no longer is king in a Latin America where complacent customers in the protected, brand-limited consumer markets of the past have been displaced by value-demanding shoppers of today's open, Internet-age markets. Customer focus and rapid-paced change are the defining conditions of twenty-first-century markets. They also determine the market environment in which smaller firms' customer service and innovative abilities are decisive competitive advantages.

Change is also turning Latin America's industrial market on its head. A telling example of the onset of a sea change in business buying habits is the process by which large firms make purchases. It is traditional in Latin America for firms to deal directly with their customary list of suppliers by hand delivered or telephoned and faxed RFQs (requests for quotations). The process is not only cumbersome and inefficient, it is also loosely controlled and vulnerable to kickbacks. As more large firms in the region go online for their buying needs, smaller suppliers will find they can reach attractive markets that were formerly closed to them. As the e-commerce marketplace is defined by the Web, buyers and sellers no longer need to be separated by national borders, size, or personal influence. As demand for general-purpose business goods grows in step with Latin America's economy, an increasing proportion of these goods will be sold online by smaller U.S. firms.

Smaller countries have also benefited for many of the same reasons by which access to the Internet has enabled smaller firms to profit by compensating for their size and lack of the economies of scale possessed by their blue-chip bigger brothers. Indeed, the smaller countries of Latin America are now able to more efficiently exploit the untapped growth potential of their domestic economies by taking advantage of internationally accessible infrastructure, technology, and financing through the Internet.

The Internet is no longer an option. Although the long-held notion of competitive advantage made possible by economies of scale is not yet dead, it is wavering. The implications of this shifting paradigm, where speed compensates for size, are pivotally important to turn-on-a-dime smaller firms looking to compete in international markets.[24] To be successful in Latin America, U.S. firms must not see e-commerce as a threat against which they are forced to play a defensive game. Rather, the winners in the race for tomorrow's Latin American markets are the ones who know that Internet time runs about seven times faster than regular clock time, and that their biggest advantage is the ability to run light and fast, realizing that if they do not make their own dust, they will have to eat their competitor's dust.

One view of this new window on the world's economy is on the screen of a computer monitor in the small, modestly appointed office of the manager of an asparagus-growing cooperative in Ica, Peru. He is searching the Web, and here is what he is looking for: reliable suppliers who could provide his farmers with hydro-cooled refrigeration components; pesticide applicators; drip-irrigation pumps and nozzles; two-wheeled tractors and pull behind equipment; service providers that can give him trade-credit financing; refrigerated containers, all-risk shipping insurance; and smaller U.S. produce distributors with whom he can deal directly to place his product in Kansas City, Denver, or Indianapolis, thus avoiding the fees and hassle of selling through the sometimes unsavory, high-volume broker-importers of Port Everglades, Florida, or Long Beach, California. Will he find your company's Spanish-language Web site? If he does find it, has it been designed to motivate and make it easy for him to do business with you? With solid planning, you will be able to answer those two questions in the affirmative, and prevent your B2B investment from becoming Born-to-Blunder.

Adapting your existing Web site to serve a Latin American market is not just a matter of snapping your fingers. In addition to the obvious need to translate text content into Spanish and/or Portuguese, you may have to adapt the visual content of your site by using photos, logos, and graphics to conform to the local culture. Of even greater consequence, however, are content considerations such as compliance with local regulations and standards, price levels, and terms of payment. Each and every one of these variables, of course, must be consistent with the business practices, currency, laws, time zone, language, cultures, and infrastructure of the countries in which you intend to do business. They underscore why the challenge of thinking globally, while acting locally, is far from being a tired cliché.

One example of the power of the Internet to ring up retail sales in Latin America is provided by the Brazilian subsidiary of General Motors. GM's Web site in Brazil is dedicated exclusively to selling its new economy size

Chevrolet Celta. By ordering online, customers can specify their new car's features and track its progress from factory floor to delivery center. Additionally, they can save money by being directly invoiced, thus eliminating taxes. Customers may also pay online, but when they do, the price they pay is the sticker price. There is no haggling in online buying. Launching its Internet sales model in late 2000, GM soon found out how potent the Internet is as a marketing tool: By 2001, the Internet sales model accounted for more than 80 percent of Celta deliveries. One reason for the success of GM's pioneering initiative was that some 65 percent of new-car buyers in Brazil have access to the Internet.

Latin American Business Opportunities—One Country at a Time

"*Tu escoges la cuchara con que te vas a dar de comer*": You choose the spoon with which you are going to feed yourself. This venerable adage alludes both to the need to make choices in life and to the need to make the right choices. It applies to business as much as to life in general. It applies to you now as you work to implement step three in the four steps to cash flow: As a first step, use the economic and industry information in this section to scan Latin America for promising trade or investment possibilities. The data have been collected from several sources and estimated by the author when sources are in conflict, and compressed into a standardized format to enable the reader to compare countries on five key business parameters. A word of caution before relying heavily on Quick Notes: Facts and fish are two commodities that are better used when fresh. Use the references mentioned to update and keep your country business facts current.

The information described below is formatted to show for each country:

1. **GDP.**[25,26] Adjusted for purchasing power parity, gross domestic product measures internal economic output. It can signal whether a market may be large enough to be interesting or small enough to escape the attention of large competitors.
2. **GDP/capita.**[27,28] Per capita income, adjusted for purchasing power, is a shorthand measure of the level of economic development and affordability of your product by the broad market. Although average income was included in Quick Notes: Country Visit in Chapter 1, it is repeated here for convenience.

3. **Economy and Industries.**[29] Use these as a guide to estimate how large a factor in an economy are the industries where you are likely to find prospective customers for your product.
4. **Best Prospects for U.S. Exports.**[30] These prospects were selected by the commercial office of each country's U.S. embassy, typically found by following an analysis of customs data, market research, and forecasting of industrial trends. For convenience, they have been divided into nonagricultural and agricultural product categories.
5. **Business Notes.**[31] This item provides you with facts, warnings, or suggestions about a country's business environment that you may find useful.

QUICK NOTES: COUNTRY BUSINESS

ARGENTINA **GDP:** $453 billion. **GDP/capita:** $11,500. **Economy and Industries:** Food processing, motor vehicles, consumer durables, textiles, chemicals and petrochemicals, printing, metallurgy, steel. **Best Prospects for U.S. Exports:** (Nonagricultural Products) agricultural machinery, equipment and parts, food processing and packaging equipment, industrial chemicals, security equipment, medical equipment and supplies, residential building materials and supplies, information technology services, telecommunication services, and management consulting services. (Agricultural Products) planting seeds, particularly those used for forage (alfalfa, clover, rye grass, fescue) and for horticultural crops, as well as food ingredients and cotton needed by the Argentine industry to expand export-oriented production of processed foods and textiles. **Business Notes:** (1) While Argentine consumer preferences have long leaned in the direction of Europe, the rapidly growing trade ties with MERCOSUR are extending the reach of many brands from Brazil, Argentina's top trading partner. Nonetheless, the United States remains its second trading partner, and consumers reflect many U.S. values and consumption patterns, as they see U.S. products as high quality and innovative. (2) In Argentina, opening a branch, instead of a legally separate subsidiary, provides no legal separation between your firm's U.S. and Argentine business, thus exposing your entire firm's assets to potential liability.[32]

BOLIVIA **GDP:** $21.4 billion. **GDP/capita:** $2,600. **Economy and Industries:** Mining, smelting, petroleum, food and beverages, tobacco, handicrafts, clothing. **Best Prospects for U.S. Exports:** Goods and services needed to support expansion in gas, oil, and secondary petrochemicals; mining; textiles; forestry and wood; and telecommunications sectors. **Business Note:** As Bolivia is landlocked, goods are usually transshipped through Argentine, Brazilian, Chilean, or Peruvian seaports. Handling delays, roadblocks, and floods can make air shipment a preferable option.

BRAZIL **GDP:** $1.2 trillion. **GDP/capita:** $6,600. **Economy and Industries:** Textiles, shoes, chemicals, cement, lumber, iron ore, tin, steel, aircraft, motor vehicles and parts, other machinery and equipment. **Best Prospects for U.S. Exports:** With the largest economy and population in South America, Brazil presents countless export opportunities, particularly in areas such as energy generation, construction, safety and security equipment, and metalworking machinery. **Business Notes:** (1) Brazil's (probably underreported) average income level can mask an impressively large purchasing power for consumer products. Using data on ownership of cars and TVs, the country's middle-class market may be some 40 percent of the population.[33] (2) Brazilians use *jeitinho* as a unique management style to resolve difficulties by circumventing obstacles or rules.

CHILE **GDP:** $153 billion. **GDP/capita:** $10,000. **Economy and Industries:** Copper, other minerals, foodstuffs, fish processing, iron and steel, wood and wood products, transport equipment, cement, textiles. **Best Prospects for U.S. Exports:** Pollution control, telecom equipment, travel and tourism, medical equipment, franchising, computer equipment, food and processing equipment, construction equipment, mining equipment, plastics machinery and resins, air conditioning and refrigeration, electric power equipment, and security equipment. **Business Notes:** (1) Geography molds business behavior in Chile. The Andes isolate the country from the rest of the continent, giving it a Pacific orientation that supports a ready acceptance of Asian products. Chile's extreme length separates it into different climate zones, each having a unique consumer profile and demand pattern; covering the national market requires distributors to maintain a traveling sales force. (2) Chileans are known for being socially conservative and ethical in their business dealings.

COLOMBIA **GDP:** $255 billion. **GDP/capita:** $6,300. **Economy and Industries:** Textiles, food processing, oil, clothing and footwear, beverages, chemicals, cement, gold, coal, emeralds. **Best Prospects for U.S. Exports:** (Nonagricultural Products) telecommunications services and equipment, industrial chemicals, travel and tourism, air cargo services, financial services, automotive parts and accessories, computer hardware and software services, oil and gas machinery and services and petrochemicals, plastics material and resins, electrical power systems, safety and security technologies and equipment, food and beverage processing and packaging equipment, medical equipment, apparel, construction and mining equipment, and pollution control equipment. (Agricultural Products) processed food, cotton, wheat, corn, soybean meal, and soybeans. **Business Note:** Because of Colombia's reputation for violence, many new-to-export U.S. firms will not even consider doing business there. Nevertheless, many savvy global companies clearly understand the country's strategic potential and are well established there. Despite its problems, Colombia ranks solidly as a member of a group of progressive, well-diversified industrializing countries. Although in the short term, some conditions are worrisome, U.S. firms looking for mid- to long-term regional positioning should focus on Colombia's record of economic stability and growth.

COSTA RICA **GDP:** $39 billion. **GDP/capita:** $9,300. **Economy and Industries:** Microprocessors, textiles and clothing, food processing, construction materials, fertilizer, plastic products. **Best Prospects for U.S. Exports:** (Nonagricultural Products) paper and paperboard, computers and peripherals, plastic materials and resins, automotive parts, agricultural chemicals, telecommunications equipment, medical equipment, construction equipment, and school and home office products. (Agricultural Products) corn, soybeans, wheat, rice, fresh fruit, processed fruit and vegetables, and snack foods. **Business Note:** Costa Rica's friendly people, pleasant climate, and law-abiding lifestyle are magnets to legions of U.S. retirees and transients. If you tarry a little in parks, hotel lobbies, or bars, you will meet too many of the latter who have a well-polished story about an investment or business deal that will pay many millions in profits tomorrow, but requires a few thousand of investment today. Beware: The other hand you feel groping in your pocket is not yours!

CUBA **GDP:** $25.5 billion. **GDP/capita:** $2,300. **Economy and Industries:** Sugar, petroleum, tobacco, chemicals, construction, nickel, steel, cement, agricultural machinery, biotechnology. **Best Prospects for U.S. Exports:** U.S. agricultural and food exports to Cuba that were only $4.5 million in 2001, jumped to $139 million in 2002, and reached $257 million in 2003.[34] In addition to increased sales of agriculture and food goods to Cuba, export growth is anticipated in wood, and medical products.[35]

Speaking to that point, Tony DeLio, vice president of marketing for the Archer Daniels Midland Company, stated, "The thing that makes Cuba an attractive proposition is that it is literally 90 miles from our shores. It's very easy for us to do business there. We sell hundreds of millions of dollars of products throughout the Caribbean. Cuba is just another stop."[36] **Business Note:** U.S. law permits U.S. companies to do business with Cuba in fields such as agricultural products and farm supplies, air charter services, artwork, cultural events, food sales, medical equipment and supplies, telecommunications, and travel services.[37] Although you are wise to avoid discussing politics with Cubans (whether in Havana or Miami), do not underestimate the power of the dollar to break down ideological barriers to normal trade relations across the straits of Florida in the near future.

DOMINICAN REPUBLIC **GDP:** $51 billion. **GDP/capita:** $5,800. **Economy and Industries:** Tourism, sugar, clothing, tobacco, construction, mining, food processing. **Best Prospects for U.S. Exports:** (Nonagricultural Products) sporting goods, recreational equipment, and mobile phones. (Agricultural Products) corn, tobacco, soybean meal, lumber and plywood, wheat, nonfat dry milk, vegetable oils, animal fat and tallow, and sweeteners. **Business Notes:** (1) In general, U.S. products are perceived to be of the best quality. (2) The government of the Dominican Republic promotes "backward linkages," projects designed to increase the local content of inputs to the country's large export assembly sector.

ECUADOR **GDP:** $39 billion. **GDP/capita:** $3,100. **Economy and Industries:** Petroleum, food processing, textiles, metalwork, paper products, wood products, chemicals, plastics, fishing, and lumber. **Best Prospects for U.S. Exports:** Telecommunications equipment and services, construction equipment, franchising, computers and peripherals, security equipment, paper products, cosmetics and personal-care products, and used medical equipment. **Business Notes:** (1) U.S. exporters and investors incur no currency risk or exchange costs in Ecuador's dollarized economy. (2) Ecuador's antiquated system of laws and arbitrary court rulings can frustrate the conduct of business. Its Decree 1038-A bars foreign firms "from unilaterally modifying, terminating, or failing to renew a contractual agreement with its local agent without just cause . . . what constitutes 'just cause' is up to the Ecuadorian courts."[38]

EL SALVADOR **GDP:** $28.4 billion. **GDP/capita:** $4,400. **Economy and Industries:** Food processing, beverages, petroleum, chemicals, fertilizer, textiles, furniture, light metals. **Best Prospects for U.S. Exports:** Textiles and textile articles, plastic materials and resins, paper and paperboard, processed foods, electric power generation and distribution equipment, telecommunications, automotive parts and service equipment, and environmental technology. **Business Notes:** (1) Salvadorians are reputed to be the most entrepreneurial businesspersons in Central America. (2) As a dollar-based economy, El Salvador presents no currency risk or foreign exchange commissions' costs to U.S. exporters and investors. (3) Major Salvadorian retailers maintain their own distribution systems and buy much of their consumer goods merchandise directly from producers.

GUATEMALA **GDP:** $48.3 billion. **GDP/capita:** $3,700. **Economy and Industries:** Sugar, textiles and clothing, furniture, chemicals, petroleum, metals, rubber, tourism. **Best Prospects for U.S. Exports:** Automotive parts, accessories, and service equipment; computers and peripherals (including motherboards, keyboards, mouses, cases, monitors, microprocessors, hard drives, color printers, scanners, CD-R/RW units, DVDs, and multimedia accessories); food processing and packaging equipment (including packaging machinery to clean, fill, and seal bottles, cans, and parts); textile machinery, equipment, and fabrics (e.g., spinning machines, sewing machines, trims, drying machines, bleaching or dyeing machines, zippers, buttons, yarn, and boxes); franchising (especially fast food, but also dry cleaning, lawn and garden, professional painters, fast shoe repair, pest control, day care and computer learning centers); electrical power systems; and computer services related to Internet/business applications. (Agricultural Products) apples, cotton, planting seeds, poultry, red meats, processed fruit and vegetables, grapes, dairy products. (Nonagricultural Products) electrical power systems; and security and safety equipment. **Business Notes:** (1) Guatemala is an excellent market for U.S. products that have high brand-name recognition. (2) Franchisors should know that when Guatemalan or other Central American investors consider a franchise, they look for a franchisor with a worldwide presence, who may be new to this region but is solidly accepted in other markets, is honorable and reputable, and provides extensive training and backup. These investors often do not know a great deal about a specific industry, but they look for known trademarks because consumers equate recognizable United States trademarks with quality. Potential franchisees are often young, wealthy executives familiar with the United States and other countries, or are large corporations that already own more than one franchise in different industry sectors, like fast food, clothing, or health.

HONDURAS **GDP:** $17 billion. **GDP/capita:** $2,650. **Economy and Industries:** Sugar, coffee, textiles, clothing, wood products. **Best Prospects for U.S. Exports:** Automotive parts, accessories, and service equipment (including engine spare parts, electrical system parts, transmission parts, suspension parts, tires, and emission control equipment); computers and peripherals (including personal computers, hard disks, keyboard units, computer monitors, server systems, modems, CD-ROM drives, printer units, and computer software and multimedia); computer software; food processing and packaging equipment; textile machinery, equipment, and fabrics; franchising; electrical power systems; and security equipment (including safes and strong boxes, charged fire extinguishers, sprinkler systems, fire and burglar alarms, and smoke detectors). **Business Note:** Honduras's small geographic size makes it practical to appoint a single representative to handle your product. Its small market size also means that a distributor will often carry a number of complementary and even competitive lines, most on a nonexclusive basis and with small inventory stocks.

MEXICO **GDP:** $920 billion. **GDP/capita:** $9,100. **Economy and Industries:** Food and beverages, tobacco, chemicals, iron and steel, petroleum, mining, textiles, clothing, motor vehicles, consumer durables, tourism **Best Prospects for U.S. Exports:** Automotive parts and supplies; computer hardware, software, and services; intermodal transportation equipment; oil and gas field equipment and services; franchising; security and safety equipment and services; water resources equipment and services; pollution control equipment; plastic materials and resins; telecommunications equipment and services; electrical power systems; building products; food processing and packaging equipment; and electronic components. **Business Notes:** (1) U.S. firms interested in capitalizing on the huge market opportunities in Mexico should keep in mind that Mexico's size and diversity is often underappreciated by U.S. exporters. It can be difficult to find a single representative to cover this vast market. (2) Although not routinely reported as a single category by the U.S. International Trade Administration, environmental products and technology services are attractive sales possibilities. Especially in Mexico City, one of the planet's most polluted cities, but also in Guadalajara, Monterrey, and elsewhere, vehicle exhaust, untreated sewage, and industrial emissions reach toxic levels. Preferential financing may be available through the U.S. Ex-Im Bank, the Inter-American Development Bank, or the North American Development Bank to promote environmental technology deals by smaller

U.S. firms. (3) NAFTA is making the legal aspects of doing business in Mexico increasingly similar to the way business is done in the United States.

NICARAGUA **GDP:** $12.3 billion. **GDP/capita:** $2,400. **Economy and Industries:** Food processing, chemicals, machinery and metal products, textiles, clothing, petroleum refining and distribution, beverages, footwear, and wood. **Best Prospects for U.S. Exports:** Agricultural commodities, fertilizer, farm equipment, food processing and packaging machinery, medical supplies, data processing equipment, electrical equipment, franchising, construction equipment, and motor vehicles and spare parts. **Business Note:** In Nicaragua, the enforcement of contracts is uneven and somewhat cumbersome, as is the enforcement of judicial rulings. The rules of the game can be changed suddenly by government proclamations or shadowy politics, significantly disrupting business planning. Despite anti-corruption efforts, bribery and requests for bribes remain prevalent.

PANAMA **GDP:** $17 billion. **GDP/capita:** $5,500. **Economy and Industries:** Construction, petroleum refining, brewing, cement and other construction materials, and sugar milling. **Best Prospects for U.S. Exports:** Telecommunications services (especially call centers), insurance services, automotive parts and service equipment; air conditioning and refrigeration equipment (e.g., commercial and home air conditioning, and industrial refrigeration), and management consulting services. **Business Notes:** (1) Consumer attitudes and many brand preferences are similar to those in the United States. U.S. television, radio programs, and magazines are all available and popular in Panama. Panamanians frequently travel to the United States for vacations, medical care, study, and business. Their buying patterns and tastes are similar to those found in the United States, so U.S. goods and services are well accepted and highly competitive in most product sectors. (2) The movers and shakers of Panama are the *rabiblancos* (white tails). They dominate business and politics as a white elite.

PARAGUAY **GDP:** $26.2 billion. **GDP/capita:** $4,500. **Economy and Industries:** Sugar, cement, textiles, beverages, and wood products. **Best Prospects for U.S. Exports:** (Nonagricultural Products) computers and components; toys; sports equipment and arcade games; audio/video equipment and media; office machines and equipment; communications equipment; and tobacco products. (Agricultural Products) soybeans, cotton, meat, and timber. **Business Notes:** (1) A significant portion of the economy consists of black and gray market activities, such as smuggling both legitimate and illicit goods to and from neighboring countries. Such transactions can complicate price schedules, commission plans, and distribution control. (2) Intellectual property rights are notoriously unprotected.

PERU **GDP:** $132 billion. **GDP/capita:** $4,600. **Economy and Industries:** Mining of metals, petroleum, fishing, textiles, clothing, food processing, cement, auto assembly, steel, metal fabrication, and shipbuilding. **Best Prospects for U.S. Exports:** (Nonagricultural Products) oil and gas field machinery; Internet services; tourism; security and safety equipment; food processing and packaging equipment; architectural, construction, and engineering services; cosmetics and toiletries; and mining equipment. (Agricultural Products) hard wheat, yellow corn, soybean meal, dairy products (whey and cheese), and pet food. **Business Note:** U.S. products are well regarded in Peru. Nonetheless, and similar to neighboring Chile in this respect, its orientation to the Pacific makes competition from Asia a significant factor.

PUERTO RICO **GDP:** $48 billion. **GDP/capita:** $12,000. **Economy and Industries:** Tourism, construction, pharmaceuticals, manufacturing. **Best Prospects for U.S. Exports:** Strong growth has occurred in the island's orders for industrial catalysts used in producing drugs, fuel oils, gasoline, organophosphorous compounds, and for parts and accessories for automatic data processing machines.[39] **Business Note:** Puerto Rico buys a great majority of its petroleum products and raw materials from U.S. suppliers. Its dollar currency eliminates all currency risks and exchange costs for U.S. traders and investors.

URUGUAY **GDP:** $32 billion. **GDP/capita:** $10,000. **Economy and Industries:** Food processing, electrical machinery, transportation equipment, petroleum products, textiles, chemicals, and beverages. **Best Prospects for U.S. Exports:** Chemicals (including agricultural), manufactured goods and machinery, transport equipment, food processing machinery, computer hardware and software (pending passage of copyright legislation), office machinery, environmental technologies, telecommunications, and medical and laboratory equipment. **Business Note:** Despite Uruguay's poor economic performance over the last few years, U.S. exporters should not overlook good business opportunities there. The country's proximity to Brazil and Argentina, combined with its manageable market size, make it a good entry point for firms considering selling to MERCOSUR. U.S. products and services are highly regarded. U.S. companies are seen as providers of high quality goods and services with a good reputation for backing their products.

VENEZUELA **GDP:** $151 billion. **GDP/capita:** $6,200. **Economy and Industries:** Petroleum, iron ore mining, construction materials, food processing, textiles, steel, aluminum, and motor vehicle assembly. **Best Prospects for U.S. Exports:** Telecommunications services and equipment, oil and gas machinery, electrical power systems, franchising, airport equipment, computer services and software, and tourism. **Business Notes:** (1) As sales support, service, and spare parts are essential to success in equipment sales, it is important to use a representative who can provide them. (2) Franchisors will find that Venezuelans are used to U.S. services and that this sector has been especially strong even during the recent economic crises.

FINDING FACT WITHIN FICTION

To err is human. It also explains why humans seem routinely prone to snatch defeat from the jaws of success. Dr. William Mayo, founder of the eponymous clinic, prayed, "Lord, deliver me from the man who never makes a mistake, and also from the man who makes the same mistake twice."[40] The myths and corrections that follow are not designed to prevent you from erring, rather, to err within Mayo's limits.

Myth no. 1: *Latin America is pretty much the same. What works in one country will work in all.*

The Quick Notes summaries in this chapter and in Chapter 1 highlight some of the differences among Latin America's countries. While the descriptions confirm the area's variety in statistical terms, they mask the more subtle differences that inhibit the transferability of business practices among its twenty societies.

Many of the differences existed long before Columbus, when the region was inhabited by indigenous populations that varied from Stone Age primitives to some of the world's most advanced civilizations. That early diversity was reinforced during the colonial era by a cultural legacy of divisiveness imported from Spain, a country of notorious regionalism, quixotic self-fixation, and feudalistic isolation. The effects of that historical disparity are magnified today as one experiences behavioral differences traceable to ethnic influences seen in the indigenous core of Bolivia, Peru, Ecuador, and Guatemala; the European flavor of Argentina, Uruguay, Chile, and Costa Rica; and the Negro presence in large parts of Brazil, Cuba, and the Dominican Republic. That historical and ethnic variety is overlaid by systematic differences in lifestyles attributable to the physical isolation imposed by one of the world's most fractured and complex geographies.

Given the ample foundations for differences in human behavior, it is no surprise that business conduct and management practices vary greatly across the region. A primary determinant is the degree to which a country has opened its markets to global competition. A case in point is Chile. Chile opened its markets in 1976, ten to fifteen years before other Latin American countries let the invisible hand of the market, rather than the visible foot of the state, guide their economies. Today, many consider that Chilean firms exhibit some of the most enlightened management practices in the region, more progressive than many firms in Central America, for example, where globalization was slower to arrive. The vast difference in Latin America's business environments and levels of managerial professionalism make it hazardous to assume a one-size-fits-all approach to the region.

Myth no. 2: *Free trade means exporting U.S. jobs south of the border.*

Do free trade agreements pull down the flush handle on the U.S. economy? Many see free trade as a downward spiral, swirling jobs away to low-wage foreign countries and draining the U.S. standard of living. Conclusive research on the issue shows a very different outcome: one that results in rising living standards for free trade countries.[41,42,43] How can hard opinions be so at odds with hard facts? The theory of comparative advantage could resolve that question, but its explanation is as tedious as a clam's night out. Moreover, it is at least two steps removed from the real answer.

The first step is when a consumer moves to the cash register with a purchase. Her mind is not on trade statistics, unemployment figures, or the product's country of origin. Her mind is on value: the product's appeal relative to its cost.

The second step is the journey the product took to the store to earn its country-of-origin mark. Did the product come to the United States after being manufactured abroad? Or was one part produced overseas and another in the United States? Or was the product mostly produced in the United States? The difference determines whether the movement of the product left all revenues overseas or if it left some cash in the pockets of U.S. workers and companies.

That difference, in turn, often depends on how much unskilled labor it took to make the product. When unskilled labor surpasses about 20 percent of production costs, companies begin to consider sourcing offshore. As unskilled labor content rises beyond that threshold, firms that do not move their unskilled functions to low-cost sites risk being priced out of the market by foreign production. Not moving today, in order to protect some unskilled workers, can mean having to lay off all employees tomorrow. Moving unskilled operations now to, say Mexico, enables companies to keep their higher-skilled U.S. workers on future payrolls. It allows firms to stay in business by keeping their competitive high-value-added functions (like research, precision manufacturing, and design) in the United States, and sending noncompetitive, low-value-added activities (like assembly) to lower-cost sites. Moreover, by engaging in shared production in Latin America, U.S. firms can retain their supplier roles. Experience shows that sourcing from Asia sooner or later means surrendering manufacturing and assembly to Asian competitors.

It is naïve to deny that the road to globalization can be brutal to those who cannot maintain their competitive pace, and menacing to those whose privileged positions depend on maintaining the status quo. But it is even more myopic to believe that the key to a strong economy is to protect the unprotectable by paying high wages for low skills. The historical record and today's reality confirm commonsense logic in showing that a strong economy rests on maintaining a trained, highly productive, and well-paid workforce. Any other alternative dooms companies to financial failure, workers to falling incomes, and consumers to low living standards.

Myth no. 3: *Free trade is destroying Latin America's environment.*

Almost all businesses tend to degrade the environment. That stark fact is evident wherever industry is found. In places like Cubatão, Brazil's center of chemical production, the air is as thick as pea soup. Yet, it is notable that the worst polluters are Brazilian, not multinational, plants. As in smog-choked Mexico City, or along the string of environmental eyesore maquiladora (assembly facility) communities that dot the Mexican side of the U.S. border, the blame can be laid at the door of poor local planning, lax government policy, and economic need.

Banning international trade will not decontaminate the world or stop global warming. Quite the contrary: If every country produced all and only the products it consumed, waste would be rife. International trade exists because of production efficiencies that are synonymous with conservation. But the environment's greatest enemy is poverty. People everywhere want to live in a healthier environment. Trade affords them the means to do so by raising their incomes. It remains a mystery why, in the words of a prominent Latin American, "[free trade] protestors have come together to save the people of developing countries from development."[44] Moreover, multinational firms—the motors of international trade—tend to be environmentally cleaner than local firms because (a) their production technologies are designed for and are attuned to global standards, and (b) the developed-country consumers of their products are more likely to penalize environmental abusers.

While industry continues to despoil Latin America's environment, international forces are at work to slow the process. In Bolivia, American Electric Power spent $5.5 million to protect millions of acres of endangered tropical forests. Brazil's Banco Axial mounted a $10 million equity fund to finance green companies in Latin America. Its ventures include a hearts-of-palm plantation in the Amazon and an organic berry operation in Chile. British-owned CDC Capital Partners focuses on socially responsible investments, having put tens of millions of dollars into agricultural and geothermal projects in Central and South America.[45]

Myth no. 4: *Latin Americans are lazy and unproductive.*

Many in U.S. industry were surprised in 1991 when Ford's assembly facility in Mexico tied with a Daimler-Benz plant in Germany for the automotive industry's annual award for quality. Since then, industry experience throughout the hemisphere proves that Latin Americans can regularly meet world-class standards of quality as well as productivity. For example, within six years of building its chip-manufacturing plant in Costa Rica, Intel doubled its investment as it saw productivity climb ahead of plan. In Brazil, Volkswagen introduced its Blue Macaw modular production system, a revolutionary partnership of subassembly suppliers that many expected would break previous industry productivity records and become the world standard during the first decade of the twenty-first century.

The issue is not that Latin Americans are incapable of producing at globally competitive levels. Rather, it is to intelligently manage their proven impressive potential for productivity. Latins work when it is time to work. When it is time to play, they play. Knowing how to manage by the Latin clock is key to raising productivity.

Myth no. 5: *Politics and corruption trump good management when doing business in Latin America.*

Not long ago this assertion would have found a solid measure of support. Prior to the 1990s, executives in Latin America spent an inordinate amount of time, energy, and (frequently off-the-books) cash maneuvering within the political system. The combination of stifling bureaucracy, corrupt officials, and the state-owned enterprises that monopolized key areas of the economy made it essential to focus daily management attention on complying with, circumventing, undermining, or swaying an unworkable structure of regulations, laws, and enforcement procedures. The demands of surviving in a political jungle left few managerial reserves available for production concerns. And as it was a seller's market, customer-centered marketing was an alien concept. Indeed, the primary functions of marketing departments involved little more than taking orders from credit-qualified customer accounts, and then dealing with the ensuing headaches of product availability and delivery.

As the protected economies of Latin America's import-substitution era gave way to more open economies in the 1990s, the prerequisite for business survival shifted from having political power to having market power. Because the primary test of market power is the ability to meet growing customer demands for world-class price, quality, and delivery standards, Latin American companies accustomed to doing business in the old way came under relentless assault from international competitors. As the wolf of globalization knocked on each door of Latin America's economies during the 1990s, its unsettling appearance quickly sorted the region's firms into two categories: (1) those that would survive into the twenty-first century because they had learned to play by the new rules of customer-focused marketing and lean production, and (2) those that had already perished or were in the process of being devoured because of their inability to gain access to the capital, management, technology, or markets needed to compete in the new global economy.

Many firms were saved from the wolf's jaws as they broke with the past and adopted top-notch management and information technology. For example, Cementos Mexicanos became a world model of productivity in the industry by managing almost all of its internal operations online. It reduced the size of its fleet of delivery trucks by using satellite systems to dispatch them to job sites, its buyers placed orders and tracked deliveries on the Net, and its managers had real-time information on inventories, finances, and sales.[46] Today, it is the world's third-largest and firstmost-profitable cement producer.

If you want to cement relationships today with firms that are destined to become tomorrow's world-class accounts, just point your marketing plan southward.

Notes

1. Robert B. Zoellick (2002), "Trading in Freedom: The New Endeavor of the Americas," speech at the *Miami Herald*'s Sixth Annual Americas Conference, October 14.
2. "Emerging Market Indicators." (2004), *The Economist*, January 10, p. 90.
3. Michelle Guevara (2003), "Window of Opportunity," *Latin Trade*, April, p. 28.
4. David Lunow (2004), "Participaciones en Empresas Latinoamericanas Vuelven a Atraer a los Inversionistas Globales," *Wall Street Journal Américas*, in *El Comercio* (Quito), January 20.
5. "Fondo de EE.UU. Compra Firma Argentina de Correos." (2004), *El Comercio* (Quito), February 2.
6. "Latin Markets Hit Their Stride." (2004), *LatinFinance*, February.
7. "Local Market's Moment." (2004). *LatinFinance*, March.
8. Hugh Dellios (2003), "Farmers See Market Wane," *Sun-Sentinel* (Fort Lauderdale), January 12, p. D1.
9. Jim Reis and Gil Cisneros (2004), "Elimination of Trade Barriers Has Been Boon to Workers, Consumers," *Chamber of the Americas* (Denver) News Bulletin, January 18.
10. Robert Zoellick (2002), "Unleashing the Trade Winds," *The Economist*, December 10.
11. Jeb Bush (2001), quoted in "Immigration Policy Under Review," *Sun-Sentinel* (Fort Lauderdale), June 10, p. A-2.
12. Carlos Adese (2003), "Lula's Early Lead," *Latin Trade*, April, pp. 31–33.
13. Jonathan Karp (2003), "Tras la batalla de Cancún, Brasil emerge con un poderoso liderazgo internacional," *Wall Street Journal Américas* in *El Comercio* (Quito), September 24.
14. David Swafford (1998), "Back to the Future," *LatinFinance*, no. 93.
15. "Manufacturers Move Out of Mexico." (2003), *World Trade*, February.
16. Sergio R. Bustos and Joachim Bamrud (1998), "Weathering the Storm," *Latin Trade*, April.

17. Mike Zellner (2003), "Securing a Shipping Seachange," *Latin Trade*, April, pp. 40–42.

18. Luis V. Dominguez and Esteban R. Brenes (1997), "The Internationalization of Latin American Enterprises and Market Liberalization in the Americas: A Vital Linkage," *Journal of Business Research 38*, pp. 3–16.

19. Mike Zellner (2003), "Internal Combustion Engines," *Latin Trade*, April, pp. 36–38.

20. "Sunset Over the River Plate" (1998), *The Economist*, June 6, p. 37.

21. Roberto Smith-Pereira (1996), "An Agenda for the New Infrastructure of the Americas," *Latin Trade*, May/June.

22. Roger A. Kerin, Eric N. Berkowitz, Steven W. Hartley, and William Rudelius (2003), *Marketing*, 7th ed., New York: McGraw-Hill/Irwin, p. 246.

23. "La Publicidad en Internet Aún No Florece." (2003). *El Comercio* (Quito), October 13, p. B1.

24. David B. Audretsch (2003), *SMEs in the Age of Globalization*, New York: Edward Elgar.

25. "Country Profiles." (2002), *CIA World Factbook 2002*, Washington, DC: Central Intelligence Agency (conversion to square miles by author).

26. *Country Commercial Guides* (various, 2002 and 2003), International Trade Administration, Washington, DC: U.S. Department of Commerce.

27. "Country Profiles." (2002).

28. *Country Commercial Guides* (various, 2002 and 2003).

29. "Country Profiles." (2002).

30. *Country Commercial Guides* (various, 2002 and 2003).

31. Author's experience and other sources (as noted).

32. Terri Morrison and Wayne A. Conway (1997), *The International Traveler's Guide to Doing Business In Latin America*, New York: Macmillan, p. 15.

33. Doreen Hemlock (2000), "Getting to Know Brazil," *Sun-Sentinel* (Fort Lauderdale), July 17, pp. D1, D2.

34. U.S.-Cuba Trade and Economic Council (2003). Retrieved June 26, 2004, from http://www.cubatrade.org.

35. U.S.-Cuba Agricultural/Wood/Medical Products Conference 2003 (2003). The GIC Group. Retrieved June 26, 2004, from http://www.gicgroup.com/cuba_trade_conf_2003.htm.

36. Nancy San Martin (2003), U.S. Exports Account for Large Chunk of Food Purchases," *Miami Herald* (International Edition), October 1, p. 5A.

37. U.S.-Cuba Trade and Economic Council (2002), "Realities of MarketCuba."

38. Morrison (1997), p. 159.

39. "Puerto Rico in Figures." (2002), Government Development Bank for Puerto Rico, www.gdb-pur.com.

40. Louis E. Boone (1992), *Quotable Business*, New York: Random House, p. 239.

41. *Globalization, Growth and Poverty* (2001), Washington, DC: World Bank.

42. Gary Burtless, Robert Z. Lawrence, Robert E. Litan, and Robert J. Shapiro (1998), "Globaphobia: Confronting Fears about Open Trade," Washington, DC: Brookings Institution.

43. David Dollar and Aart Kraay (2002), "Spreading the Wealth," *Foreign Affairs*, January/February, pp. 120–133.

44. Ernesto Zedillo [President of Mexico, 1994–2000] (2003), in a speech at Quinnipiac University, April 29.

45. Jennifer Galloway (2000), "Clean, Green, and Latin," *Latin Finance*, April, pp. 24–26.

46. Doreen Hemlock (2000), "Surging Mexican Cement Giant Goes High-Tech," *Sun-Sentinel* (Fort Lauderdale), December 18, p. 6.

Part II

WHY AND HOW LATIN AMERICANS DO BUSINESS DIFFERENTLY

In business, as in war, understanding the terms of engagement is the first step toward winning the battle. But make no mistake about it: Business in Latin America is conducted under different terms of engagement than you will customarily encounter in the United States. Understanding the different terms of engagement, and how they can affect you, is the pivotal factor controlling the success or failure of your Latin American business venture.

Differences between Latin American and U.S. approaches to doing business flow from differences in regional mind-sets. These differences, in turn, can be most easily understood and used to your advantage if they are considered as springing from two separate, but continuously interacting forces: history and culture. High-quality studies conclude that history and culture are the fundamental determinants of national well-being and the conduct of business.[1,2] Even though the line dividing these intertwining forces is seldom sharply defined, history and culture represent conceptually legitimate, as well as comfortably familiar categories into which a large and complex body of information may be conveniently partitioned for easy understanding.

Thus, Part II is organized around the roles that history (see Chapter 3) and culture (see Chapter 4) play in shaping the terms of business engagement in Latin America. The aim, in these two chapters, is to provide a working understanding of the different mind-sets that are at the front line of business engagement between U.S. and Latin American executives. Toward that end, Chapters 3 and 4 draw judiciously from a massive body of literature on Latin American history and culture, selecting and describing the forces that make sense from a business perspective. Thus, the intent here is not to extract a full-core sample of the geology that underlies the terrain on which business forces engage one another in the Americas, but to convey a swift impression of the overall lay of the land. Only by understanding how your new Latin American business associates think, live, and do business will you be able to engage them under the most advantageous terms.

Notes

1. Lawrence E. Harrison (1992), *Who Prospers? How Cultural Values Shape Economic and Political Success*, New York: Basic Books.

2. David S. Landes (1998), *The Wealth and Poverty of Nations: Why Some Are So Rich and Some So Poor*, New York: Norton, pp. 4–11.

Chapter 3

The Historic Legacy

CIVILIZATIONS IN COLLISION

What should we call that historic footfall on a Bahamian beach that was destined to shake the entire earth? That 1492 event could scarcely qualify as a discovery to the tens of millions of native souls who already inhabited the Western Hemisphere. Indeed, their Asian ancestors may have preceded by 30,000 years[1] the appearance of any European in what came to be called the New World. Nor does the label encounter adequately capture the extraordinary scope and magnitude of the epochal reverberations set in motion by that first European landing.

Nothing comes close to describing how the simple occurrence of that first Spanish footfall hit our planet with the force of an asteroid. Trade patterns were shifted forever, while age-old social and economic systems were turned upside down and inside out throughout the Old and the New Worlds. The impact of the Europeans' arrival was as jolting, massive, and unceasing as are the tectonic collisions that continue to thrust the snow-capped Andes high above the steamy Amazon basin.

As with those seismic collisions, the early and ongoing effects of the Iberian people colliding with the indigenous societies of the Americas resembled a forcible rape more than a consensual union. The sheer violence of that savagely invasive encounter gave rise to a complex cultural topography that is still evolving. The historical perspective taken here focuses on describing how cultural collisions and blending caused the business environments of the two Americas to evolve in markedly divergent directions.

Among the countless reasons given to explain the different business environments, none is more compelling than the ways in which differences in market systems shape differences in business mind-sets. The mind-set determined by market structure pervades the spectrum of business decision making, spanning issues as elemental as competitive positioning, corruption, distribution strategy, customer service, target-market selection, quality management, organizational structure, and share value.

Historical incidents provide us with a visible record of invisible economic processes. The challenge is to track those invisible processes through time, discovering in them the forces that shape the way business is done today and that define the way it will be done tomorrow. The historical record is purposely telescoped in this chapter, limiting the incidents described to those directly relevant to whether markets are inward looking and protectionist, or outward looking and open. As the difference in orientation accounts for the most durable differences in business practices in Latin America, the distinction will keep our story concise and to the point.

1492–1981: SELF-DETERMINATION IN CHAINS

During most of Latin America's first 490 years of existence, business practices were shaped by inward-looking, government-regulated markets that contrasted with the laissez-faire business policies then evolving in the United States. Three intertwined forces were responsible for steering Latin America toward the state-controlled economic path that would diverge so sharply from the market-controlled economy of the United States: (1) the tenacious heritage of the region's colonial past, (2) its postindependence oligarchies, and (3) its long-standing love-hate relationship with the United States.

The Cultural and Institutional Imprints of Colonialism

The paths taken by colonialism left deep imprints that survive today to uniquely mark the cultures and institutions of Latin America.

The Cultural Legacy of Colonialism

Through the mysterious workings of an unexpected destiny, our New World society was catapulted into existence from a springboard of exotic circumstances. Not since the birth of Christ had the course of human history been so irreversibly redirected as it was in 1492. To understand the effects of that long-ago event on the ways of doing business in Latin America today, you must first appreciate the very different natures of the four cultures that collided in the New World.

1. *The Iberian.* Spain and Portugal had the distinction of remaining the last battlefield in Europe where the Christian Crusade continued to be waged against the Muslim infidel. As the rest of Europe entered the Renaissance and embraced religious freedom and individual worth, Spain and Portugal established a church-state absolutist authority as a divinely inspired mechanism to carry out the religious war against the Godless Moors. The inseparable institutions of war and religion that had defined the medieval Christian world throughout Europe during the Middle Ages continued unabated in the Iberian peninsula. It was in 1492 that the fusion between the Roman Catholic Church and the feudal authority that had been building in Spain for eight centuries reached a historic fulfillment. As if that year were a coiled spring suddenly released, the world saw unleashed in Spain a climactic series of events, occurring in rapid succession, that was to shape the destiny of nations and men for the remainder of recorded history. The compression limits of history were surely tested as, in that single fateful year of 1492, Spain:

triumphed in its ten-year siege of Granada, the last Moorish stronghold in Europe, thus achieving the final goal of eight centuries of crusading.

watched as Columbus set sail for the Spice Islands of the Orient and later blundered haplessly into the unimaginably greater wealth of the New World.

consolidated, under the single rule of Ferdinand and Isabella, the five independent kingdoms that made up the core of what was to become the modern Spanish state.

sent its pope, Alexander V, to direct the Holy See in Rome as the pontificus maximus. One year later, that compliant church leader granted Spain exclusive rights to conquer the New World, west of Portugal's possessions.

expelled from its territory the Jews who had survived the fires of the Inquisition, many of whom would soon follow Columbus to the New World as Christian converts.

> produced the first grammar of a romance language. Its author, Antonio de Nebrija, would comment prophetically that language was the most powerful weapon of empire.

The confluence of these events had the effect in Spain, and to no lesser a degree in Portugal, for analogous reasons, of prolonging the momentum of the crusade mentality, making the conquest of the New World pagans simply an extension of the conquest of the Islamic Moors. As in that earlier epoch, Spain and Portugal committed themselves wholly to securing the Americas for God and for king. Their zeal to defend the religious doctrine was viewed as nothing less than defending the cause of civilization in its age-old struggle against barbarism. The nobility of their cause left no latitude for non-Christian beliefs.

To maintain the purity of the faith in the colonies, Spain permitted no one to migrate who was not Christian and a loyal citizen. Spain's strict emigration policies produced a far more homogeneous group of European settlers than did England's policies, which caused the lands of the future United States to be settled by diverse groups of English, French, German, Danish, Dutch, Chinese, and other nationalities. The difference between Spain's and England's policies stemmed from the different aims they had for their respective American possessions. As Spanish America was already inhabited by civilized peoples whose numbers exceeded the population of Spain, there was little reason to encourage massive emigration. Spain simply needed to reorganize the way the new colonies' wealth was being exploited by replacing the native ruling class with loyal Spaniards. In the English colonies, a different set of conditions dictated a different emigration policy. The small population of Stone Age natives and scarce deposits of mineral wealth found in its colonies shaped the Crown's need to send large numbers of hard-working Europeans to convert the vast wilderness into agricultural land. The manufactures needed by that large population of farmers would then create a captive market for the products of English industry. Accordingly, England set no restrictions on the number, the nationality, or the religion of emigrants to Anglo America.[2] It could hardly have been foreseen at the time that those differing colonial policies created attitudes toward manual labor, individual achievement and worth, and civic responsibility in Anglo America that would diverge sharply from those that evolved in Spanish America.

In colonial Latin America, it was unrealistic to believe that life outside of a feudal, militaristic Christianity could exist. Today, we feel the same way about the existence of a civilized society without an organized national economic and political structure. Such pervasive and uncompromising intolerance helps to explain why, in Spain and Portugal, there remained much greater popular acceptance of autocratic and feudal rule than in the rest of Europe. Iberian claims to nobility were invariably traceable to the bloody exploits of some ancestral soldier who had wrested by force lands that he then settled and ruled. The exalted figure of the soldier led to contempt for manual labor and a readiness to resort to military means to achieve political ends. The glorification of the exploiter left neither compassion for the exploited nor support for the rule of impartial law. In addition to engendering the cult of an authoritarian military, Spain's and Portugal's mediocre records as economists and statesmen were also transferred to the New World, thus perpetuating for almost five more centuries a legacy of feeble economic and political institutions. That legacy is fundamental to understanding why that first Spanish footfall on a remote Bahamian beach was to doom all further economic and social advance of the New World's indigenous peoples that, over the previous 30,000 years, had evolved into such remarkable civilizations as the Inca, the Maya, and the Aztec.

2. *The Indian.* Indian, as a term to describe the native residents of the New World, is used advisedly. While Indian has no unusually pejorative connotation in English, the term *indio* in Latin America (at least implicitly) refers to an uneducated and socially inferior individual. To avoid being offensive, *indigena* (indigenous) should be used.

Living indigenous traditions in countries such as Bolivia, Peru, Ecuador, Guatemala, and Mexico form the cultural cornerstones of modern life in these countries. Pre-Columbian feelings of harmony with nature and stoicism clashed with the Iberian drive for wealth and domination under the triple-threat banners of God, Gold, and Glory.

Nevertheless, the pre-Columbians' intimacy with the forces of nature in no way diminished an intense interest in distant commerce by native inhabitants of the New World. Numerous surprising discoveries found throughout the Americas attest to a long-established, remarkable trading prowess. Archeologists have unearthed from ancient Peruvian tombs artifacts fashioned from turquoise traced to the U.S. Southwest, emeralds from Colombia that had been used ritually in Mexico before the time of the Aztecs, and amber from the Dominican Republic buried in pre-Inca Andean sites.

But even the local trading patterns found in modern times in Latin America are the surviving features of a far-distant past. Today, the open-air markets held in the region's small towns and villages have their origins in age-old networks of interlocking village markets. Highland buyers of one commodity, lowland cacao beans, for example, were producers and sellers of another commodity, potatoes, and spirited haggling would take place as the terms of exchange were settled. Because local markets also functioned as a place to exchange gossip and the news of the day, they became centers of social activity for natives who led otherwise isolated existences. The indigenously flavored institution of open-air markets is a common and colorful mainstay of the Latin American lifestyle. It shapes the instruments and instincts with which Latins approach business situations. Consequently, it is therefore not surprising that today, many Latins are gregarious and move naturally and effortlessly along a spectrum of roles: at one moment bargaining aggressively, at another displaying an infectious sense of humor, and at yet another serving as gracious hosts. Anglos who have not been exposed from such an early age to the same freewheeling marketplace atmosphere may at first be disconcerted as their Latin opposites shift fluidly back and forth between roles seemingly scripted for different business and social situations.

3. The Mestizo. The most visible and prevalent social evidence of Iberian conquest are the descendants of European conquistador fathers and Indian mothers. The hybrid child of the Old and New Worlds soon became the dominant element in the social fabric of Latin America. Today's factory worker, national president, small farmer, army general, barber, cabinet minister, taxi driver, corporate CEO, artist, university professor, or physician is most likely to be a mestizo. Exceptions to mestizo dominance in Latin America today are found in the countries of Argentina, Uruguay, and Chile, societies in which, prior to the massive waves of European emigration that began in the mid-nineteenth century, peoples of mixed European and Indian blood also constituted the majority.

During three centuries of colonial rule, mestizos were viewed as combining the worst traits of the Iberian and the Indian and deplored as being deceitful, lazy, and unstable. Unrecognized by his father and raised neither as an Indian nor as a European by his mother, the mestizo yearned to be part of the world of wealth and status in which his European blood-father lived. The ferment of a century of wars of independence and civil uprisings gave him that opportunity. Between the early nineteenth and early twentieth centuries, he won status by moving upward into roles of military and political leadership. As he gained power through allegedly liberal revolutions, the mestizo partially displaced the criollo (of Spanish blood, but born in the new world) oligarchies and took over their businesses and property, their European ways, and their disdain for the Indian.

4. *The Negro.* Of the some 12 million Africans brought to the Western Hemisphere between 1500 and 1850, the greatest number went to Latin America.[3] Brought chained and branded as chattel to both Anglo America and Latin America, the Negro arrivals occupied the social status of slaves in both societies. Over time, it became common for the Negro in Latin America to gain his freedom peacefully and become integrated with the rest of society. By contrast, the Negro who won freedom in the United States, was segregated from white society.

That does not mean that there was and is no color-based prejudice in Latin America. Rather, it is differently defined, based on the amount—rather than the mere presence—of color. In slave-era Latin America, the pure Negro was regarded as inferior, but every drop of white blood raised his status. That tradition continues today in countries like Brazil and the Dominican Republic, where most of the populace can claim some Negro ancestry. In those societies, nearly imperceptible differences in skin coloration are the central determinant of one's position within the social hierarchy. The converse applies to the United States, where Negroes were an easily identifiable minority and possessing a single drop of Negro blood was sufficient to taint one's social status.[4]

The Institutional Legacy of Colonialism

Spain's colonization of the Americas was an enterprise of epic proportions. The costs of maintaining the sword and the cross as the two front lines of conquest were sizable. To finance the immense expenses of its military and missionary advances in the New World, Spain organized her new colonies as cash cows. They were exploited as captive subsidiaries with the aim of providing for their own operating costs and of paying dividends to the Crown. In keeping with their status as cash-cow subsidiaries, the colonies' huge surpluses were drained off to support the royal treasury, rather than reinvested to further their own economic development. Saying, "Get gold, humanely if possible, but at all hazards—get gold,"[5] King Ferdinand succinctly expressed the executive summary of colonial Spain's equivalent of a business plan.

Spain imposed pervasive controls over virtually every aspect of commercial activity in the colonies. If you wanted to export cacao, for example, you would have to grow it in Venezuela. Sugarcane could only be raised in the Caribbean. Chilean colonists were not permitted to raise tobacco, but could grow wheat.[6] Five hundred years ago, Spain's efforts to control every minute detail of economic life in the colonies gave rise to five durable institutions that shaped the business system of the New World. Although today they are gradually yielding to the forces of globalization, those institutions—statism, civil law, corruption, personalism, and the cult of power—still survive as the strongest strands of connective tissue that join together a common business culture found throughout the republics of Latin America. Let us trace the origin of each of these historic strands, and the path it has taken to arrive at today's business practices.

1. Statism. Just as the visible legacies of the Iberian conquerors survive today in imposing churches, plazas, and fortresses, so has the less-visible imprint of statism lasted into our own time. While in the United States, the capitalist government's role is to provide an environment to stimulate market-driven, bottom-up economic forces, in statist Latin America the role of government has been to control the economy through top-down mandates. Rigid, Crown-controlled monopolies curbed the ability of private business initiatives to respond to market opportunities. Then, and for most of the 500 years thereafter, private enterprise was assigned to a seat at the back of the bus. Where statism has held sway, private enterprise and economic growth have suffered. By transferring its feudal version of statism to the colonies five centuries ago, Spain forged an antibusiness mold that still shapes the perceptions many Latin Americans have of the private sector.

Spain's bias against private enterprise had its roots deeply entrenched in the soil of elitist tradition. The condescension accorded to business activity is reflected in the etymology of *negocio*, the Spanish word for business (*negocão* in Portuguese). *Negocio* is derived from *negación del ocio*, literally "negation of leisure." The word reflects the classic Greek belief that nothing of creatively redeeming value can be achieved in the absence of leisure. In contrast to the Anglo concept of business (busy-ness) as the antithesis of leisure, the cultural attitude reflected in the Spanish and Portuguese languages is indicative of a predisposition to view those who engage in the practice of business as pursuing ends that are somehow intellectually empty, socially suspect, or ethically bankrupt. Over time, the Iberians' arrogantly elitist disdain for business became the cornerstone of

Latin America's popular scorn for capitalism. It is ironic that the antibusiness (and antimanual labor) attitude of an elitist European aristocracy became the anticapitalist and anti-U.S. ideological rallying cry of Latin American populists. The emotionally inflated economic nationalism and contempt for capitalism they espoused discouraged the very international trade and investment that held the key to alleviating Latin America's massive poverty.

By allowing politicians and bureaucrats to control the business of the New World, Spain let slip between its fingers the wealthiest windfall discovery of all time. By wasting its New World bonanza on frivolous consumption and dynastic wars, Spain forfeited the opportunity to invest productively in developing its economy at home. Having coupled political paralysis with economic incompetence, Spain became the pauper of the major Old World empires by the early years of the seventeenth century and created an enduring image of economic ineptitude, prompting commentary like the following: "A City friend has confided to me the secret of his successful investment policy. Never, he says, invest in a country which has been previously governed by Spain. This principle has kept him out of trouble."[7] Spain's anti-free-enterprise posture was transferred to Latin America where state-run economies yielded a bitter recipe for bloated payrolls and inefficient companies, saddling consumers with overpriced, shoddy goods, and choking off individual initiative. The resulting economic sclerosis reinforced and perpetuated the spectacle of poverty that has plagued the human condition in Latin America for centuries.

2. *Civil Law and the Legal Labyrinth.* The legal system and institutions that are familiar to Anglo executives are not the same ones practiced in three-fourths of the rest of the world, including Latin America. Whereas the English colonists carried with them the common-law system practiced in England, the Iberian conquerors brought to the New World the Napoleonic Code version of the Roman civil law system that had been developing in Europe for almost twenty centuries. In this manner, two very distinct systems of law developed in the New World: common law in Anglo-America and civil (or code) law in Latin America.

A key difference between civil law and common law is that under the former, the presumption of a right to act always rests on a judicial ruling, in other words, the limits of what is permissible are predefined under a strict code of legal behavior. Under common law, it is presumed that a right to act exists unless otherwise restricted by law. As the codified norms of what constitutes legitimate action under civil law seldom change, over time civil law becomes increasingly distant from currently accepted behavior. Common law, on the other hand, is founded on a continually unfolding series of rulings that constitute recent precedent, thus enabling the law and human behavior to evolve along parallel tracks.

Because legislation under civil law is considered to be all-embracing, a Latin American lawyer will first search for arguments in the statutes, then in scholarly commentary on the statutes, and finally in specific cases. In contrast, a U.S. common-law lawyer will first look to cases, then to statutes. The primacy of legislated statute under civil law reduces the discretionary authority of judges who, in many Latin American countries, take office soon after graduating from law school and passing a lenient qualifying examination.[8] Enjoying more power than judges are prestigious legal scholars, whose influential written opinions may represent a major factor in the success and cost of a legal action.

The sheer number of regulations and rules in a civil law system means that legal actions that would be straightforward and uncomplicated under U.S. common law can be onerous in Latin America. Even the simplest document must be notarized and attached with the appropriate paid stamps, seals, and signatures. Paperwork invariably takes more time to complete than in the United States. One study, for example, showed that the process of getting the permits to set up a small business in Peru took 289 days. The regulatory requirements for the same business in the United States were obtained in one morning.[9] Another study revealed that among seven major world regions, the number of procedures and the time required to enforce contracts was greatest in Latin America and the Caribbean.[10]

The obsession with formal procedures turns a petty government bureaucrat into a king in the realm of ludicrous paper shuffling that both Anglo and Latin executives find exasperatingly inefficient and venal. But because these archaic bureaucratic requirements must be strictly satisfied, a thriving cottage industry of *corredores* (paperwork runners) and *tramitadores* (bureaucracy fixers) has existed since the sixteenth century to shorten the permit cycle. These solutions to the inefficiency problems, of course, are paid for by fees that become a necessary cost of doing business, thus merely replacing a large waste of money with a somewhat smaller one.

In that virtually every conceivable human act has already been spelled out under civil law codes, contracts tend to be shorter than under common law. That does not make civil law contracts any less subject to careful review by a qualified lawyer whose role should be to make the legal provisions and implications of your deal formal and crystal clear from the outset. For example, not all Latin American countries allow their citizens to maintain unauthorized accounts outside of the country. As a result, you must be cautious about agreeing to make payments outside of the country of your Latin American associate. Special caution should also be exercised in defining what constitutes an act of God as a basis for excusing nonperformance. While an earthquake could be a pardonable event for not meeting a production delivery or contract deadline in both the United States and Latin America, the same symmetry may not apply if a workers' strike caused the delay. Latin American laws are so protective of labor that a nonperforming party might well prevail in a Latin American court with the argument that it was beyond the reasonable ability of management to avoid the strike and its consequences.

Given the rigidity of the colonial civil law system, it was virtually impossible to accomplish any productive economic undertaking if one acted in full compliance with the law. Indeed, sixteenth-century colonial officials, knowing the irrelevance of Crown laws to the reality of life in the colonies, commonly operated under the maxim: "Obedezco, pero no cumplo" (I obey, but I do not carry out). The colonial practice of maintaining an inflexible, but unenforceable system of rules encouraged the widespread disregard and selective application of the law that has plagued Latin America for centuries. The ongoing practical effect of that lengthy tradition can be seen today in Latin America's highly evolved, almost innate sense of *olfato político* (political nose, or "smarts"). It is that nose for politics that enables Latins to know, in any given situation and at any given moment, where the constantly shifting line is drawn that separates written law from real law that is being enforced. Because of the play in the steering system that guides the course taken by real law, you should rely on local counsel to avoid potentially costly surprises. For example, a licensing agreement may need to be creatively structured to defend a company's patent or copyright if the courts may not be relied upon to protect intellectual property.

While litigation can be a viable, cost-effective means for a company to protect its interests in the United States, it is usually a less-satisfactory option in Latin America. The likelihood of delays in congested court systems, low tort recoveries, high potential for "losing" files, and absence of a discovery process, can make one wary about bringing lawsuits in Latin America. If differences cannot be settled amicably, then mediation by a party known to and respected by both sides should be attempted. Because both placation and mediation may fail, it is advantageous to write into your agreement a clause that provides for dispute resolution under the jurisdiction of a U.S. court or arbitration process. Prior to relying on that clause, however, you should verify that the decision of the U.S. court or arbitration panel will be recognized and enforced in Latin America.

Many disputes can be avoided simply through a clear understanding of key differences between common-law and civil-law terminology. For example, U.S. executives looking to set up joint-venture operations in Latin America may step off on the wrong foot because of a misinterpretation of what the term corporation signifies under civil law. Under common law, a corporation is a sovereign creation. As such, it is common for legal counsel to be in attendance during its establishment, and extensive clauses to protect the parties are written into the formal agreement. Under civil law, however, a corporation is simply a product of an agreement between two or more parties. The Spanish term *Sociedad Anónima* (anonymous society) expresses the confidential partnership nature of a relationship based on personal trust, rather than on legalistic formality. The resulting contrast in interpretation can create unwanted conflict when, in an attempt to put an agreement in place based on the rule of law, U.S. executives surround themselves with lawyers. The presence of so much legal firepower at a meeting presumably intended to cement a relationship based on mutual trust may not be understood by Latin American executives. They may be justified in feeling that there would be no more need to bring a lawyer to a meeting between trusted friends than there would be to use legal counsel in a meeting between husband and wife, unless one of the spouses was not acting out of trust.

As Latin American courts have often favored the rights of a lender over those of a stockholder (particularly if a minority, foreign stockholder is involved), some experienced investors have structured an innovative financial mechanism to protect a minority equity position. To establish their investment as debt, instead of equity, they exchange their cash injection for bonds convertible to voting preferred stock of the Latin American firm. As the bond issue carries covenants (e.g., a minimum liquidity ratio of 2:1) that Latin American firms would not ordinarily meet, the investor is in a legally tenable position to declare the borrower in default. The ability to pull the rug out from under their majority partners' weak or unscrupulously managed operation at any time levers minority investors into a controlling position at the same time that it increases the security of their principal and current cash flow. Later, when propitious to do so, investors can exercise their option to become shareholders.

3. Corruption. A common challenge to doing business in Latin America is learning how to detect and respond to the sometimes flexible ethical standards of those with whom you must do business. While especially prevalent in government procurement, revenue collection, and permit-issuing functions, corruption is difficult to countenance anywhere. The money that lines a corrupt official's pocket could otherwise have been invested in education, health services, or infrastructure to bolster economic productivity and social well-being. The lack of official integrity is additionally damaging because the mere image of corruption keeps away the legitimate investment needed to bring Latin American companies and economies into the global mainstream.

Although business profit is often the victim of corruption, profit orientation is also its source. As profit margins grew narrower under the pressure from competitive world markets in recent years, the high cost and risk of making payoffs became less affordable. Because it takes two to tango, as bad business practices drove out good ones, firms that refused to be party to dishonest transactions stayed out of markets where payoffs were required to do business. While multinational firms had the luxury of being able to leave one country and relocate operations in another, the far more numerous smaller local firms were under pressure to go along with bribes demanded by sticky-fingered officials. Because most Latin American firms lack the luxury of having an alternative to living with corruption, the unavoidable operating reality they face should serve to moderate the voices of those who would criticize them for being more willing to use bribes than would U.S. firms.

The profit opportunities created by the appalling inefficiencies of state-owned enterprises (SOEs) were an especially fertile field for corrupt officials to demand payoffs or kickbacks. The sky-high duty rates that protected SOEs created strong incentives to smuggle foreign-made goods into local black markets where quality-starved consumers would pay premium prices. The key factor underpinning the smugglers' success were customs and law enforcement officials who agreed to turn a blind eye in exchange for a portion of the illicit profits.

Neither Anglo Americans nor Latin Americans enjoy being shaken down by petty bureaucrats or powerful political figures. But, among Latin Americans, corruption at both levels of public office came to be widely, but grudgingly, countenanced for different motives. Contributing to tolerance for corruption at the lower levels of government was the fact that payoffs performed an income-redistribution function. Bureaucrats, clerks, and police officials were usually paid low wages because they were politically or socially blocked from gaining higher-paying jobs in the public-sector hierarchy or in family-controlled firms. Hence, the proceeds from payoffs supplemented their meager salaries, making it possible to afford their lower middle-class existence. As those who used frequent public services belonged to the privileged class of wealthy landowners or industrialists, receiving a payoff from the powerful was sanctioned by social justice. Viewing payoffs as a mechanism to redress the sprawling inequalities of income distribution in Latin America had a ring of legitimacy in a society where the rich regularly evaded paying taxes and the poor had little access to social benefits.

As an Anglo business executive, your refusal to make a payoff may trigger outrage on the part of the public official who solicited it. Moral disdain and hostility are common, understandable reactions when a Latin official attempts to put the bite (known in Spanish by its literal equivalent, *mordida*) on them. Offending a public official by curtly rejecting his modest (at least, to him) request for a gratuity may be only marginally more productive than provoking an armed terrorist by insulting his religion or questioning his parentage. It is more fruitful to view the occasional expectation of a gratuity as belonging to the same moral category as tipping waiters. In each case, you are supplementing the low wages paid by their employer.

A different ethical norm attaches to payoffs made to high-level government officials. Wholesale corruption existed in colonial times in Latin America and was quietly tolerated at the uppermost levels of government. The reason it was tolerated is qualitatively different than the rationale for sanctioning corruption at the lower levels. During colonial times, a bankrupt Crown routinely granted public offices to the highest bidder in auctions held under the supervision of the viceroy. It was implicitly understood that the winning bidder had the right to recoup his investment. Therefore, once installed, the new officeholder's first priority was to use all means possible (short of daytime looting) to accelerate his payback. The attitude that an official was tacitly entitled to charge others for access to the prerogatives of his office was normal for the time and helped to perpetuate the popular view that authority was a license to steal.

So it happened that generations of Latin Americans grew up with the view that corruption was a natural condition of power, and it was normal for anyone in a position of authority to expect a payoff in return for bestowing favors. While Latins may understand and be resigned to the reasons for corruption among low-level bureaucrats and high-level public officials, they do not do so without protesting. Indeed, heated complaints about pervasive government corruption and the outrageous behavior of greedy officials often approach the status of a national pastime. At odds with today's broad public displeasure with the murky financial behavior of public officials, is the telling fact that no simple translation exists in Spanish for accountability. Awkward efforts to coin an equivalent exist, such as *obligación de rendir cuentas* (obligation to render accounts). But the inability of the Spanish and Portuguese languages to produce a succinct, one-word description to express an expectation of transparency and honesty in financial dealings testifies to a mind-set still hobbled by a centuries-old toleration of impugn authorities.

It is an unpleasant fact that ethically offensive people will be found in public offices in both Latin America and in the United States. The incidence of corruption among public officials in Latin America, however, is less than one would believe. Nonetheless, if you do business in Latin America, you come to terms with the simple truth that you find unsavory characters occupying low- and high-level positions there more often than in the United States. Moreover, the distinction between low-level and high-level bribery is more sharply defined in Latin America. While having to pay gratuities to gain the cooperation of low-level bureaucrats is a routine cost of doing business in parts of Latin America, payoff decisions involving higher-level authorities are weighed by a different set of ethical and legal norms. In the realm of ethics, your decision about whether to make payoffs to high-level officials is a moral choice; thus, it is a discretionary decision subject to your own personal standards. In the legal realm, however, the act of bribery is much less ambiguous. Making payoffs to high-level foreign officials or political figures is strictly prohibited by U.S. law, and can trigger criminal charges against your company and against you personally.

The U.S. Foreign Corrupt Practices Act (FCPA) of 1977 prohibits any U.S. firm's employees or agents to pay any foreign government official, political leader, or political candidate to gain or retain business by influencing that individual's discretionary decisions. The FCPA does not, however, bar payments made to (usually lower-level) public officials to expedite normal transactions, such as providing security services, issuing work permits, or loading perishable goods into a refrigerated hold in a timely manner. In brief, the FCPA allows you to speed or ease routine transactions by oiling the smaller cogs of bureaucracy. But beware of trying to lubricate the big wheels to gain a business advantage, such as a contract award. Disgruntled losing bidders can smell grease a continent away and may be delighted to report to U.S. authorities their suspicions of a U.S. competitor's bribe to win business. Even if such suspicions are unfounded, the expenses entailed in legal defense, disruption to operations, and negative publicity could be ruinous for smaller companies. The surest way to avoid being blindsided by the FCPA is to develop a written code of ethics, educate all your employees and agents about what it means, and ensure that accounting system controls are in place to detect trouble.

4. *Personalism*. The institution of personalism in colonial Latin America has its roots in the feudal system of land tenure and patrimony that has prevailed in Spain and Portugal since the eighth century. That durable system was transferred virtually intact to the New World.

Just as a drunk uses a lamppost for support instead of illumination, the Iberians used religion as a rationale to justify their feudal-like depredation of the Indians. As the conquest advanced, new lands wrested from the Indians, along with the right to exact labor tribute from them, were granted to the conquerors. The labor tribute was awarded to compensate the landowners' cost of bringing the Indians to a Christian salvation.

By gaining simultaneous awards of land and cheap Indian labor, the valuable mining and agricultural potential of the land could be exploited. Because those cash cow concessions were granted by royal favor, being part of a network of influential social and family alliances was critical to success. As one's official position in the colonial hierarchy was directly related to one's personal position in the colonial social order, there was no separation between the person and his prerogative to exercise the authority of his position. To this day, business relationships in Latin America are predicated on in-group personal relationships. One does business with members of the same social class and with friends whom one can trust, a practice that is encapsulated in a popular business maxim: "A good deal for my friends, the law for my enemies."

As a result, organizations in the Spanish and Portuguese colonies were highly centralized and staffed on the basis of know-who rather than know-how. Except at the pinnacle of these steep pyramids of power, lines of communication were vertical, from subordinates to their *patrones* (masters). Organizations were rigid and incapable of engendering horizontal information flows, or delegating decision making and responding flexibly—hallmarks of today's competitive flat-form organizations.

Iberian personalism was a system built on oppressive regulations enforced by entrenched bureaucrats, responsive only to their *patrones*. Public service was an unknown concept. Indeed, the public rendered service to the officeholder in exchange for favors, not the other way around. Authority within such a system was exercised for personal privilege, and common people were subjects who had to obey, rather than citizens who could claim rights. The resulting fusion of economic and social power among the elite lives on as a system of concentrated wealth, making income distribution in Latin America the most unequal in today's world.

5. *The Cult of Power.* The origins of divergent attitudes toward political authority in Latin America and the United States reach much further back in history than the colonization of the New World by Europeans. The advanced indigenous civilizations encountered by the Spanish were stratified societies, organized around powerful castes of noble birth. In contrast, the natives that English colonists found on the North American frontier were more democratic societies, fragmented into small groups, and governed by consensus.[11] Oddly, dissimilar as were the attitudes toward authority held by each of the New World native groups, each was to find that its own attitude matched the attitude of the Old World invaders who were to become their respective masters. As an accident of history, those self-reinforcing pairings would have far-reaching effects.

One of the first effects of those contrasting social attitudes was felt in the economic realm. The Spanish were able to force the Indians to work in the mines because those Indians already were accustomed to rule by an iron hand. As no similar class-based tradition existed among the more egalitarian tribes of the North American frontier, attempts made by English settlers to subjugate them to labor servitude met with failure.

As power was transferred from the conquered to the conquerors in Latin America, the indigenous authority structures remained largely intact, the primary change being the substitution of native autocrats for the Iberian variety. To maintain their faraway system of colonial autocrats under centralized Crown control, the Iberian monarchies found it essential to decentralize authority in the New World. Appointees to all key posts were selected by Iberian emperors. The possibility that any colonial authority would accumulate too much power was blunted by the checks and balances flowing from the jealousies the rival appointees felt toward one another and toward higher-ranking appointees in the colonial administration.

The cost of centralizing control at home by decentralizing control in the New World was high. The power struggles set in motion by atomizing authority among and within the political, military, and judicial realms laid the groundwork for the heavy-handed dictators, inefficient economies, and arbitrary individual rights that have darkened so much of Latin America's history. Not surprisingly, micromanagement and information hoarding are still more commonly practiced than are delegation and empowerment in Latin American organizations.

Reinforcing the tradition of rule by an absolute monarchy was the Iberian philosophic legacy of natural law. Under natural law, if a ruler acts unjustly, the citizens have a right and duty to rebel. As every citizen feels empowered to adjudicate any law, a built-in disposition toward anarchy results.[12] That tendency helps explain why, until recent times, Latin governments were more often overthrown by force than overhauled by votes. It also explains why Latins, to protect themselves against their own penchant for anarchy, were willing to tolerate strong rule as a necessary evil.[13] So it was that "the faithlessness of politicians [and] the faithful stubbornness with which people seek to believe"[14] made betrayal synonymous with political life for centuries. Democracy is a fledgling experiment in a region that remembers when every man was his own political party, idealistic rhetoric obscured venal reality, and the force of custom legitimized the custom of force.

Independence: Revolution from the Top

Early in the nineteenth century, independence from Spain and Portugal had little effect on the economic and political life of most Latin Americans. The movers and shakers behind independence were the Creole (born in the colonies) elite who acted to wrest the monopoly of trade and high public office held by the dominant Peninsular class (born in Spain or Portugal).

The postindependence power struggle among the Creole elite gave rise to the rival liberal and conservative political movements that, to this day, vie with one another to impose their own economic policies. What movement represents which policy can be confusing to Anglos because the labels used to describe them in the United States do not signify what they mean in Latin America (and, for that matter, in Europe). In general, liberals were members of the commercial class who supported free trade, foreign investment, and minimal government interference in the economy. Clinging to colonial traditions, the conservatives were more nationalistic, supporting protectionist economic policies to shield local producers from foreign competition.

The Birth of Import Substitution Industrialization (ISI)

While power changed hands between liberal and conservative political factions for much of the latter nineteenth century and until about 1930, economic policy in most of the region was dominated by liberals. But, for economies dependent on exporting a narrow range of raw materials to meet the demand of the high-growth markets of the United States and Europe, the Great Depression that gripped the world in the 1930s was a death sentence. The liberal era ended abruptly as world demand for Latin America's sugar, meat, wool, coffee, copper, and other primary products plummeted. Turning away from outwardly oriented trade policies, Latin America embraced the conservative gospel of becoming self-sufficient in the industrial goods it previously had imported from the United States and Europe, paid for with the earnings generated by its raw material exports. That inwardly oriented policy came to be known as Import Substitution Industrialization (ISI), and it continued long after the Great Depression ended. As the developed economies focused on fighting World War II, industrial output was diverted from peacetime uses, international commerce shriveled, and Latin America was cut off from normal trade flows. High world prices for manufactures, combined with low prices for primary goods helped ISI policies continue after the war ended in 1945. But the greatest postwar impetus for Latin America's infatuation with ISI was the pronationalist fervor that grew in the 1950s, and made ISI dominant until 1982—the onset of the Lost Decade.

What was ISI's effect on business strategy? Because competition based on price, quality, and customer service was almost nonexistent in Latin America during ISI's closed-market reign, the consumer-oriented marketing that became king in the United States during the latter twentieth century was unnecessary in Latin America. Industry was plagued by poor infrastructure, rigid labor codes, unreliable suppliers, and corrupt bureaucracies. The trick for managers was simply to get product to the plant's shipping dock, even if that process regularly took place with the finesse of a blind butcher. ISI trade barriers kept out most foreign products (and also many foreign cultural influences). As protected monopolies, State Owned Enterprises (SOEs) and large family-owned companies made shoddy products, sold them at inflated prices, and relied on product-starved consumers to beat a path to their door. It is no mystery why, even now, a commonly used Spanish term for marketing is *ingeniería comercial*, or commercial engineering. The term connotes the primacy of producers and the low priority assigned to consumers. The business mind-set forged over a half-century of ISI-era economic policies is only slowly giving way to modern management practices. For that reason, you should know what signs to look for (see Table 3.2 later in this chapter) when you assess the business mind-set of Latin American executives. The traditional (ISI) and the modern mind-set often coexist among and within the region's firms.

Personalism and the Family-Owned Business

Your first impressions of the business system of Latin America are unlikely to produce many high amazement-level surprises. You will note, for example, that financial institutions are similar to, and may well be branch operations of banks you deal with in the United States. Moreover, you will find that chambers of commerce and trade associations operate along familiar lines. Furthermore, you will recognize that the legal forms of business organization are roughly analogous to structures used in the United States. But as your experience accumulates, and you peel back the surface layers, you may find that your first impressions were misleading.

A unique and pervasive feature of the Latin American business system is the prevalence of family-owned firms. The family business flourished as an institution well-adapted to survive in a closed society that trusted only in-group members and in a legal system that offered few property guarantees to outside investors and traders. As that originally closed-society institution gives way to the modern open-market environment, the function of family-owned firms in Latin America today reflects a spectrum of management attitudes ranging from traditional to modern. When you find yourself meeting with executives displaying the traditional inclinations, it will be useful to recognize their managerial peculiarities, and to estimate whether those peculiarities will (a) fade into the background as the traditional firm adapts to the competitive exigencies of modern management practices, or (b) remain as vestiges of a managerial Jurassic Age that can put a firm on the endangered species list.

Meet the family. If you deal at any length with a traditional family-owned business, you will come to understand its strengths and weaknesses. Not surprisingly, each stems from the same underlying condition: ownership and management control held in the same hands. Family control of ownership and management endows a business with undeniable advantages:

- Family owner-operators know their business upside-down and inside-out because they grew up in it. That level of intimate knowledge is seldom observed among the footloose managers of publicly held firms in the United States who move from company to company as job opportunities of the moment beckon.
- Conflict-of-interest and managerial opportunism, occasioned by separation of management and ownership are precluded, allowing objective reinvestment to be made in long-term growth.

- Because the family's of reputation and power are so reliant on the success of the family business (that usually bears the family name), the family will give its all to ward off any threat to survival in troubled times.
- If the company is not unionized, labor-management relations are likely to be harmonious. Long-time employees may enjoy favored compadre (trusted retainer) relationships with the family *patrón*.
- While particular transactions are geared toward generating short-term paybacks, overall family goals are long term. There is little incentive to rig earnings, and the complementary short-term and long-term goals impose a conservative, nonspeculative perspective on planning.
- As family companies are not publicly held, their activities, performance, organization, and plans are not a matter of public record. The resulting opacity makes it difficult for competitors or tax authorities to gain access to sensitive information.

These strengths have made Latin America's traditional family-owned firms enduring institutions. But other traits have left them especially vulnerable to survival threats during times of rapid change. In today's competitive environment, the chief weaknesses of traditional family-owned firms are outlined below.

- While the scale of the family-owned business can become quite large, its scope is limited by the size of the family and the interests and capabilities of its individual members.
- Decision making is informal, intuitive, and oriented toward daily operations of a nonstrategic nature.
- In their dealings with stakeholders such as suppliers, customers, employees, government officials, and other family members, family managers tend to mix rational decision making with emotional judgments.
- As a consequence of weak strategic planning, traditional family businesses become more reactive than proactive to changes taking place in their operating environment.
- If the primary incentive to maintain the firm's viability is family prestige, that motivation is not likely to be enough to achieve breakthrough innovations or lean management practices.

- The organizational structure that evolves in a traditional family firm is more indicative of the power positions and interests of individual family members than it is of the firm's key functions or competencies.
- Reluctance to divulge operating results to nonfamily creditors and investors blocks access to capital.

At one time, the traditional family firm was well suited to a stable, but weak competitive environment in which threats to the family business arose locally. In that confined setting of interlocking political, social, judicial, and business networks, the family could resolve difficulties by exercising its personal influence. In competitive global markets, however, capital, technology, and management trump family influence as determinants of success.

Capital, technology, and management, as requisites of success, can create a scenario that favors a prospective U.S. buyer, supplier, or licensor who begins serious discussions with a family-owned firm. If the U.S. firm is slow to understand the nature of the Latin firm's long-term needs, it may inadvertently forfeit an auspicious opportunity. The possibility of developing a close relationship with a U.S. firm offers the traditional family-owned firm a means to overcome any or all of the three constraints that limit its future growth. Your firm's ability to help a Latin partner overcome its capital, technology, or management constraints could give it low-cost access to a future that will pay dividends long after the profit from the initial transaction has been booked.

1. Capital. Latin American capital markets have traditionally been weak mechanisms from which to transfer private savings into productive uses. Runaway inflation made fixed-income instruments a poor choice for savers to maintain the purchasing power of their cash reserves. Small investors faired no better with equity holdings: Corrupt judges and civil-law statutes seldom favored minority shareholders. The playing field is still tilted against smaller outside investors. Take, for example, Brazil's law that allows a firm to issue up to two-thirds of its equity capital in nonvoting shares, thus giving control to insiders holding only 17 percent of stock.[15]

Company cultures of secrecy also placed small investors at risk. As managers of family-owned firms resist disclosing financial results to outsiders, nonfamily stakeholders are left in the dark about matters concerning operating performance or wrongdoing. An undoubtedly frequently true story is told about the Latin patriarch who maintained three sets of books on the family business. The first was kept for investors and bankers. It showed stunning results: Profits almost equaled gross revenues, the current ratio was astronomical, the plant was operating on a 24/7/52-week schedule to work off its huge order backlog. A second set of financials was kept for the tax authorities. It reflected a financial near-death experience: Massive losses had accumulated over the firm's 100-year history, even customers who never intended to pay had stopped buying, and the owner had to exit the building late at night through an unlighted side door, taking different routes home to avoid being assaulted by angry creditors ("Could the examiner find it in his heart to lend the owner $5 for lunch?") The third set of books, of course, reflected the firm's true condition, and was furtively removed from beneath the mattress at night for the owner to examine in secrecy.

Savings and realty. Given the disadvantages of being a small holder of debt or equity, three common means survive to manage finances. The first, used by those of limited resources or financial sophistication, is whimsically called *banco colchón* (mattress bank). Those practicing this option simply convert their local-currency savings to U.S. dollars. They are betting on the greenback's loss of purchasing power being less than that of pesos held in a local savings account and earning a negative rate of interest.

Despite today's mild inflation rates, converting pesos into U.S. dollars continues to be an option used by small savers, a factor that supports dollarization policies. But two better alternatives are open to the bigger-league players with whom you are more likely to deal. One alternative is to invest in real property. The widespread exercise of this option helps explain why realty in Latin America often sells at prices higher than comparable property in the United States. Despite its relatively high cost, investing in property was and remains a popular alternative in a traditionally agricultural society where land ownership is an important source of social prestige and personal satisfaction.

Accommodation Accounts. The final alternative is to move liquid assets outside of the country. While foreign remittance limitations have eased considerably in Latin America, tax evasion and hiding wealth are still strong appeals to quietly shift profits abroad. These are lures that could directly affect you as a U.S.-based supplier or buyer. The Latin firm plays this game with a willing U.S. partner by adjusting transfer prices. Cooperative vendors or buyers over- or under-invoice Latin firms. The difference between the real value and the invoice value of the transaction is deposited by the U.S. company into an accommodation account controlled by the Latins and, presumably, kept safe from the prying eyes of home-country tax authorities. The ruse allows profits to accumulate abroad that would otherwise have to be declared as taxable income and, often an even more important factor, be recorded at home as wealth. The motive to hide wealth is strong in countries like Colombia, Mexico, and Venezuela where sophisticated kidnappers select their victims on the basis of their wealth as reflected in the "confidential" records of banks and official agencies.[16]

Should you accede to your Latin buyer's or supplier's request to set up an accommodation account? Your decision will probably hinge on both ethical and legal concerns. While ethical concerns may be a subjective matter, legal concerns entail four concrete deliberations. First, keep your end of the deal aboveboard. Do not engage in any off-the-books transactions. This precaution will help insulate you from being attacked, or raising the eyebrows of skeptical executives, directors, or law enforcement officials. Second, be aware that the profit you have been instrumental in transferring out of Latin America may have been moved onto your own company's books as taxable income. This shift in the origin of the income could invite the attention of two tax authorities: (1) the Latin American fiscal enforcers who may find you or your firm guilty of acting as a conspirator to evade tax liability, and (2) the U.S. Internal Revenue Service (IRS) that, in applying Section 582 or other relevant sections of the U.S. Tax Code, may deny your accommodation account deposits as allowable business expense deductions. Third, you may become liable for federal money-laundering charges. Fourth, if your Latin American buyer or supplier is a political figure or a state-owned enterprise, you or your company could face criminal charges under the 1977 Foreign Corrupt Practices Act (FCPA). In sum, agreeing to set up an accommodation account should not be done capriciously. Consenting to an accommodation request is not always a cost-free means to gain good guy status with your Latin counterpart and could trigger painful consequences for both you and your company. Your decision about whether to engage in such an arrangement should be made only after consulting with legal counsel in the United States, in the country of your Latin American associate, and in the country where the account would be located.

Investment Groups. A unique group arose in Latin America during the nineteenth century as a direct consequence of both the personal character of business relationships and the inability of family firms to obtain capital through the normal channels of debt and equity financing. This body was composed of banking, industrial, and trading enterprises, and came to be called an investment group. Investment groups have functioned in most Latin American countries to channel savings within the private sector toward investment opportunities. They remain today as private sector alternatives to government-financed experiments in socialist capitalism.

Through membership in an investment group, a family firm gains access to outside capital that enables it to grow more rapidly than if it had to rely solely on retained earnings. The need and opportunity for more rapid growth became a significant factor in Latin America during the nineteenth century as production technologies became more complex and capital intensive. As a cluster of financial, commercial, and industrial firms acting through interlocking ownership, the investment group emerged to accommodate new growth needs. It became the dominant private-sector force in most of Latin America by the late twentieth century. By having access to capital from a member bank within its group, a family-owned manufacturing firm can get the working capital and investment it needs to build inventory and modernize its plant as it gears up production for world-class buyers. Such capital injections are seldom available at arm's length with a local commercial bank limited to short-term credits based on a conservative estimate of the liquidation value of pledged assets.

You can find that dealing with a member firm of an investment group can be a satisfying experience. Your firm's high credit standing, reputation for honesty, and positive letter of introduction from a U.S. correspondent of the investment group's anchor bank can open doors that would otherwise be closed to outsiders. Those doors may lead you to the Latin American equivalent of business utopia: forthright negotiations, simple closings, and on-time payments.

Technological and managerial barriers to growth can also mean opportunities for you when Latin American firms wish to expand into new areas, but lack the requisite resources to do so.

2. Technology and Management. As Latin American economies grow, demands are placed on family firms that can outstrip their ability to respond with internal resources. The resulting performance gaps occasion the need for outside capabilities to meet the challenges of new product and process technologies, new markets, new sources of inputs, or new logistical systems. As a U.S. supplier or buyer of proven competitive success, your firm may be seen by the Latin American firm as a means to extend the latter's technological or managerial reach. Many U.S. suppliers or buyers have found this scenario to be a rewarding opportunity to enter into joint ventures or strategic alliances entailing licensing, market representation, or exclusive supplier relationships.

A final suggestion when dealing with family firms: Avoid the mistake of underestimating their abilities just because they may appear managerially or technologically unsophisticated. Remember, the Titanic was built by professionals, the Ark by amateurs.

ISI: Yesterday's Economic Blessing, Today's Management Curse

Size matters. At least it has in Latin American economic performance. Imagining that the law of comparative advantage could be ignored, small countries that continued ISI policies in the 1950s learned in the 1980s that they had sacrificed competitiveness at the altar of nationalism. Falling into the trap of thinking they could be efficient in producing most of the goods they consumed, they found that scale disadvantages condemned them to being efficient in none. The lofty duties that protected high-cost local industry from cheap imports created an artificial economy that, in turn, created artificial rules of business.

The ISI era continued in Latin America much longer than it was necessary or helpful because it coincided with recordlevels of macroeconomic performance. During the decades of the 1950s, 1960s, and 1970s, Latin America's gross domestic product advanced at an average annual rate of nearly 6 percent, far outpacing the growth of the industrialized countries, and only slightly behind that of Asia's fastest-sprouting economies. Prospects seemed especially bright during the 1965–1980 period when manufacturing surged ahead at annual gains averaging 7 percent. As if foreshadowing a dark period to come, however, inflation during the same years averaged over 30 percent, and export gains were meager.[17]

The region's rapid growth in output and inflation was driven internally by subsidies to bloated state-owned enterprises (SOEs) and by entry into the money economy of massive numbers of migrants from the ISI-impoverished countryside to the city (ISI's effect was to transfer wealth from efficient agriculture to inefficient industry). The internal motors of industrialization were fueled externally by cash flows from a growing sea of foreign debt. The ability of the region to repay that debt was rooted in the assumption that prices for its exports would steadily rise. While lenders and borrowers watched those prices fall as the glut in oil and other commodities accumulated in 1981, the scene was set for the tragedy of the Lost Decade that moved center stage in 1982.

The Arrogance of Authority

Latin America's fractured geography, combined with the fractious nature of its independent people, produced local caudillos (strong men) throughout the region. As caudillos expanded their dominion by crushing or making alliances with neighboring caudillos, they became national dictators. Rule by armed force became the normal pattern of authority in Spanish America for 150 years after independence. It was not until the 1980s that more of the region's citizens lived under democratically elected governments than under dictatorships.

Today, all of Latin America except Cuba is a technical democracy. While democracy does not guarantee good rule, an open political system is the natural ally of an open economy. Working in unison, free elections and free markets undermine corruption, and reinforce the foundation of a prosperous economy. Those effects make good sense for society and for business. Indeed, doing business under today's elected governments does not require a sharp nose for the nuances of politics. As today's democratic regimes tend to be more technically oriented than their repressive predecessors, being right on policy is more vital to executives than being right on politics. That is why the best rule for involvement in Latin American politics is not to be involved.

The Tangled Histories of Two Americas

The centuries-old background of European military and religious conflicts set the course heading for the relationships that the English and Iberian settlers in the Americas would follow. Largely detached in the colonial era, those relationships often became conflictive after independence, and did not change greatly until the Lost Decade that began in 1982. That period marked a course change toward economic pragmatism, albeit one in which Latin America now is taking a more adamantly independent stance.[18] But whether conflictive or cooperative, the histories of the United States and Latin America have always been intertwined, and it is those interlaced threads that will continue to knit their destinies together in the future. This section explains how the distinct origin and evolution of the Western Hemisphere's two dominant cultural realms created differences in the ways that business is conducted. Later, I will discuss how the gap between the two is narrowing in response to forces set in motion during the Lost Decade.

The View from North to South: Shifting Latitudes and Attitudes

"Welcome to Latin America. Please set your watches back 50 years." These words formed a favorite greeting one of my 1960s-era U.S. bosses would use to welcome visitors from corporate headquarters to our Latin American subsidiary. The intention of his favorite one-line welcome was not to demean the people or the culture of the country in which the subsidiary was located. Rather, it was to warn visitors to be prepared for the different business practices and operating standards they would soon witness.

The View from South to North: The Shifting Image of the U.S. Corporation

Hardly praiseworthy were the corporate citizenship records of many U.S. companies that began migrating to Latin America in the late 1800s. The infamous habit of U.S. companies to become cozy with autocratic regimes remained evident for a half century. U.S. corporate comfort with the stable, controlled country environments provided by Latin American dictatorships fueled U.S. "banana diplomacy" policies that backed many brutally repressive despots. Powerful U.S. companies were often beyond the reach of local authority and could act with disregard to formal law.

But a 1960s incident exemplifies how times changed that immunity: Auditors working in a Latin American country's office of corporate income-tax collections supplemented their meager official salaries by soliciting bribes to "correct" the returns of firms that had underpaid their income taxes. To decide who would win the chance to exact the largest payoff, auditors would auction among themselves the rights to examine the returns of those delinquent firms they judged to be the juiciest prospects for extortion. I was pleased to learn that, among the largest companies operating in the country, only two had received no bids: my own U.S. employer and another U.S. multinational. The firms eliciting the highest bids, because they were deemed to be the largest evaders, were all locally owned. At least among that country's tax auditors, it was implicitly believed that corruption was a domestic product, not an imported behavior.

That incident is not an isolated example. Contrary to populist demagoguery, the ethical behavior of U.S. firms now operating in Latin America is generally exemplary. Taxes owed are taxes paid, contracts are won on the basis of competitive offerings rather than bribes, workers are treated honestly and rewarded for productivity, and firms follow a hands-off policy toward local politics. The relatively transparent and clean operating policies now practiced by the great majority of U.S. firms make them model citizens of the Latin America corporate community. It would be naïve to presume that those laudable practices are inspired solely by an elevated sense of civic duty. The truth is that, in the twenty-first century, long-term profits come from being perceived as a good corporate citizen.[19] Testimony that long-held feelings of resentment, envy, and jealousy of the United States are softening can be found in a remark recently made to me by a left-leaning Latin intellectual: "The only thing worse than being exploited by U.S. multinational corporations is not being exploited by them."

The growing acceptance of U.S. firms during the latter decades of the twentieth century was not based merely on their ability to deliver sorely needed capital and technology to Latin America, but on their undisputed lead in management. U.S. planning and decision-making methods have become the world's benchmark. Even the most outspoken socialist cannot seriously question the marketing, finance, and production prowess demonstrated by U.S. management. As Latin American executives become familiar with smaller U.S. firms, they gradually realize that good management is not correlated with firm size. As a result, smaller U.S. firms and Latin firms of all sizes have begun to strike deals together, many of them rooted in expectations that interactions with the former will strengthen the management capabilities of the latter.

That same motivation drives many Latin Americans to attend management seminars or to enroll in one of the many U.S.-style MBA programs being offered in the region. By the close of the twentieth century, differences were fading as business and political leaders in the two realms of the Americas found common ground on which to build trade alliances to pursue rapidly expanding opportunities in global markets. But to take that step forward, Latin America had to take two steps backward, suffering a ten-year lesson that its past policies of protectionist isolation incurred while the rest of the world was becoming a Global Village.

1982–1991: THE LOST DECADE—SYSTEM SHOCK AS A DOUBLE-EDGE MACHETE

As a lesson in how to drive economic development in rapid reverse, few examples can beat the backward race record set by Latin America during its Lost Decade of 1982–1991. By 1982, misguided ISI policies had propelled the region's debt to eight times its 1973 level, causing billions of dollars of private capital to take flight to safer regions. By 1990, per capita income had plunged, slashing middle-class purchasing power to 1972 levels. As angry street mobs demanded more money, weak governments were quick to print it. The double-digit inflation rates of previous decades soared to triple digits in the early years of the Lost Decade, then raged to quadruple and even quintuple digits during its later years.[20] Interest in the executive seminars and business consulting I was conducting in Argentina, Brazil, Mexico, and Peru shifted away from quality control, productivity improvement, and export marketing, and toward solutions for dealing with hyperinflation.

The wake-up call for the region began in 1982 as the shock waves of Mexico's default on its $80 billion debt spread throughout Latin America and beyond. The "tequila effect" signaled that ISI's financial bankruptcy had caught up to its ideological bankruptcy. The cascade of financial crises that followed fueled a series of economic, social, and political upheavals that were forever to alter the region's business landscape.

The Death Agonies of an Era

Since independence, the march of economic history in Latin America has been a succession of left and right steps as conservatives and liberals exchanged power. During the Lost Decade, it became clear that protecting inefficient industry was out of step with the march of globalization. By the Lost Decade's end in 1991, most of a desperate Latin America had committed to open markets, free trade, deregulation, and rolling out the red carpet for foreign investment—a policy program called neoliberalism.

It was no coincidence that the end of the Cold War coincided with the end of Latin America's Lost Decade. Latin Americans muted their more extreme expressions of anti-U.S. sentiment, and turned their attention toward the enviable economic record of their neighbor to the north. They asked the obvious question: Why had the economic performance of Latin America lagged so far behind that of the United States? Answers to that question could fill libraries. Significantly, the question spawns self-doubt among many Latins, as evidenced by a popular Brazilian saying, "If we had been colonized by the English and not the Portuguese, Brazil would be rich like [the United States]."[21] Table 3.1 summarizes the key historical factors that have made the economic and political paths taken by the two great cultural transplants of the New World diverge so sharply.

Table 3.1
Historical Basis of Contrast between the Economic and Political Systems of the United States and Latin America

Historical Factors	United States	Latin America
Colonial emigration policy	Unrestricted as to nationality and religion	Limited to Roman Catholics loyal to Crown
Profile of European colonists	Farmers and tradesmen. Arrived with wives or families, prepared to settle permanently.	Peasant soldiers. Sought to return home after making a quick fortune. Intermarried with native women.
Profile of indigenous inhabitants	Loosely organized, egalitarian. Small population.	Complex and stratified social structure. Large population.
Population growth	Rapid	Initially negative, then slow
Primary labor force	European colonists	Indigenous and African slaves
Religion permitted	Any Christian denomination	Roman Catholics only
Independence significance	Popular revolution against economic and political oppression	Changed only lyrics of economic tune, same elitist musical score
Access to power	Through impartial law	Through personal patronage
Responsibility for one's welfare	Individual	*Patrón* and in-group
Hiring and promotion criterion	Performance and skills	Family and social background
Social governance basis	Rule of law	Rule of men
Primary role of military	Defend against external threat	Defend against internal threat

Rediscovering the Americas 500 Years after Columbus

By the end of 1991, the curtain was falling on both the Cold War and on the Lost Decade. Nineteen ninety-two was a year in which not only had the worst social agonies of the Lost Decade been put to rest, but it was also a year that belonged to an era that was unlike any other in the region's history. By 1992, the major features of the economic environment that had typified Latin America during the previous sixty years had disappeared. Nationalistic resistance to foreign investment gave way to free capital flows, controlled economies evolved toward open trade and deregulated markets, and compulsive expansions of the money supply yielded to disciplined anti-inflationary measures.

In the political sphere, except for Cuba, dictatorships had been replaced by popularly elected regimes. After 500 years of economic and political tyranny, Latin America had learned that it could not join the future by protecting the past. Neoliberalism and democracy had become the hemisphere's watchwords by 1992.

Bumps and Turns in the Road from Closed Economies to Global Markets

The fiscal and monetary belt-tightening that most of Latin America had practiced during the Lost Decade was beginning to pay off during the decade of the millennium transition. From the 1980s to the 1990s, the growth in per capita GDP was higher in Latin America than in any other developing region in the world. During that same period, the proportion of trade in the region's GDP grew from 25 to 30 percent, and levels of child mortality, child labor, and illiteracy fell sharply.[22] Positive results encouraged policymakers during the 1990s to launch a raft of economic policy reforms. While expectations for the prosperity the new policies would bring were high, that raft of reforms had yet to reach the opposite shore by 2004.

Indeed, the combination of Latin leaders having oversold the immediacy of neoliberalism's benefits and the too-slow implementation of the full scope of its policy implications are the probable reasons why there is growing disappointment in the region with free-market economics.[23] Hopes for progress in Latin America have foundered before. Still, the evidence routinely mounts that these early years of the twenty-first century are part of the pivotal period in a massive and fundamental transformation of Latin America's tradition of on-again, off-again economies.

The basis for optimism about business prospects is glimpsed in the hundreds of microlevel effects that can be traced directly to macrolevel reforms made during the millennium transition. A case in point is Argentina's experience with deregulation. Major cost savings for business were achieved between 1991 (the last year of the Lost Decade) and 1996 (the fifth year of the millennium transition). During that short transitional period, unit manufacturing costs fell by 16 percent. These impressive production gains were helped by savings of 67 percent in the cost of port containers, 26 percent in electricity, 20 percent in water and sewage disposal, 30 percent in postal rates, and 43 percent in ocean freight.[24]

The powerful forces of improved competitiveness unleashed during the millennium transition are loosening the viselike grip of the way business has traditionally been conducted in the region. So transforming is this change that when seasoned "Old Latin American Hands," whose experience in the region dates to an earlier period, attempt to do business as usual, they often land on their faces instead of on their feet. As there is no way to un-ring the bell of history, the sweeping shifts that have taken place in recent years are likely precursors of greater future change. That possibility makes it essential to understand how the fundamental changes brought about by the millennium transition affect business practices in Latin America. Therefore, the following paragraphs discuss how shifts in the forces shaping the region's business system are altering that system, and, along with it, the conduct of business.

Dollarization

Doing business outside of the U.S. dollar environment has always made international business an uncertain proposition. That uncertainty is gradually disappearing in Latin America as several countries adopt the dollar as their local currency. For decades (beginning in 1904), Panama was the sole Latin American country to dollarize. In 1991, Argentina inaugurated a currency board as a hybrid approach to dollarization. While economic mismanagement forced Argentina to discard its Law of Convertibility ten years later, its Central Bank had maintained a dollar reserve equivalent to the number of pesos in circulation, which tamed soaring inflation and boosted business and investment for many of those years. Foreign exchange risk vanished again as Ecuador replaced its local currency with the dollar in 2000, followed in 2001 by El Salvador. The jury is still out on deciding whether dollarization will be a cure-all or toxic medicine for financial policy. Nevertheless, in 2004, Guatemala and Nicaragua were considering exchanging their own local currencies for the greenback.

Statism Yields to Capitalism

Most companies and senior managers in Latin America today were raised in a controlled economy. Their backgrounds can be a handicap. Using yesterday's controlled-economy market rules to do business in today's open markets is akin to playing night golf with meatballs on a crocodile farm. In controlled markets, the state regulated key business variables such as retail prices, contract enforcement, input quality and cost, the type of products sold, the production technology used, the amount of profits remitted abroad, and the role of labor in company decisions. Because politicians and bureaucrats controlled the economy, the key to business survival was to influence those government officials who wrote and enforced the rules of the game. Thus, executives focused on nurturing friendly contacts in local and national power circles who had the *palanca* (leverage) needed to put a company on the inside track. When combined with decrepit infrastructures, political controls created a distorted business reality that forced companies to assign priority to influencing or circumventing government policy and to struggle with supply and production bottlenecks. After dealing with political and production headaches, executives had little time or will to worry about raising customer satisfaction levels. The misguided policies and official corruption that marked controlled economies widened the gap between the private and public sectors. Executives were prone to thumb their noses at rules that they saw as having been made solely to undermine business or exact a payoff.

Among the worst offenders of efficient business practices were, and are, state-owned enterprises (SOEs). The bloated payrolls and rigid, inward-looking organizational cultures typical of SOEs are the antithesis of what is required to become customer oriented and cost competitive. The policy pill most widely prescribed to treat the stubborn competitive paralysis of many Latin American SOEs is privatization.

Privatization

After almost 500 years of sliding down the slippery slope of state-controlled markets, Latin America's economies hit bottom in the Lost Decade and began to climb the opposite bank by adopting the belt-tightening programs advocated by the International Monetary Fund (IMF). The element of those structural adjustment measures that had the most direct and dramatic effect on the conduct of business was the privatization of large numbers of SOEs. Airlines, railroads, sea- and airports, telecommunications, cigarette and food manufacturing, tourist resorts, and even a Mexican nightclub were among the gamut of public enterprises that Latin American governments turned over in whole or in part to private capital.

The demise of the SOEs as public institutions was a microlevel sequel to the death of ISI at the macroeconomic level. Privatization was driven primarily by the prospect of fiscal benefits. By selling unprofitable SOEs to private investors, governments would no longer have to drain treasuries to bail out losers; hungry budgets would be fed by tax proceeds received from enterprises that had become profitable under efficient private management; and the combined benefits of sale proceeds, savings from not having to support operating losses, and new tax revenues could be applied to reduce the massive foreign debt and increase spending on desperate social needs at home.

Privatization is gradually lowering the wall of distrust and misunderstanding that has always strained relations between the public and private sectors in Latin America. As financial objectives displace political objectives in the former SOEs, Latin American industry is gaining competitive strength through sane capital investment, updated technology, professional management, and direct access to export markets. In the process, the role of the state is becoming more cooperative, rather than confrontational, toward private enterprise.

The pace of privatization in Latin America, however, has not been uniform. Chile, its earliest major adherent, and Mexico have undergone the most extensive privatization reforms, while Argentina has followed not far behind. As the reforms proceed to the smaller economies, they are invariably supplemented by legislation that encourages foreign investment, protects contracts, clarifies procedures for settling disputes, safeguards property rights, encourages new ventures, and reduces corruption. Because such reforms threaten money-spinning status quo sinecures, their advance is slowed by influential vested interests.

The new business-friendly governments moved on several fronts to help revitalize economic growth. Getting out of business itself and turning over SOEs to private investors was an early, major victory in the battle against economic sclerosis. Then, beginning during the mid-1980s and gaining momentum in the 1990s, many of the region's governments complemented their privatization initiatives with the creation of export processing zones marked by up-to-date infrastructures, compliant labor relations, liberal import privileges, and low taxes. Progressive governments also made giant strides to reduce the paperwork burden imposed on foreign firms by setting up *ventanillas únicas* or "one-stop windows." These are offices in which the red tape and permits required by multiple official agencies for exports or new investments can be processed in a centralized location, saving a great deal of time, headaches, and, of course, payoffs.

Narrowing the Civil–Common Law Gap

Corporate governance can improve no faster than the legal environment in which corporations operate. A key force of the millennium transition has been the movement of Latin American legislation toward narrowing the gap between yesterday's obsolete legal norms and today's business needs for a supportive legal system.

An important topic in which civil law and common law once differed greatly, but may now be slowly converging, is tax law. As import duties and export taxes are reduced or eliminated, national budgets are increasingly financed by income taxes and value-added taxes. The United States is the model for the former, Europe for the latter. The U.S. Internal Revenue Service has been a strong influence on training Latin tax officials in matters of policy, audit, and enforcement. While income-tax evasion was blatant just fifteen years ago, it has steadily dropped since the beginning of the millennium transition. Nonetheless, a trend is building toward generating government revenues more from value-added taxes than from income taxes. Whereas autonomous tax examiners used to pocket with impunity the settlements they negotiated with taxpayers, governments now find that the more straightforward value-added tax system lends itself to less perfidy between taxpayers and tax collectors. Taxation under the VAT system is less complex because a firm's tax liability is simply a flat percentage of its sales adjusted for the tax amounts that had been paid previously throughout the value-added chain of vendors supplying it with inputs. A major benefit of the VAT system is that it tends to be self-enforcing: It is in the interests of suppliers and manufacturers to keep customers honest about reporting true invoice values.

There are signs that another fundamental convergence between civil and common law may be underway in Latin America. In 2001, for example, Bolivia inaugurated a penal code that, in a sharp departure from normal civil law practice, exhibits strikingly common-lawlike features. The new legislation creates a prosecution service that is independent of the police, permits oral evidence to be heard in an open-court setting, and most radically, makes the presumption that the defendant is innocent until proven guilty.[25]

Corruption on the Defensive

People who did a great deal of business in Latin America prior to the 1990s knew that government corruption was a pervasive and unavoidable fact of business life. Bribery would flourish wherever there was an import duty to be levied, a routine permit to be signed, or a government purchasing contract to be awarded. Trying to conduct business in those times without engaging in bribery was like trying to nail Jell-O to a tree. But times are changing. Research shows that as countries become more exposed to global trade, adopt more open markets, and become more democratic, they also experience lower levels of corruption.[26,27] Latin America is no exception. So, while *la mordida* (the bite) is still the Achille's heel of the rule of law in Latin America, there are encouraging signs that "the bite" is weakening.

One such sign is a broad movement to simplify Latin America's complex and ambiguous legal systems. Ecuador is a recent example. Its National Association of Businesspersons (ANDE: Asociación Nacional de Empresarios) advocated reducing the number of the 52,774 legal norms that were on the books in 1997. ANDE argued that such a chaotic proliferation of often contradictory laws (many were centuries old) created a confusing legal environment that was fertile ground for bureaucrats to interpret, apply, and enforce at their own discretion. Rather than falling on deaf ears, as would have been typical in the past, ANDE's initiative received strong support from the country's legislature and press. As a result, Ecuador's new constitution includes an innovative provision to empower a committee to codify and reconcile law.[28]

A similarly hopeful sign is seen in the changes taking place in the administration of import duties. Customs corruption used to be ubiquitous. The saying, "Closed borders mean open palms," reflected its intensity. I saw an example of this turnaround while working in a Central American republic during the Lost Decade. Policymakers were concerned about the damaging image being projected abroad by widespread (and well-founded) rumors of rampant corruption in that country's customs service. To resolve the issue of low incomes as the alleged root of the problem, legislators passed a resolution, offering to immediately and retroactively increase the salaries of customs officials by up to three times. To qualify for the raise, however, the officials would be obliged to annually disclose the results of audits of their personal finances. The disclosure provision was imposed because it was difficult to explain how officials earning average monthly salaries of less than $200 could live in opulent homes and drive luxury cars. Few citizens were surprised when not a single customs official opted to accept the seemingly generous raise.

During recent visits to that same country, I learned that corruption in the customs service had dropped greatly. That happy event did not happen because of a politically inspired movement to reform the service by paying corrupt officials more. Rather, the duty-driven corruption declined in response to the fall in the tariff barriers that sustained the high duty rates. When duty rates were reaching 100 percent or more, an importer-friendly customs officer with a flexible sense of ethics could live off the fat of the land. He could accept an undervalued export invoice, or change a product's tariff classification to a lower duty rate, or ignore a few extra cartons of merchandise that somehow also had escaped being included on the shipper's packing list. But when duty rates edged down to 20 percent, much of the fat had fallen from the bone. And when they slipped to 5 percent, even most of the bone disappeared. As globalization lowered tariff barriers across Latin America, one of the great blessings it bestowed was the decline in customs corruption. With few exceptions, the process of clearing customs on arrival in any Latin American country today is less painful than the lengthy, frustrating, and frequently extortionate experiences that prevailed prior to the millennium transition.

While payoffs to customs agents have declined markedly, corruption has not disappeared entirely. The comment of a Canadian manager summarizes an experience that many U.S. businesspersons have had in Latin America, but are reluctant to talk about: "[Having to make payments to move cargo at airports] doesn't bother me at all. There is a cost for us to do business in Buenos Aires. That's why we hire agents. They're to make the friends, and we're to pay the bills."[29]

What about corruption connected to government purchasing? If you wanted to sell to the government, which is still today the largest single buyer in any Latin American country, you had to build the cost of *la mordida* (the bite) into your bid price. Even though thousands of corrupt SOEs have been privatized, it would be naïve to claim that corrupt officials and bureaucrats have disappeared from government purchasing offices in Latin America. It is more accurate to say that the routine, daily corruption that exists today is less prevalent and less blatant than it used to be. Instead of being able to touch and taste bribery as in the past, you now just smell it.

Prior to the millennium transition, the rule of thumb for winning Latin American government contracts was that the larger the project, the larger the payoff. Today, the typical public tender process is decidedly more clean and transparent. Bid documents are adequately advertised, although you may need to pick up the bidder's package in person at a designated government office and have cash or a counter check drafted on a local bank to pay for the document copy fee. On the date and at the place and time specified, sealed bid envelopes are collected from the bidders, who are physically present, opened in full view, and their contents announced publicly.

So, is there a catch? Well, even though the tender bidding process has become more open today, bidders can still pull the key levers that control award decisions by influencing the technical specifications written in the tender document. Being influential in the procurement process at an early stage is an advantage. Firms may underbid their services at the project identification, definition, design, or engineering stages. Any profits they forego at these early stages may be offset by the gains from being in a position to specify a set of project standards that tilts in their favor, and places competitors at a disadvantage for the final construction or purchasing award.

A less-legitimate variation on this same theme is to cultivate the goodwill of the government technicians responsible for specifying contract standards. Two recent developments make "friend-of-the-pen" approaches more difficult. The first is the increased oversight and auditing of the bid process on the part of bilateral (e.g., U.S. Agency for International Development) and multilateral (e.g., Inter-American Development Bank) donors that fund large projects. The second, and potentially more far-reaching constraint, is the vastly greater access to project information available to alert competitors and media reporters through the Internet and other publicly accessible sources. Freely obtainable information is the most powerful deterrent available to curb corruption, bolster competitive markets, and encourage clean and open business dealings. Happily, these are also the very conditions that create the potential for small business to thrive.

Personalism versus the Cult of Democracy

Latin America had turned an important corner by the 1990s. Five centuries of authoritarian rule had been replaced by popularly elected governments in most countries. Whether democracy proves to be a historic anomaly or an irreversibly established institution, replacing bullets with ballots is a giant step in the right direction, and its presence is a strong boost for business growth and investment security. Latin Americans are learning that if it was difficult to attain freedom in the market arena without having freedom in the political arena, it is virtually impossible to have political freedom without market freedom. They have placed their bets on the proposition that political reform will catch up to economic reform. As popularly elected leaders replace dictators, rule by law is replacing rule by men. In the process, democracy is deposing large-scale crony capitalism, and economic power is passing to smaller firms that compete on the basis of customer service, ethical practices, and creative initiatives.

20–21 VISION: THE PRESENCE OF THE FUTURE

Kierkegaard lamented that life could only be understood backwards, but must be lived forwards. But even if in hindsight our understanding of Latin America has not always been a perfect 20-20, we are not condemned to be blind to the future. We can claim some prescience by virtue of knowing that Latin America looks to the future with 20-21 vision: It sees its experience with twentieth-century policy failures as a lesson to guide wise policy in the twenty-first century. Signs that the Latin American policy genie is out of the bottle, and that there is no easy way to put it back in, include these indicators of fundamental shifts in the region's historical record:

- Business-friendly governments
- Growing adherence to democracy and the rule of law
- Poverty and extreme poverty, respectively representing 48.3 and 22.5 percent of the region's population in 1990, had fallen to 43.9 and 19.4 percent by 2003[30]
- Commitment to free trade and open markets
- Deregulated and consumer-oriented markets
- Legal systems geared for smaller businesses
- Less tolerance for corruption
- Improving telecommunications and road, port, and air transportation infrastructures

These landmark shifts argue that the historic transformation sweeping Latin America is creating a range of business opportunities that has never been more varied, or more favorable to small U.S. firms.

The Persistence of the Past

Like chewing gum sticking to the bottom of a shoe, the business habits acquired during Latin America's protectionist past adhere to its present, slowing its progress toward the future. A reality of doing business in the early twenty-first century is encountering relics of the twentieth century controlled-market mind-set that still guide the thinking of a generation of Latin executives whose management behavior was formed in the glory days of ISI. Firms still mired in that tradition will find it tough to compete against modern industry practices. Latin firms that have one or both feet stuck in the past face an uphill climb to survive in today's global economy. Occasional nudges by experienced U.S. executives can help push them out of that rut. The key is for U.S. executives to recognize the signs and to know in which direction to nudge their Latin partners. The willingness of Latin executives to climb on board the modern management train is a solid indicator of any firm's future prospects. For that reason, be wary about hitching your wagon to any firm that seems stuck in the rut of obsolete management practices.

Table 3.2 summarizes the signs of tradition-bound companies, contrasting their management behavior with that of modern, globally competitive organizations.

Finding the Shoe That Fits

There is little question about the overall direction of change in Latin America's business environment. The reality of the ongoing transformation is mirrored in the evening news, in daily company operations, and in the content of management-development seminars. Larger questions concern the different rates at which modern innovations are being transferred between and within countries. These questions reflect the tug of war between tradition and globalization, and attest to the reality that one cannot make a baby in a month by getting nine women pregnant. But the most incisive questions are rooted in the growing realization that competitive markets are needed to break the power hold of the old elites and that, in the process of trading crony capitalism for market capitalism, there is no one-size-fits-all set of policies for doing business. At the regional

Table 3.2
Contrast in Business Practices between Modern and Traditional Companies

Business Practice	Modern (Open-Market) Pattern	Traditional (ISI, Protected-Market) Pattern
Production planning	Produce for demand	Produce for inventory
Intra-organizational communication	Delegated decision making, vertical and horizontal information flows	Top-down decision making, vertical information flows
Organizational structure	Few management levels, stays flat as organization grows, flexible response	Steep pyramid, gains management levels as organization grows, rigid response
Organizational divisions	By integrated product lines, defined by final markets	By specialized function, defined by internal priorities
Personnel selection	By merit, past performance	By family or social standing
Labor force	Trainable for multiple functions	Low skills, limited to specialized functions
Productivity measure	Total cost of each product, zero-defects quality standards as target, benchmarking practiced	Cost of each function (production, marketing, etc.), tolerant of defects, unaware of industry best practices
Research and development	Innovative. Viewed as essential to competitive performance	Imitative. Practiced on a limited, as-needed basis
Technology choice	Product and process optimization, carefully selected	Product imitation, process adaptation; adopted with limited information
Organizational focus	Market orientation	Production and political orientation

level, management models that have worked in the United States and elsewhere must be adapted to fit conditions unique to Latin America. At the country level, strategies tailored to fit Brazil, for example, will seldom fit Nicaragua. At the corporate level, it is obvious that privately owned, smaller firms will play a larger role in the new economy than will the state-owned, mega-monopolies of the past. The access of those smaller firms to capital, modern management, technology, and markets is *the* pivotal factor in the region's economic future.

That same factor is also the key to understanding the rapidly expanding business opportunities being made available to smaller U.S. firms. Just as the fall in tariff barriers has opened Latin American markets previously closed to trade, advances in transportation and communication technologies now make it practical and profitable for smaller firms in both realms of the Americas to do business with each other. The similarities between Anglo American and Latin American smaller firms in terms of operating scales, company cultures, project time horizons, and product types make them natural business allies.

The Future Is Now

Benjamin Disraeli wrote that the key to business and political success was to understand the times in which one lives. What that wise statesman failed to pass on to us was the instruction manual on how to do it. Historians tell us that momentous turning points in the course of human events are seldom apparent to those living in them at the time they are taking place. The lack of awareness that people have of the historic processes and moments in which they live is akin to the fish's indifference to the water that surrounds it. This analogy may help to explain why the growth in smaller-business opportunities that have appeared in Latin America over the last decade may be one of the best-kept secrets of the new millennium. By turning the page on a five-century tradition of an inward-looking mind-set rooted in an indigenous and Iberian feudal past, Latin America has opened a new chapter in global integration. From today's first reading of that emerging text, it is apparent that the millennium transition was a turning point for U.S.–Latin American business relations. This historic period created the opportunity that gives smaller U.S. firms access to the lucrative international deals that a close-fisted destiny had previously bestowed only on large multinational corporations.

Notes

1. Brian W. Blouet and Olwyn N. Blouet (2002), "Historical Geography of Latin America," in *Latin America and the Caribbean*, 4th ed., Brian W. Blouet and Olwyn M. Blouet, eds., New York: John Wiley, pp. 51–96.

2. John Herman McElroy (1999), *American Beliefs*, Chicago: Ivan R. Dee.

3. Frank Tannenbaum (1962), p. 46.

4. McElroy (1999).

5. Peter L. Bernstein (2000), *The Immortal Metal That Once Ruled the World*, New York: John Wiley, p. 8.

6. P. C. Roberts and Karen LaFollette Araujo (1997), *The Capitalist Revolution in Latin America,* New York: Oxford University Press.

7. Christopher Fildes (1988), "Spanish Chestnut," *The Spectator*, November 19, p. 22.

8. K. S. Rosenn (1988), "A Comparison of Latin American and North American Legal Traditions," in *Multinational Managers and Host Government Interactions*, Lee A. Tavis, ed., Notre Dame: University of Notre Dame Press.

9. Hernando de Soto (1986), *El Otro Sendero*, Lima: Instituto Libertad y Democracia.

10. "Doing Business." (2004), *The World Bank.*

11. McElroy (1999).

12. R. Morse (1964), "The Heritage of Latin America," in L. Hartz, ed., *The Founding of New Societies*, vol. 123.

13. Emilio Willems (1975), *Latin American Culture*, New York: Harper and Row.

14. Alma Guillermoprieto (1994), *The Heart That Bleeds*, New York: Alfred A. Knopf, p. 54.

15. "Looks Good on Paper." (2003), *The Economist*, September 20, p. 73.

16. Barbara Wall (2000), "In Latin America, Unease Grows," *International Herald Tribune*, October 10, p. 3.

17. Economic Commission for Latin America (1997), *Annual Report 1996*, Santiago.

18. Christopher Marquis (2004), "Latin American Allies of the U.S.: Docile and Reliable No Longer," *New York Times*, January 9, p. 1.

19. "Who's Responsible?" (1999), *American Demographics*, December, p. 17.

20. Economic Commission for Latin America (1997).

21. "Paradise Lost." (2003), *The Economist*, February 22, p. 5.

22. David de Ferranti [World Bank vice president for Latin America and the Caribbean] (2004), "The Unfinished Agenda," *LatinFinance*, March, pp. 79–80.

23. Ernesto Zedillo [President of Mexico, 1994–2000] (2003), in a speech delivered at Quinnipiac University, April 29.

24. "International Notes." (1998), *Forbes*, September 1, p. 18.

25. "Trial and Error." (2001), *The Economist*, June 30, p. 57.

26. Wayne Sandholtz and William Koetzle (2000), "Accounting for Corruption: Economic Structure, Democracy, and Trade," *International Studies Quarterly*, vol. 44, pp. 31–50.

27. Shang-Jin Wei (2000), "Natural Openness and Good Government," *National Bureau of Economic Research* working paper, June.

28. John D. Sullivan (2000), "Anti-Corruption Initiatives from a Business Viewpoint," Sixth Annual Harvard International Development Conference, Cambridge, MA, April 8.

29. Courtney Tower (1998), quoting Michael Gallant in "Greasing Palms Makes Cargo Fly," *The Journal of Commerce*, May 30, p. 21.

30. "Pobreza e indigencia en América Latina." (2004), *El Comercio* (Quito), January 21.

Chapter 4:

Using Cultural Literacy to Hone Your Competitive Edge

Deep cultural undercurrents structure life in subtle but highly consistent ways that are not consciously formulated. Like the invisible jet streams in the skies that determine the course of a storm, these currents shape our lives; yet their influence is only beginning to be identified.[1]

CULTURE AS CAPITAL

Business everywhere is a race to beat the competition. To compete, you need enough financial capital to leave the starting gate. In addition to the financial capital, you need enough human capital to be able to run the race and cross the finish line. But in Latin America, you will not even be allowed on the track until you have the right kind and the right amount of cultural capital. Cultural capital can be as good as cash. You should not leave home without it. It is the surest means you have to earn trust. And trust is the most potent advantage you have to close today's deal, and go on to book new and repeat business. On the upside, cultural capital is a priceless competitive asset that costs little to acquire. On the downside, the cost of not having cultural capital to put into play can be ruinous. Two propositions show the pivotal role of trust in making profitable deals happen in Latin America:

Proposition no. 1: *Rock-Bottom Price + Bell-Ringer Product = Sale*

Proposition no. 2: *Reasonable Price + Satisfactory Product + Customer's Trust = Sale*

Proposition no. 1 describes a world that never was or will be. The premises underlying it are rooted in the "simplifying" assumptions that you had to learn to pass Economics 101. It is a flawed approach to doing business anywhere, especially in Latin America. It presumes that buyers are vendor neutral and will instantly issue a purchase order to any new supplier whenever that supplier offers a lower price or a better product. Those who failed to lure a loyal customer away from a competitor simply by offering what they believed was a better deal know that it takes more than a neat and tidy blackboard theory to land a new account. The sterility of economic theory flies in the face of human behavior when an unknown anybody representing an unknown brand of an unknown company located in an unknown place, tells a prospect to abandon a supplier who has cultivated his trust over many years.

Proposition no. 2 mirrors the reality known to executives that are experienced in opening markets in Latin America. Veterans of successful Latin American marketing campaigns know that you do not have to engage in either cutthroat pricing or offer bell-ringer products to prosper in Latin America. But, it is essential to reassure customers that they can rely on the assurances you make because they are backed by your own personal integrity. When you motivate customers to buy only from you because you are trustworthy, you expand the envelope of what qualifies as an acceptable price and product. That is why trust is such a precious currency in Latin America. Wise executives will try to earn, conserve, and invest it with the same discretion that controls their other financial decisions.

You Cannot Afford to Ignore Your Customer's Cultural Roots

Anthropologists know that individuals who share a common culture also tend to exhibit similar personality traits, attitudes, and beliefs. That makes culture the chief determinant of the way individuals view the world about them, relate to others, and make decisions. Any force that has such an armlock on business decisions is worth understanding. Use the information that follows to jump-start the process of making culture work for you.

What You Don't Know Can Hurt You

The cultural dissimilarities that evolved over five centuries have made the Anglo American and Latin American business systems diverge widely. Nonetheless, the thrust of globalization over the last twenty years is steadily nudging the traditional business systems of Latin America toward convergence with modern Western systems. As the curtain rises on the new millennium, elements of both traditional and modern cultures coexist in Latin America. Your sales and earnings performance can hang on knowing how to discriminate between the old and new ways, and on knowing how to make them work together to your best advantage.

The O'Neill Maxim: Tip O'Neill rose from obscurity to become Speaker of the House of Representatives by practicing a simple rule: "All politics is local." The former Speaker's rule for success in the political arena applies with equal force to the international trade arena, where "all business is local." Putting that rule into practice is easy: Know your territory, and never believe anyone who says, "People are alike and do business the same way everywhere." Blindness to local differences in culture can lead otherwise able executives to write ethnocentric checks that their firms cannot afford to cash. Opening your eyes to local differences not only opens the door for your firm to profit, it enables you to profit from the peculiar win-win arithmetic of becoming culturally literate: In the process of adapting to another culture, you do not subtract from your own culture, you add to it.

The Millennium Transition

John Herman McElroy draws an analogy between the evolution of a culture and the formation of a path.[2] He reasons that the first person to traverse a new landscape chose a route that seemed the most expedient course for the existing conditions. Later travelers followed that pioneer's track because they believed it would lead them where they wanted to go. Over time, that initial track evolved into a plainly marked path that all travelers now follow. Its constant use has confirmed it as the right course. Cultural traditions are formed similarly. Each generation takes on as its own the beliefs and values of the prior generation. As the established way of life is successively imitated over repeated generations, its behavioral patterns steadily take on the force of a mandated tradition. It is only when the original, formative conditions undergo obvious and threatening changes that the culture, like the path, becomes amenable to change. At the dawn of a new millennium, Latin Americans now see that the path markers they followed for 500 years are no longer taking them where they want to go. As they seek new paths, they are revolutionizing the way business is being done in the Americas.

The following two sections provide insights into Latin American culture from a U.S. business perspective. The first views how Latin American organizations are run and how decisions are made within them. The second views how culture affects the workings of the marketplace in Latin America. For convenience, these two perspectives are described from the viewpoint of a U.S. seller interacting with a buyer in Latin America. Even if your business in Latin America is not exporting, but importing, investing, licensing, or finding a strategic-alliance partner, these sections contain the tips you will need to put profitable deals together south of the border.

LATIN AMERICAN BUSINESS CULTURE: PROFILE OF MANAGEMENT AND ORGANIZATIONAL BEHAVIOR

When you arrive in Latin America from the United States, you instantly notice that you have crossed more than a mere national border. You have entered into another realm. You are assailed and invigorated by the strange sights, smells, and sounds of this new reality. So varied and intense are the changes in these unfamiliar surroundings that your senses are overwhelmed. The obviousness of these surface contrasts masks a deeper truth: The forces underlying the business opportunities and challenges you will find in Latin America are not to be seen in the outward expressions of this new environment. Rather, the forces driving your business destiny are embedded in the more subtly sensed differences in traditions, values, and expectations. A veteran of many Latin American business campaigns sums it up this way: "Ignore what you can see" (i.e., the sun, sand, and other attractive distractions), "and pay attention to what you can't see" (i.e., the invisible cultural forces controlling human behavior).

This section discusses the cultural forces that shape the realm of human conduct where what you can't see is key to how Latin American organizations and managers behave. Even though that realm is invisible, what happens in it is as real as bedrock and can make the difference between your venture's success or failure. To find your way in that invisible realm, think of it as being charted by seven guideposts. Knowing how to read the guideposts will give you the cultural literacy equivalent of night-vision goggles, letting you see the opportunities and avoid the traps to which your culturally illiterate competitors will be blind.

Seven Guideposts to Latin American Business Culture

Culture is the paintbrush of the mind. It colors the way we view the world. The worldview of one culture is never arbitrarily different from another. Rather, it reflects the many forks in the path of human experience, where each has taken a different turn to set its own cultural course. The major ways in which business cultures of Latin America and the United States have diverged can be traced to seven pivotal turning points. This section describes the guideposts that identify the turning points, and traces the different courses taken by the region's two business cultures.

The first three of our guideposts are described by Geert Hofstede in his rigorous research on culture-determined management attitudes.[3,4] Hofstede found that more than 50 percent of differences in managers' attitudes were due to national culture, a proportion far greater than was explained by managers' profession, gender, race, or age. Hofstede's study included thirteen Latin American national cultures, each of which displayed its own profile of attitudes. For simplicity, the thirteen cultural scores have been reduced to one Latin American composite. While using a composite measure creates a loss of descriptive precision for individual national cultures, the high level of similarity within the Latin American country cluster allows you to use that synthesis to portray broadly how Latins view the world around them and behave in accordance with that view.

1. Power Inequality. Called power distance by Hofstede, power inequality reflects the degree to which less-powerful individuals in a society accept that power is distributed unequally. Cultures that rank high in power inequality tend to concentrate decision making, so that decisions of consequence have to be taken at the top. Hence, managers from countries that rank high in power inequality tend to seek decision-making approval from superiors more often and on more issues than do managers from lower-ranking countries. That approval-seeking process often delays progress on key decisions that must be taken within the short time frame of a business trip or a production timetable. These delays frequently frustrate executives from the United States, where power attitudes are lower.

(The scale below and those that follow show how Latin America and the United States rank on key cultural measures. For purposes of comparison, they also show the cultures that rank highest and lowest on each measure.)

POWER INEQUALITY RANKING

(Highest-Hierarchy)			**(Lowest-Equality)**
1	17	38	53
Malaysia	Latin America	U.S.	Australia

Social Implications. The rankings above show that relative to the typical Anglo, who tolerates authority, the average Latin respects authority, accepting as a given Latin America's large differences in power. These different attitudes translate to different management styles. In the United States, managers are seen as problem solvers. In Latin America, managers are seen as experts. In the United States, a good manager would refer an employee to a knowledgeable authority when the employee's task involved resolving a problem outside the manager's own expertise. In a traditional Latin American firm, a manager behaving in the same way would be deemed incompetent. Similarly, the readiness of a U.S. manager to roll up his sleeves and get his hands dirty to resolve an immediate problem on the factory floor would be admired by his superiors, peers, and subordinates. In the traditional Latin American work setting, the same behavior might harm the manager's career. His superiors may question the social pedigree of anyone so ready to dirty his hands. Peers may fear his example, alarmed that his behavior could set a bad precedent. Subordinates might lose respect for someone whose low self-esteem would dispose him to engage in such a menial task. In traditional Latin organizations, one shows respect for authority, for example, by addressing people formally and observing differences in status.

Anglos have long rallied around the banner of meritocracy. Their lower power-inequality ranking conditions them to view power as a privilege that must be acquired by legitimate means and used responsibly. They frequently are uncomfortable with whatever they perceive to be unfair or demeaning treatment. The tolerance for high power-inequality typical of traditional Latin societies plays a role in the ordinary citizen's feeling of being powerless to correct an overbearing or abusive authority and, thus, of being reluctant to rock the boat. To an Anglo, a frustrating example of this hesitancy to alter the established order could be the unwillingness of a smaller distributor to take aggressive steps to increase market share. The reluctance to act forcefully may stem from not wanting to confront the market leader face-to-face if the smaller distributor perceives that the market leader occupies a higher position in the local business or social hierarchy.

Rather than feel smugly superior because of their lower tolerance for power differences, Anglos should examine the flip side of the power-inequality coin, which reveals some appealing features of high power-inequality behavior. For example, in Latin America's hierarchical societies, children are raised to be obedient to their parents. The view of parents as authority figures spills over into the workplace where the hierarchy of unequal power relationships is considered a part of the natural order, and subordinates expect to be told what to do, ideally by a benign paternal figure. The Latin's hierarchical perspective is at odds with attitudes commonly held in the United States, where children are encouraged to develop and exercise their own free will. Anglo children learn early on to treat their parents as equals (or even inferiors). While Latins may acknowledge the creativity value of the U.S. freewill mandate instilled during childhood, they also view the drugs, promiscuity, and materialism that plague U.S. adult society as its unhealthy behavioral extensions.

Managerial Implications. Because of the emphasis placed on equality in the United States, it is not surprising that Anglo workers expect to be consulted about how to perform their jobs, and view hierarchy in the workplace as intrusive. It follows that participative management styles are widely practiced and that flat, rather than steeply pitched, organizational structures are common in the United States. Because work routinely bypasses managers, power-tolerant Anglos tend to believe that hierarchical structures exist within organizations to help organize decisions and facilitate information flows. In contrast, power-respecting Latins are inclined to view the purpose of a pecking order as a mechanism that lets each member of the organization know who has authority over whom.[5]

The compatibility between participative management approaches and the cultural attitudes held by low power-inequality Anglo managers explains the more widespread use of Theory Y leadership practices in U.S. firms. In many U.S. firms, a manager's operating decisions commonly incorporate the experience and opinions of the employees who will carry out her decisions. The popularity of the Theory Y approach is predicated on providing employees with the responsibility and freedom to make work-related decisions that, in turn, will cause them to be more productive. Essential to empowering employees is ensuring that they are aware of the planning decisions made by superiors.

That level of employee empowerment is seldom practiced in traditional Latin hierarchies.[6] Decisions involving routine matters are regularly made by Latin managers. Subordinates are not encouraged to contribute to those decisions or to be made aware of them directly. Research supports that trait. A study comparing managerial behaviors in twelve cultural regions of the world showed that Latin American managers at all levels regarded being considerate to employees as relatively unimportant.[7] As a consequence, employees in traditional organizations work only in the way that management instructs them, because delegating decisions to lower-level employees undermines authority, creating discomfort and uncertainty.

Given the centralized structure of decision making in Latin American organizations, there are likely to be only a few people in a traditionally managed firm who have the clout to decide if a firm will buy your product. These key decision makers are the people with whom you want to be in contact. Going straight to those with purchasing authority will yield better results than beginning with mid-level, technically qualified employees who understand your product, but who have no authority to make the buying decision. Once you have established rapport with the decision maker, you will be sent to the technical side of the house to verify if your product is what the firm needs. This makes your sales campaign a two-stage test. First, you must clear the personal relationship hurdle. Only then will your product be submitted for technical evaluation. Trying to reverse the sequence by selling to the engineers first, then waiting to get referred to the top can cost you much lost time and effort in a traditional Latin American company culture.

2. *Structure-Need.* Hofstede referred to this cultural variable as uncertainty avoidance. It describes the degree to which unknown situations, lack of predictability, or unclear rules create discomfort in individuals. People from cultures with high structure-need tend to be uneasy if discussions posted on a meeting agenda move into new territory or unforeseen directions. It is common for them to resist innovative or "out-of-the-box" solutions, or trying to run when they believe that walking will also get them where they want to go.

STRUCTURE-NEED RANKING

(Highest)			**(Lowest)**
1	18	43	53
Greece	Latin America	U.S.	Singapore

Social Implications. Despite their high score on structure-need, Latin Americans are entrepreneurial. However, their risk-taking ventures have to meet a higher than expected rate of return than similar projects would in the United States. The typical U.S. risk-taker's attitude of nothing ventured, nothing gained is reversed in Latin America. Their attitude toward new ventures is: nothing gained nothing ventured. That maxim summarizes Latins' unwillingness to commit resources to a new project until most of the risk has been squeezed out, sometimes through capitalizing on influential personal contacts or making well-placed bribes.

Managerial Implications. Latins' high propensity to avoid uncertainty may seem obsessive to risk-taking Anglos. Whereas Anglos are likely to be open to uncustomary ideas, Latins are more inclined to resist change, a frustrating trait to U.S. managers bent on raising performance by updating marketing, management, production, or financing practices. Efforts to streamline work practices are often blocked in Latin America because employees set a high priority on career stability and are protected by rigid work rules, seniority benefits, and severance penalties. Relative to Anglo employees, Latins tend to place greater emphasis on retaining and consolidating their present position than on being promoted to a higher position.

Latins' need for structure in the workplace follows naturally from habits formed in childhood. Latin children are taught to adhere to traditional ways of doing things, and that what is different can be dangerous. The tendency to avoid uncertainty encourages Latins to seek both written and informal work rules, narrowly standardized job descriptions, and the security of seniority. Anglo managers in Latin America are often frustrated by the restraints imposed by customary practices when they seek to impose cross-functional training and work policies, eliminate obsolescent work rules, reduce the number of supervisors or management levels, or discharge employees for poor performance. Anglos view procedures and policies merely as guidelines that may be broken if the deviation can be explained as being best for the company. Latins view those same procedures and policies as absolute, the sacrosanct foundation of the organization's strength and, not incidentally, their own job security.

The higher need of Latins for structure makes them more susceptible to fatalism than Anglos, who believe that people should take charge of their own destiny. The Latins' predisposition toward fatalism is reflected in the ubiquitous use of the Spanish word *ojalá* (may God be willing), that consigns one's destiny to an uncontrollable external force, making it illogical to accept too much personal responsibility for future outcomes. If, for example, a delivery date is missed or a cost overrun occurs, a Latin manager responsible for the failure may strenuously try to externalize the blame, finding excuses for nonperformance in everything, except himself.

In Latin America, where high structure coincides with high power-inequality, organizations tend to evolve into what Hofstede calls "pyramids of people."[8] Each pyramid is largely independent from the other pyramids within the organization. Within each of these feudal-like fiefdoms, lines of communication run vertically instead of horizontally. Each subordinate will jealously shield sensitive information from his coworkers, sharing it only with the patrón (sponsor) to whom he owes his job. It is no mystery why the lack of horizontal information flow within the pyramids, and the information vacuum between the autonomous pyramids makes traditional Latin organizations inefficient and slow to respond to market changes or competitive threats.

The Latin American business organizations that are most susceptible to the paralyzing effects of high structure-need coinciding with high power-inequality are family-owned firms and state-owned enterprises (SOEs). As the wave of globalization sweeps over these organizations, their competitive survival is predicated on becoming more efficient through updating and streamlining their operations. In the case of family-owned firms, the two most common modernizing methods are upgrading the managerial skills of family members or hiring professional management from outside the family. One result is that business school enrollments in Latin America at undergraduate and MBA levels are breaking historical records as both of the modernizing methods are implemented. In the case of SOEs, the privatization impetus continues to transform an array of formerly bloated, inefficient, and often corrupt government-run railroads, seaports, petroleum refineries, telephone systems, cigarette factories, and the like into lean, consumer-friendly enterprises.

In Latin America's public sector, the combination of high structure-need and high power-inequality creates bureaucrats who may appear to Anglos as obsessed with details, perhaps to show their authority, even while occupying relatively minor positions. No matter how inane a bureaucrat's request for documentation or data may appear, it is essential not only to comply, but to do so with a smile. If you do not treat minor, detail-fixated functionaries with a deference bordering on worship, you may learn painfully that their ability to become a thorn in your side is out of all proportion to the modest stations they occupy in life.

Resistance to change often combines with a reluctance to cooperate with strangers, creating a mind-set that blocks efforts to make traditional Latin firms more responsive to customers. A case in point is a common complaint voiced by U.S. firms that wish to link their automated supply chains to Latin suppliers or distributors. The Anglos' job is difficult because traditional Latin managers prefer to rely on telephones and faxes to process transactions on a person-to-person basis. Such manual processing adds to costs at the same time that it slows down the flow of goods through the supply chain. One solution has been to install electronic data interchange terminals at suppliers' or distributors' facilities as a first step toward integrating them into a Web-centered, supply-chain application.

3. *Social Orientation.* At one extreme of this dimension is individualism, defined by the degree to which a culture promotes the role of the individual over that of the group. The opposite of individualism is collectivism, which describes cultures where individual rights are subordinated to the welfare of the group.

SOCIAL ORIENTATION

(Individual)		**(Group)**
1	42	53
U.S.	Latin America	Guatemala

Social Implications. No national culture ranks as high on individualism as the United States. Our natural tendency to project our own values onto other societies can turn our unnatural degree of individualism into a cocked gun, aimed to shoot us in the foot when we do business in Latin America. Consider, for example, that most of today's management theories and concepts were made in the U.S.A. during the last fifty years, in a place and time period in which assumptions about high individualism limited their relevance to the group-oriented cultures of Latin America. Hence, three rules that effective Anglo executives have used as guides for business conduct in Latin America are:

1. To know what they do not know about culture-driven differences in behavior,
2. To realize that business practices based on U.S. experiences may not apply outside of the United States, and
3. To assume that Latins will be perceived to behave unpredictably.

As members of the most individualistic culture in the world, Anglos are weak on loyalty to employers, groups, communities, coworkers, relatives, and spouses. Anglo individualism involves fewer people in making decisions. So time and effort to get projects moving is usually less time consuming than in group-oriented Latin organizations. The tendency of individualists to make decisions rapidly and to respond swiftly to changing situations has been pivotal in explaining U.S. industry's record level of creativity, and the resulting power of the U.S. economy.

Latin American attitudes toward individualism vary widely among groups belonging to the same organization. One study surveyed attitudes toward individualism and equality among 2,192 managers and workers in twenty Venezuelan organizations. It found that workers were extremely more collectivistic and more tolerant of unequal power distribution than were managers.[9]

Collectivism assigns individuals to in-group or out-group membership. This makes affinity circles a critical force in shaping how business is done in Latin America. Latin social relationships are like concentric circles with individuals and their nuclear and extended linear families occupying the two center-most circles. Moving outward, the next circle includes cousins, aunts and uncles, spouses of siblings, and in-laws of children. Beyond that third circle is a fourth that includes close friends, and a fifth that could include teamates from sports teams, trusted work colleagues, or schoolmates. Subsequent circles enclose everyone to whom there is a degree of obligation or trust based on shared affinity for a family, social class, locale, profession, or institution. All others lying outside of one's affinity system are strangers to whom one feels neither moral obligation nor considers trustworthy or deserving. That detached attitude leads to nepotism, tax evasion, littering, environmental neglect, and reluctance to cooperate to achieve a common goal.[10] It also helps explain the passiveness that some Latins display to the grinding poverty that surrounds them, and also, the region's weakly developed tradition of public charity.

Individuals within Latin societies may move from one affinity circle to another, but people located outside the circles pattern will remain strangers until they can establish themselves within it. If you are on the outside, you must find a way to position yourself within one of the circles to gain the personal trust that is a prerequisite to doing business productively. One of the surest and most direct ways to winning in-group status is to be introduced by an in-group member. Here are some means to gain in-group membership on at least a probationary basis:

- Have a letter of reference written on your behalf by a U.S. bank that has a correspondent relationship with a reputable bank in your Latin prospect's locale.

- Take advantage of the bond provided by a common affiliation such as a membership in Rotary International or a religious organization.
- Participate in a trade show or mission sponsored by the U.S. Department of Commerce or your state's export promotion agency. Those functions typically enjoy the prestige of being hosted by U.S. embassies.
- Make as many personal contacts as possible. Get out of the office. Call on clients, suppliers, and competitors. Take every opportunity to make your face known to the widest possible range of businesspersons, chamber of commerce officers, industry association officials, government bureaucrats, media reporters, and civic leaders.

Managerial Implications. Collectivism emphasizes workplace harmony. When combined with high structure-needs, the ingredients are present to create a middle-management weakness frequently found in Latin American organizations. Performance choke points can be traced to yes-men who fail to advise their superiors when something goes wrong on the job, or when they know that their superior's decision is mistaken.

The individualism-collectivism gap between the United States and Latin America affects how salespeople are assigned to territories. In the high-individualism United States, salespeople are often reassigned because a new territory may need to be developed by one of the company's experienced professionals. Because customer loyalties are to the product and the company, the appearance of a new salesperson is not likely to disturb the client-vendor relationship. A different outcome may occur in a high-collectivism Latin setting, where the constant nurturing of rapport between buyer and seller is critical to keeping customers loyal. In Latin America, you run the risk of losing key accounts if you regularly rotate salespeople.

Social orientation also has a strong effect on the way personnel are hired. The hiring policies of most U.S. firms stress bringing on board the best-qualified applicants because of their technical expertise. Job candidates submit résumés emphasizing their professional skills, achievements, and education. Not surprisingly, hiring the best-qualified candidates is also the first concern in traditional group-oriented (collectivist) Latin American firms. The criteria of what constitutes best-qualified for Latin American positions, however, will center more on the applicant's family background, social class, or loyalty to an influential executive, because these are key indicators of a candidate's in-group status and, thus, trustworthiness. The ability to get along with coworkers, of course, is another price of entry to membership in the collegial in-group. Hence, candidates for responsible positions within traditional Latin organizations will focus on cultivating influential employees. So it is no mystery why personal relationships often take precedence over performance in Latin organizations. As a result, Anglo executives who set "getting the job done" as a priority can find it vexing when they must penetrate the barrier of personal relationships before they can approach performance issues.

Given the sharply different emphases on hiring and promotion criteria, it is no mystery why Anglo and Latin managers may see one another's personnel policies as misguided. Anglos disdain the nepotistic practices of Latin firms, believing that such policies undermine morale, democracy, and ultimately, financial performance. Group-oriented Latin managers, on the other hand, believe that the only candidates that can be trusted in responsible positions are those that are known to other responsible employees, or that have proven their trustworthiness in other organizations known to share company values. The moral force in collective societies that ties employees and companies together blurs the dividing line between personal lives and work lives. It is common for large companies in Brazil, for example, to:

> help employees with personal financial problems. For example, because of a lack of public social services, employees may have an illness in the family which puts them in a precarious financial position. The personnel departments of large Brazilian firms regularly provide assistance to employees in such a situation, thus mitigating the impact of employees' problems on the functioning of the firm.[11]

To support their position, Latin managers can point to ample evidence attesting to Anglos' lack of loyalty, as shown by their high turnover in employment, social, and matrimonial relationships. In short, the Latin model of employer-employee relationship is based on the premise of mutual moral obligations. That noble view clashes with the cold and calculating Anglo model wherein employees view their skills and knowledge as marketable commodities, and look to sell them to the highest bidder.

The traditions of long-term employment at the same company and loyalty to one's group can be obstacles when trying to recruit managers in Latin America. Prospective candidates for a job will seldom be open to the overtures of a headhunter unless the hiring company has a well-respected name in the business community. Candidates must feel comfortable that the confidentiality of the search process will safeguard their identity. For that reason, advertising an open position in newspapers may not yield the highest-quality candidate for the job. More effective recruiting is done by directly and personally inviting a prospective hire to discuss a job possibility in confidence. That approach should be made by a trusted family member, friend, or professional associate, and it should be made outside of the candidate's place of work. Because many qualified candidates are financially satisfied with their current positions, they are likely to place a high priority on the quality of the new project. Nevertheless, the minimum salary increase a candidate would expect to get in order to jump companies would be 15 percent, with smart negotiators initially asking for a 30 percent hike.

4. *Universalism-Particularism.* Closely related to Anglos' high sense of individualism is the belief that rules come first, loyalty to friends second. Anglos place great trust in the rule of law to get what they feel they deserve. Collectivist Latins tend to put group loyalties first, the rule book second. Subordinating impersonal rules to personal loyalties is called particularism. Its opposite is universalism, the belief that the same set of standards should apply uniformly to everyone.

Latin American particularism can be traced to an age-old characteristic of human behavior in Spain. There, according to Spanish philosopher José Ortega y Gasset, the feeling of particularism found its origin within the individual himself, expressed in the notion that each man is his own political party.[12] It is a tendency that Cervantes immortalized in the epic work, *Don Quijote de la Mancha*, and one that makes it admirably common for Latins to appreciate the normality of a moment in which a humble youth may recite his own poetry as he shines shoes at a bench on the plaza. Particularism permits outsiders to practice nonthreatening idiosyncracies, but refuses to grant them social equality.

As the ability to move a profitable deal forward may hinge on gaining the approval of a high-level company or government official, U.S. executives in Latin America often see at close range how in-group members, such as friends or relatives, are treated more favorably by someone in authority. In a study on how culture-based differences affected ethical decisions, some 15,000 managers in forty countries were surveyed. They were asked to respond to the following situation:

> You are riding in a car driven by a close friend. He hits a pedestrian. You know he was going at least 35 miles per hour in an area of the city where the maximum allowed speed is 20 miles per hour. There are no witnesses. His lawyer says that if you testify under oath that he was only

driving 20 miles per hour, it may save him from serious consequences. What right has your friend to expect you to protect him?

a. My friend has a definite right as a friend to expect me to testify to the lower figure.
b. He has some right as a friend to expect me to testify to the lower figure.
c. He has no right as a friend to expect me to testify to the lower figure.[13]

The results of this study are used as a proxy to classify cultures by the extent to which judgments and rules are influenced by personal loyalties (particularism) or impersonal law (universalism). The figure below shows the percentage of respondents from Latin America and the United States (Yugoslavia and Norway are included to mark the low and high extremes of the scale) who responded to "b" or "c."

RULE ORIENTATION

(Loyalty = Particularism)		(Law = Universalism)	
12%	45%	78%	90%
Yugoslavia	Latin America	U.S.	Norway

Among U.S. managers, 78 percent rejected friendship (option "a") as their primary decision criterion, whereas only 45 percent of Latin American managers would have placed rule by impersonal law before rule by personal loyalties. The contrast in results does not mean that Anglo managers are more trustworthy. Indeed, a Latin viewing the same results could conclude that Anglos cannot be trusted because they would not be willing to help out a friend in need. The results show that the domain of legal rigor in Latin America is constrained by the radii of trust that define the affinity circles mentioned earlier. They also suggest that favoritism enjoyed by in-group members can play a large role in determining who gains a competitive advantage in particularist cultures.

What are the lessons that can be learned about doing business in a particularist culture?

1. As a source of competitive advantage, core competencies can count less than close personal relations with customers.
2. Unless your situation is exceptional, avoid the Anglo penchant for going it alone. There is simply no way to overstate the value of locally well-connected, reliable associates who know the ropes.

3. The habit of universalistic executives to depend on intricately written contracts to define the rules of a business relationship is at odds with the loosely written, short agreements and personal trust that particularist Latins use to bind an agreement. Latins may regard a lengthy, tightly written contract, especially one that includes penalty clauses, as an indicator that in-group trust is missing. Thus, they will feel little personal obligation to adhere to the terms of the agreement.

5. *Communication.* Listen to Latin America's silent language. Communication is a contact sport in Latin America. Hearty embraces, kissing on the cheek, standing closely together, pats on the back, tugs and squeezes on the arm, two-arm handshakes, energetically expressive arm, hand, and facial gestures, and dancing body movements used to supplement spoken words are standard fare in the warm personal encounters practiced among Latin Americans.

But the physical gestures that are so common in Latin America are only one means of expression in the broad dimension of nonverbal communication that experienced travelers know to vary widely across the globe. Cross-cultural researchers distinguish between explicit (called low-context) and implicit (called high-context) styles of communication.[14] Explicit communication styles depend heavily on transmitting the meaning and content of messages through words. Although not as plainspoken as the Swiss, Anglo Americans say what they mean, and mean what they say because they are low-context communicators and use spoken language to convey meaning. In high-context cultures, much of the message is carried by often subtle, nonverbal cues. This explains why, compared with low-context Anglos, high-context Latins rely on the silent language of subtle signals to convey their messages. Those signals are important cues for you to note, and may include indicators such as the kind of clothing being worn, facial expressions, hand and arm gesticulations, posture and stance, eye contact, office size and trappings, lapel pins, educational titles and certificates, the use of silence, eating habits, and displays of family and social affiliations.

CONTEXT RANKING

(Low-Explicit)			**(High-Implicit)**
1	4	9	11
Switzerland	U.S.	Latin America	Japan

As low-context communicators, Anglos invest little time in preliminary social exchanges, preferring to advance rapidly to the business at hand. The art of the deal takes longer in the high-context culture of Latin America, as business cannot be conducted effectively until trust levels are established and the parties build personal bonds by getting to know one another. In explaining the way members of a high-context culture communicate with one another, Hall describes a process practiced by traditional Latins:

> They talk around the point. [They] think intelligent human beings should be able to discover the point of discourse from the context, which they are careful to provide . . . The United States, having its roots in European culture which dates back to Plato, Socrates, and Aristotle, has built into its culture assumptions that the only natural and effective way to present ideas is by means of a Greek invention called "logic."[15]

The deductive communication process Hall describes is frustratingly bewildering to U.S. executives accustomed to building ideas inductively. The inductive communicator moves from specific issues to the general framework, building the structure of the discourse piece by piece and premise by premise from the ground up until the edifice enclosing the deal's elements is complete. When an inductively precise Anglo engages a deductively open-ended Latin who is attempting to build the structure of the transaction from the roof downward, it is not surprising that the patience of both parties will be tested. As a result, the intended deal may never come together in the middle.

The Latin focuses his immediate attention on the overall relationship that binds the parties together. He asks himself: Is the right chemistry present to build strong personal bonds between the individuals and does there exist enough strategic fit between the companies to expect the relationship will have long-term potential? In contrast, the Anglo's concern is about closing today's transaction. The Anglo may believe in the abstract that the possibility exists to build a roof in the future that could be supported by strong personal and strategic ties. Yet, the Anglo also believes that it is premature and pointless to invest much time in talking about the design of the roof until the foundation, formed around the cornerstone of the first transaction, has been set firmly in place.

Communication differences between Anglos and Latins also extend to advertising. In low-context cultures like the United States, advertising tends to have a high factual content. In high-context cultures like Latin America, the advertiser is more likely to use symbolic or emotional content to arouse the consumer's interest.[16]

6. *Space and Time.* Why do Anglos and Latins often fail to connect as business associates? The answer may be that they inhabit different realms of space and time. While many humorous anecdotes allude to that space-time separation, it is a real and serious cultural factor that has sabotaged countless deals.

My Space or Yours? Personal space is a cultural feature that varies markedly between Anglos and Latins. It is the physical distance that seems appropriate to maintain when two people are conversing. If the distance separating two conversationalists is too great, the Latin may feel that the Anglo is aloof or indifferent. If the distance is too little, the Anglo may feel that the Latin is intimidating or brash for having invaded his personal space. Anglos project a protective bubble that surrounds them at a distance of about twenty-four inches. If the bubble is broken by anyone accidentally approaching too closely, the intruder is expected to apologize, saying, "Excuse me." If the bubble is broken intentionally, the invader's closeness makes them feel uneasy, they will back away in order to reestablish their customary zone of comfortable separation.

For the Latin, a physical proximity of about eight inches is a communication prerequisite. If a conversational partner is further away, the Latin will move to close the gap. If not interacting within his eight-inch comfort zone, the Latin feels the two conversationalists might as well be shouting across a valley at one another and cannot achieve any meaningful understanding. Given their different perceptions about what constitutes proper personal space, Anglo and Latin conversationalists may follow a predictable dance movement. Their dance steps are not complicated: Feeling threatened by the Latin's closeness, the Anglo steps away; feeling denied by the Anglo's retreat, the Latin moves to narrow the gap; the Anglo withdraws again; the Latin moves in, and the strange shuffle continues until one or both of them lose interest, patience, or stamina. The lesson for the Anglo is not to retreat. Doing so repeatedly will put off the Latin who perceives it as discourteous or shifty behavior.

It's About Time. It is no secret that Anglos and Latins have different views about time. The Anglo's notion of time is linear, or monochronic. He is systematic, sequential, punctual, and reluctant to waste time, because "time is money." Latins have a polychronic, or cyclical view of time, believing that, like the repetition of the natural seasons, there will always be another opportunity to do tomorrow what was put off today. The Latin's agenda is filled with multiple and conflicting activities, a jumbled program that preordains (and thus excuses) schedules that cannot be kept, meetings that are interrupted, and personal and business priorities that are constantly reshuffled.

It is a mistake to think that the Anglo places a higher priority on time than does the Latin. It is more instructive to understand that each has a high regard for the value of time as a finite resource, but chooses to apply it to different ends. Fundamental to the Anglo belief that time is money, and that no time should be wasted in getting down to business, is the Protestant ethic that encourages hard work, admonishing that the Devil works through idle hands. In contrast, the Latin believes that in the broadest view, the essence of a successful life is to learn to enjoy the passage of time. Applying this view to the realm of business, the Latin sees the purpose of time as a means to judge if a potential business colleague may be trusted and if a warm personal relationship can be developed.

While punctuality is somewhat more widely practiced now than in the past, particularly in private firms, it still has not become a Latin American competitive advantage. If your appointment with a Latin government official is scheduled for 9 A.M., you should arrive on time. But you should not be disappointed if you are placed in a holding pattern in a waiting room, where the others present know that the only difference between 9 A.M. and 11 A.M. is that the latter is two hours closer to lunch. To prepare for this familiar contingency, always bring a book or something to work on, so that your wait will not be unproductive. Of course, the consequences of a late appointment are that all of your subsequent appointments will get backed up. For this reason, experienced U.S. executives schedule fewer appointments per day during a Latin American business trip than when traveling in the United States, Europe, or Japan. When you are finally received by the Latin official, avoid appearing irritated at having had to wait. No matter how exasperated you may feel, you must act genuinely pleased to see the Latin and appear attentive to the social exchanges and extraneous discussions that almost inevitably precede the main business topic.

You may find it consoling to learn that the issue of flexible time standards can cause as much disruption to Latins as it does to schedule-precise Anglos. The wedding band of the wife of a Honduran executive is forever inscribed with a date that precedes the date of their betrothal by seven days. Asked why there is a one-week mismatch between the true date and the inscribed date of the wedding, she offers a simple explanation: "Pablo and I wanted to be certain that the jeweler would have our ring ready in time for the ceremony." Having estimated that tardiness costs the country almost 5 percent of its annual GDP, an Ecuadorian civic group launched a national punctuality campaign in October 2003. Given top billing in the media, the campaign inauguration almost had to be delayed because of the late arrival of its principal backer—the president of the country.

As a social guideline, know that if you are invited to a Latin's home for dinner at 8 P.M. (your invitation will likely read 20:00 hrs because Latin time is based on the twenty-four-hour clock), it would be a mistake to show up right at eight. Your host will be surprised and possibly upset, because he did not expect you before 8:30. At the arrival time specified in the invitation, he will probably be bathing or making last-minute preparations for the event.

7. Formality. The region's historic ties to European elitism and continued separation by class lead Latin Americans to stress social customs and business protocol. Their emphasis on hierarchy accents formality in personal interactions. It is an attitude that contrasts with more casual U.S. executives that, having a weaker sense of social tradition, prefer to dispense with ceremony, and place today's profit ahead of yesterday's custom.

Education and Titles. Formal education is more highly esteemed in Latin America than in the United States. Possessing a postsecondary degree confers respect, and is reflected in multiple forms of personal titles. If your Latin associate has earned a title through formal education, it is imperative that you refer to him by that title. The most common one is *Licenciado*, referring to a trained lawyer or to one who has completed a formal university program. Most business school graduates will use this title. Abbreviated as *Lic.*, it is the safe title of choice to use when you are not certain what level of education your Latin associate has attained. *Ingeniero* is the second most-frequent professional title you are likely to encounter, and refers to a graduate engineer. An *arquitecto* is a trained architect. Occupying the top of the hierarchy of educational titles is *Doctor*, a title that is sometimes appropriated by those who consider themselves well educated, but who may not have earned the corresponding Ph.D.

Age. While the energy and creativity of youth is valued in the United States, the wisdom and experience of age is venerated in Latin America.

Therefore, it may not be a good idea to send your fast-track young manager to Latin America to pursue that hot new deal with a high-level officer of the Latin American firm. Senior Latin executives are used to being catered to by younger yes-men of mixed technical proficiency, in whom they seldom confide. Because of age-based stratification in Latin organizations, their senior executives ordinarily prefer to deal with other senior executives, and may be offended by younger envoys sent by a U.S. company.

Meals and Manners. Perhaps more business transactions are nourished at restaurant tables than at conference tables. To the casual observer, business meals in Latin America seem to have less to do with business, and more to do with a convivial procession of dishes and drinks accompanied by lively conversation ranging from sports to current events, and art and music to ribald humor. The purpose of the meal's varied gastronomic and conversational fare is to get to know the person with whom one is dealing. It is easier for decorum-conscious Latins to gauge the social caliber of Anglo executives in a casual environment, where good food and ample drinks could make the latter drop their guard, than in a more inert office setting. It is in the less-restrained ambiance of a restaurant that Latins can test if prospective business associates are "their kind of people."

To help you pass the Latin's test of social pedigree, you should be aware of some mealtime customs. The most frequent business meals in Latin America are breakfast and lunch. Breakfast is gaining ground because it can be a healthier, less-filling meal (appealing to Latins' recent greater concern with physical fitness) and does not break up the work day as much as lunch. Nevertheless, lunch still remains the premier Latin meal. Taking place between 2 P.M. and 5 P.M., lunch is a convivial affair, with liberal amounts of food and drink.[17]

You should avoid discussing any business topic at meals, unless it is broached initially by your Latin colleague. If it is necessary to bring up a business issue, wait until dessert has been ordered. You should also avoid discussing host-country politics and problems, U.S. foreign policy, or religion. Safe topics are children, local cultural and historical features, sports, hobbies, and travel. When it is time for the bill, the person who made the invitation, usually the seller, pays.

Latins will observe your eating behavior and table manners as indicators of your breeding. While eating the way your mother taught you to eat will usually allow you to pass muster, some tips may help raise your final score:

- Keep your hands exposed above the table, but do not allow your elbows to touch the table.
- Order your meal in a decisive manner; avoid prolonged searching of the menu. If in doubt, order the same dish that your Latin colleague orders. Avoid ordering anything that is messy or difficult to eat, and could distract from the easy flow of conversation.
- Fork etiquette is a germane topic. Latins are curious about the Anglo's use of the fork at meals. Whereas the fork always remains in the left hand of right-handed Latins (and Europeans), it is passed back and forth between the Anglo's left and right hands. This peculiar shuffle begins with the fork in the Anglo's left hand as he holds the knife in his right hand to cut. Finishing the cut, the knife is laid to rest on the right side of the plate. Then the fork is shifted to the right hand. From that hand food is introduced to the mouth. The odd five-stage cycle is completed as the fork is reintroduced to the left hand. To add to the Latin's wonderment about why there is any need for a fork to ever have to leave the left hand, the tines of the Anglo's fork, when introducing food to the mouth, are always pointed upward, in a position opposite to the curvature of the palate and tongue. With practice, you may learn to adapt your fork management habits, an adjustment that will make you appear less strange to Latins and, incidentally, will make your dining more efficient.

Dress. Jackets and ties are appropriate for business in the cooler mountain and higher-latitude locations in Latin America. In most of the humid tropics, the guayabera (pleated light-cotton shirt worn outside the pants) is the garment of choice among executives. Your sartorial score will suffer if you show up in shorts, even for informal social meetings. For those occasions, khakis or jeans and an open-collar sport shirt are appropriate fashion.

Table 4.1 is a synopsis of how cultural differences shape management differences in the Americas. The risk of overgeneralizing is great when compressing a large body of information into a small amount of space. Accordingly, the reader should be aware that Table 4.1 describes prevalent behaviors, excluding anomalies in which U.S. managers mirror behaviors common some forty-or-more years ago and Latin American managers exhibit modern practices. Nevertheless, the table previews the nascent, but unmistakable trend of Latin American firms as they evolve from a traditional to a modern management model.

Table 4.1
Contrast in Management Practices between the United States and Latin America

Characteristic	Anglo American (Modern)[a]	Latin American (Traditional)[b]
Rationale for income and authority differences	Individual merit—a mailroom clerk can rise to become CEO	Family background and formal education credentials
Decision-making process	Structured participation, delegated to lowest competent level. Information is systematically shared.	Centralized, concentrated at top. Impulsive, autocratic. Information is compartmentalized
Decision makers	People who know the most	People who rank the highest
Attitude toward work, employer, competition	Live to work. Loyalty to self. Use information cooperatively to enhance own performance, earn promotion.	Work to live. Loyalty to patrón. Hoard information to consolidate self in current position. Avoid conflict.
Responsibility	Employees are self-starters, don't expect company to look after them.	Employees expect close supervision, paternalistic supervisors.
Hiring criteria	Demonstrated performance	Family or personal ties to company
Purpose of hierarchy in organizations	To define problems, then delegate task authority to resolve them.	To define holders of authority, then attempt problem-solving tasks.
Position in hierarchy	Indicative of unequal abilities	Indicative of unequal roles
Organization chart	Reflects information flows needed for key operating functions.	Reflects personal interests or power relationships of key family members.

Table 4.1 (*continued*)

Characteristic	Anglo American (Modern)[a]	Latin American (Traditional)[b]
Delegation	Performance expectations are assigned with discretionary authority.	Task functions are assigned with symbolic authority.
Model boss	Expedient communicator	Benevolent dictator
Performance evaluation	Employee accepts accountability.	Critical feedback resented.
Task performance	Do whatever must be done to perform task, be willing to get hands dirty.	Some tasks are too menial or undignified for one's position.
Activity modality	Accomplishments and "doing"	Personal relationships and "being"
Planning process	Long term. Proactive for predictable contingency scenarios. Premise: Future can be controlled. Formal, deliberate.	Short term. Reactive to volatile environment. Premise: Destiny is preordained. Unstructured, impulsive.
Policy decisions	Formally stated	Not stated
Records	Data must be accurate.	Accuracy subordinated to convenience.
Logical perspective	Inductive, action oriented, factual	Deductive, analytical, conjectural
Time orientation	Present activity is the means to future accomplishment. Time commitments are taken seriously.	The future is subordinate to the past, the past is subordinate to the present. Deadline dates are initial estimates.

[a]Anglo American characteristics describe practices common to U.S. firms operating in the modern, high-productivity sector of their respective industries.

[b]Latin American characteristics describe practices common to Latin American firms operating under traditional (ISI) management norms.

LATIN AMERICAN BUSINESS CULTURE: PROFILE OF MARKETPLACE BEHAVIOR

Consumer Behavior—Then and Now

Although it seems paradoxical, only 30 years ago, the market in Latin America for middle-class consumer goods was mostly limited to upper-class buyers. The absence of a sizable middle class in Latin America reflected the region's claim to having the world's most unequal income distribution. A massive lower class, an exceptionally wealthy upper class, and scarce numbers in the middle barred any pretension of economic equality. While glaring income inequalities still remain infamously intact, middle-class numbers have multiplied in the years since the Lost Decade. As beneficiaries of the open-market policies of the 1990s, a rising wave of middle-class consumers swept through Latin America's marketplace. These new consumers sought to satisfy their pent-up demand for world-class goods and services. They were fed up with the inferior products imposed on them during the long era of protectionism—they had money and wanted to spend it. Marketers who understand the key differences between U.S. and Latin consumers and the ways in which their buying patterns are converging, can expect to perform well as the region's consumer-goods markets swell to catch up and keep up with global growth.

As the role of the family dominates consumer buying patterns everywhere, and family roles differ in the two Americas, consumer buying behaviors also differ in the two markets. Consider, for example, the foremost position of the family at the center of the Latin's system of affinity circles. Strong Latin family bonds make it traditional that, as parents grow old, they will live with and be taken care of by their adult children. While that same tradition of parental care was once prevalent in the United States, it is uncommon today as weaker family ties and greater geographic mobility decree that parents take responsibility for meeting their own needs. One effect of that rising trend is the explosive U.S. demand for retirement homes and long-term-care insurance. That same demand is not yet widespread in Latin America. Except in the region's largest cities, where extended family ties are breaking down and Western behavioral patterns are displacing traditional ways, senior-care facilities and services are still virtually unknown.

But while the domestic market for senior care in Latin America was a long-shot just five years ago, a small but expanding number of U.S. senior citizens are now buying vacation and retirement homes there. Senior-friendly locales in Mexico, Costa Rica, and elsewhere have special appeal to this affluent market. Already, adult communities and assisted-living facilities are springing up. The forces of demography, geography, and economics are auspiciously aligned to make Latin America an appealing proposition for growing legions of aging U.S. baby boomers. Significantly, a parallel market for senior services (referred to as *tercera edad*—third age) is beginning to grow in or near the region's major urban centers as the influence of globalization alters social behavior within the family institution in Latin America.

The role of the family in consumer markets is also influenced by the more dominant role of males in macho Latin American societies. One illuminating study compared the average number of decisions made by spouses in Venezuelan and U.S. families when purchasing consumer items. Table 4.2 shows the tendency of Latin males to share less authority with their spouses than U.S. males when both couples made purchasing decisions for the same products.

Avoid Making Experience Something You Get after You Need It

Procter and Gamble spends a lot of money on market research and still launches duds in its pursuit to place first-to-market products. An example of the opposite approach is the one taken by Volkswagen in Brazil, the last place in the world where the company still makes the venerable VW van. While considered a vehicular anachronism in most of the world, the classic van is the workhorse of choice in Brazil for postal workers, contractors, ambulance drivers, convenience-store operators, and mobile-food vendors.[18] If your firm has neither a large market-research budget nor a large market-flops reserve, it should heed a lesson from nature: Sometimes the early bird does get the worm. But observe the less-exalted, but well-fed second mouse. It has learned important lessons about how to avoid first-mover risks in the quest to gain share in the perilous cheese market.

For the smaller company planning a new-to-market product launch, a deliberately gradual, moderate-cost entry is the prudent course. As Latins have high brand loyalty, the key to profit is to find the right tune and keep playing it, not to get the band to play a new song. Then, when you and the market are in harmony, follow up with a speedier, higher-investment product rollout. That second-mouse strategy can produce the same even-

Table 4.2
Latin America's Macho Marketplace

MEAN NUMBER OF PURCHASE DECISIONS BY PRODUCT TYPE		
Product	**U.S.**	**Venezuela**
Automobiles		
Husband	2.59	4.16
Joint	3.06	1.42
Wife	0.41	0.40
Furniture		
Husband	0.41	1.16
Joint	3.41	2.71
Wife	2.23	2.16
Life Insurance		
Husband	2.65	3.38
Joint	1.23	0.55
Wife	0.15	0.05
Major Appliances		
Husband	0.98	1.97
Joint	3.21	2.10
Wife	0.85	0.93

Source: Robert Green, and Isabella Cunningham (1980). "Family Purchasing Roles in Two Countries," *Journal of International Business Studies*, Spring–Summer, p. 95.

tual market position and profitability as the early-bird approach, but at substantially less cost, risk, and embarrassment.

Less-experienced U.S. firms, however, occasionally rush headlong into a new deal, assuming that the way they do things at home is the world's best practices. Given how difficult it is to survive in the hard-hitting competitive environment of the United States, it can be easy to assume that our way is best. But acting on that assumption can catch us between the jaws of a painful trap in Latin America.

On the one hand, we are trapped because we are right. Let us suppose that the U.S. way is the best way. In that case, the danger of putting it into practice in Latin America is that it may threaten vested local interests. While those local interests may be operating with outmoded industry practices, they could be in a powerful position to force us out, if they see us as a threat to their cash cow. Here is an example: A U.S. transportation firm in a Central American country was interested in brokering freight services between smallish shippers of winter vegetables and tramp steamers that charged a fraction of the international freight rate pegged by the large, scheduled conference carriers. The investment was so low and the profit potential from sharing in shippers' savings so high, that the proposed venture smelled like a trap. It was. Some discreet nosing around revealed that the local agencies of the large carriers were entirely able and ruthlessly willing to pull the political levers necessary to block the U.S. interloper from obtaining the business permits necessary to set up shop. As a result, the rug was pulled out from under a potentially lucrative new business initiative.

On the other hand we are threatened because we are wrong. This is the more frequent experience: The would-be innovator discovers there are good reasons for the way things are done locally. If he does not adhere to the local practices, he could receive a costly lesson in the reason for their existence. Look at this example: A U.S. manufacturer of construction equipment centered its export-marketing campaign on the ability of its products to reduce labor costs—a promotional theme that it had used successfully in the U.S. market and that competitors were not emphasizing at that time in Latin America. It was not surprising to anyone familiar with Latin America why the product bombed in a region saturated with dime-a-dozen, low-skill laborers of the type the equipment was intended to replace. But the story ends happily. After licking the wounds inflicted by its initial market failure, the manufacturer revised its promotional theme. This time, the sales campaign emphasized the financial cost savings available by reducing job times. Contractors were quick to respond to the savings made possible by shortening cash-to-cash cycles in a hyperinflationary financial environment where, if one was fortunate enough to find a lender, annual interest rates on construction loans exceeded 600 percent.

Moral: Being bold is not always the best strategy. Eagles may soar, but weasels don't get sucked into jet engines.

Understanding the New Latin American Consumer

As you travel in Latin America, you will see centuries-old behaviors that are disappearing before your eyes. These changes will powerfully influence the final consumers of your product, what they buy, how much they are willing to pay, and how they buy. But do not be fooled into believing that the swiftly paced changes you see are being felt throughout the economy. The pace of change in the region is greatly uneven. In the traditional sectors, change does occur, but at a glacial pace. The rate at which a sector undergoes change is proportional to the degree to which it is subject to the forces of globalization. These forces shatter traditions and smash resistance to change by striking on two fronts: taste and price.

Like a fortuitous astrological junction, consumer taste preferences and production cost pressures are in favorable alignment to give U.S. companies a potential advantage over competitors from virtually anywhere. Knowing how to play these two forces can propel your company to a position of strength in Latin America.

Taste

How taste preferences are formed, and how opinion makers are swayed are still murky subjects in marketing. But ringing up sales depends on knowing why some products and brands sell more readily than others in Latin America. The simple truth is that the United States is the primary influence on tastes and preferences for consumer and industrial products in Latin America.

Regional similarities. The Gap, Nike, Levi's, McDonald's, and even Taco Bell are top brand franchises in Latin America. How have these brands been able to command so much awareness and loyalty so far from home? It is plainly because the mystique of U.S. trends and fads spreads as rapidly to Latin America as it does to Cleveland or Kalamazoo. The United States transmits tastes and shapes product preferences among Latin America's consumers through movies, the Internet, tourism, and TV (a monthly cable fee of $12 can bring many more channels into a Latin home—including pirated pay-per-view channels—than the household could possibly watch).

Make no mistake, you may still find vestiges of anti-U.S. political sentiment in Latin America. But even the anachronistic handful of park bench nationalistic fanatics are preaching their anti-imperialist doctrines behind FosterGrant sunglasses, sporting stone-washed Levi's, sipping a Diet Coke to wash down slices of Domino's Pizza, and distributing Xeroxed propaganda flyers. Surely the culture of the Big Mac has outstripped the most ambitious of any imperialist conspiracies alleged to be hatched in the CIA or Pentagon. A sixty-something journalist friend in Buenos Aires confided to me, with some bitterness, that "My generation venerated European culture. Paris, Rome, and London were the places of our intellectual dreams and were the standards against which we measured not only our aesthetic, fashion, and culinary inclinations, but also our buying habits when we went shopping. Nowadays, my grandchildren dream only about Hollywood, Miami, and New York." And, he might well have added, in today's age of e-commerce, his grandchildren do not have to travel to the United States to buy music, software, books, training courses, or clothing. The United States comes to them on the Internet. Online demand is being exploited in ever-increasing numbers. In 1999, some nine million Latin Americans had used the Internet. By 2000 that number had grown to 14 million. In 2001, about 24 million Latins were online in their homes, schools, or offices. In 2002 nearly 40 million Latins were online.

Another promotional tool, direct mail, is meeting with growing success in Latin America as postal systems grow more dependable and mailing lists more reliable. Growth in the numbers of consumer and business product marketers show that direct mail has become cost-effective in delivering promotional messages. Direct-mail response rates in Latin America reach levels at least equal to, and often higher than the more advertising-saturated U.S. market.

Regional differences. But product preferences generally oriented to the United States by no means signify that there are not great differences in tastes within Latin America. Some examples: Consumers in warm Caribbean climates favor sweet-tasting orange soda, but temperate-zone Argentines prefer their orange soda to taste more like orange juice, as it does in Europe, from where Argentines still take many of their purchasing cues.[19] Mole sauce, a perennially popular favorite in Mexico, is a slow seller anywhere else in Latin America. *Pupusas*, the national dish of El Salvador, are virtually unknown in any nonadjacent country. Guayabera, the pleated and comfortable cotton shirt that is the de rigueur business uniform in much of coastal Latin America, is considered appropriate only for dentists in sweltering San Salvador. Boxed cereals, consumed in Mexican cities as a breakfast food to be eaten with milk, are used more commonly as snacks in Central America. Hair-straightening products sell well in Santo Domingo, but are not on the shelves in Santiago. Coffee, the most-consumed caffeinated beverage in Mexico, Central America, and the northern parts of South America, runs a distant second behind tea and tealike maté in Argentina and Uruguay. Body armor, armored car conversions, and personal security products sell well in Colombia and Mexico, but are in low demand in Chile, Costa Rica, Paraguay, and Uruguay. Industrial and construction equipment, priced to reflect the cost of complying with U.S. environmental and safety standards, often sells more easily in Mexico than in Brazil. Cleaning products show wide national differences in per capita usage: The average Ecuadorian, for example, buys only 50 percent as much powdered detergent as a Peruvian, but buys 265 percent as much hand soap as a Venezuelan, and 41 percent of the chlorinated bleach purchased by a Peruvian.[20] Incidentally, package color exerts a strong influence over what brand of detergent Ecuadorians buy: Research has shown that Ecuadorian consumers consider yellow too strong and can damage clothes, blue is too weak and gets nothing clean, but detergent in a yellow package with blue highlights is perceived as the best.[21]

Price

Geographic proximity, historical ties, and cultural similarities combine to give U.S. sellers a price advantage in Latin American markets. The lower expenses U.S. firms incur in advertising, credit, freight, inventory, pre- and post-sale services, insurance, and tariffs can give U.S. companies a potent cost edge that European and Asian rivals find hard to beat. That is why, year after year, Latin American imports from the United States exceed those from any other country by wide margins. Its greater total market share does not mean the United States always leads in every product in every Latin market. But research confirms the favored image that U.S. products enjoy in Latin America's most important markets. For example, a study of 2,000 consumers in Argentina, Brazil, Chile, and Mexico showed that in seven of eight categories, U.S. products ranked as having the best overall quality at a given price.[22] Preference for U.S. products means that if your price, design, quality, warranty, and delivery are reasonable, the cost savings you may have in production, overhead, and logistics will translate to larger market share and/or profit margins.

The Singer Sewing Company seems to have struck the right pricing model to sell quality electric sewing machines in Latin America's largest market. Singer knew that seamstresses and tailors across Mexico were stitching away on the same foot-powered machines used by their grandparents. Owning a new sewing machine was an impossible luxury that they could only dream about, because Mexico, like the rest of Latin America, was a cash-only market for millions of working-class consumers. To tap into the huge lower-middle-class market, Singer offered a lease-purchase plan to circumvent the liquidity barrier faced by customers who have income, but no access to credit cards or bank accounts. Thanks to strong personal pride and low transient rates, Mexican buyers go to great lengths to avoid defaulting on monthly lease payments, thus avoiding the shame that would befall them if their machines were repossessed. That threat of social stigma kept repossession rates down to 2 percent. Knowing the income patterns and cultural behaviors of a ripe market and devising a matching purchasing strategy worked well for Singer. Mexican sales of the firm's sewing machines and white goods went up by 500 percent within five years of offering the leasing plan.[23]

Another cost-oriented marketing success can be found in Peru's telecommunications market. Thousands of mothers bought their children cellular phones that are rigged to receive calls only. These devices let mothers locate their children without spending much money or time calling around to their children's friends. If children wish to make a call, they can do so by buying prepaid debit cards. The combination of caller-pays and prepaid fees have enabled the Peruvian telephone company to tap into the revenue streams of market segments that, because of those customers' marginal credit standings, would otherwise have been inaccessible.

Distribution

It is not surprising that the distribution system used to bring modern, world-class products to Latin consumers is undergoing remarkable transformations. Prior to the millennium transition, the bulk of the region's retail sales were through mom-and-pop *tienditas* (small stores). As most customers walk to these neighborhood stores and carry their purchases home, decisions regarding package size and ease of handling are paramount in merchandising strategy. These crowded shops have such limited shelf space that point-of-purchase promotional materials often are hung from tall ceilings to take advantage of the stores' vertical dimension. While the *tienditas* are still favored places to buy staples in residential neighborhoods, the top destinations for today's middle-class shoppers are the malls, category-killer stores, supermarkets, and discount outlets. These modern, United States and Western Europe look-alike retail formats are commonplace in today's Latin American cities. But they only began to lose their novelty status ten years ago and were virtually unknown thirty years ago.

Changes taking place in the distribution system go hand-in-hand with changes being seen in the profit margins of high-quality sellers in today's more price-conscious Latin American markets. It would be natural to assume that price-based competition would become more prevalent as Latin markets become more open, and local prices fall to be in alignment with international costs. The reality of what happened in Latin America, however, parallels what occurred in U.S. and Western European markets. Smart sellers found that the formula for success in Latin America's consumer markets is similar to what has worked repeatedly in modern markets: To maximize profit, price should not be set as a function of cost, but as a function of the consumer's perception of value. That awareness is shifting the game strategy of Latin consumer marketing away from price-cutting, and toward managing consumers' perception of value. By offering customers a bundle of product benefits tailored to meet their needs, a seller makes it more difficult for them to draw price comparisons between its brand and a competitor's.

The broad factors that influence consumer perception of value are no different in Latin America than in the United States. Only the details change. Strategies designed to strengthen the appeal of product performance, branding, design, packaging, advertising, and the like have universal appeal and can displace price as the top buying motive for value-oriented consumers. Good marketers know that by shifting consumer focus from price to value, unit profit margins can be increased without having to suffer a proportionate drop in sales volume. This strategy seems to work in all Latin markets, including the least affluent. For example, I noted during a recent visit to Nicaragua, one of the region's most battered economies, that two packaged breakfast cereals were offered at widely disparate prices. Whereas the Central American brand was priced at twenty-three cents per ounce, the well-advertised Kellog's box was tagged at thirty-four cents per ounce. Interestingly, while the listed ingredients showed the products to be almost identical, the store manager told me that the high-ticket import was moving off the shelf at the same rate as the local inexpensive brand.

CONCLUDING TIPS

As a U.S. executive doing business in Latin America, you are constantly exposed to new cultural behaviors. Your reactions to these unfamiliar ways can take either of two forms:

1. Cultural Dominance. This view assumes that U.S. practices are superior, and are the right way to do business. In the past, U.S. managers took this approach because there was no other model to

challenge it. The arrival of strong European and Japanese firms, and the advent of professionally managed Latin American organizations is challenging the primacy of the U.S. management model.

2. Cultural Synergy. This perspective assumes that there is the U.S. way, and there is the Latin American way. There is no right way. The view is predicated on a solid grasp of both management models and the cultural forces that underlie them. It foresees that the best elements of each culture will combine to create a new system of management that could transform Latin America into a world-class competitive force.

I have written about the competitive need to adjust U.S. viewpoints to the cultural perspective of Latin America. It would be folly to finish this chapter without issuing a warning: Never go native. While it is surely good business to adapt some of your surface behaviors to the Latin milieu, once you begin to relax core standards, you set both feet on the slippery slope of mediocrity. If allowed to continue, small infractions of principles gather momentum, soon becoming the operating equivalent of a migraine headache on steroids. If you lose sight of the finish line, it makes no difference what horse you saddle or how you ride. Do not compromise your ethical or performance standards. The only people who make money by bending over backwards are acrobats.

Notes

1. Edward T. Hall (1981), *Beyond Culture,* New York: Doubleday, p. 12.

2. John Herman McElroy (1999), *American Beliefs,* Chicago: Ivan R. Dee.

3. Geert Hofstede (1980), *Culture's Consequences: International Differences in Work Related Values,* Beverly Hills, CA: Sage Publications.

4. Geert Hofstede (1991), *Culture and Organizations: Software of the Mind,* London: McGraw-Hill.

5. André Laurent (1983), "The Cultural Diversity of Western Conceptions of Management," *International Studies of Management and Organization,* vol. 13, no. 1–2, pp. 75–96.

6. L. J. Bourgeois III and Manuel Boltvinik (1981), "O.D. in Cross-Cultural Settings: Latin America," *California Management Review,* Spring, pp. 75–81.

7. B. M. Bass et al. (1979), *Assessment of International Managers: An International Comparison,* New York: Free Press.

8. Geert Hofstede (1980), "Motivation, Leadership, and Organization: Do American Theories Apply Abroad?" *Organizational Dynamics,* Summer, New York: American Management Association.

9. Elena Granell de Aldaz (1997), "Cultura Gerencial y Organizacional en Venezuela," *Debates IESA: Gerencia y Cultura*, vol. 3, no. 2, pp. 33–45.

10. Lawrence E. Harrison (1992), *Who Prospers? How Cultural Values Shape Economic and Political Success*, New York: Basic Books.

11. A. M. Jaeger and R. N. Kanungo, eds. (1990), "Management in Developing Countries," London: Routledge, p. 292.

12. José Ortega y Gassett (1922), *España Invertebrada*, 2nd ed., Madrid: Espasa Calpe.

13. C. Hampden-Turner and F. Trompenaars (2000), *Building Cross-Cultural Competence*, New Haven: Yale University Press, p. 16.

14. Edward T. Hall and Mildred Reed Hall (1987), *Hidden Differences: Doing Business with the Japanese*, Garden City, NY: Anchor Press/Doubleday.

15. Edward T. Hall (1983), *The Dance of Life*, New York: Anchor Press/Doubleday.

16. Edward T. Hall and Mildred Reed Hall (1990), *Understanding Cultural Differences*, Yarmouth, ME: Intercultural Press.

17. The relaxed pace of the traditional Latin American lunch break is succumbing to the pressure of fast-paced Anglo habits. In tropical locations, the hot and humid climate was good reason for dedicating afternoons to leisurely pursuits, chief among which was the large afternoon meal preceding the siesta. To adjust work schedules to the demands of the climate, employees traditionally began their workday at 8:00 A.M., left for lunch at 1:00 P.M., and returned to complete their shifts during the cooler hours from 5:00 P.M. to 8:00 P.M. Because air conditioning today makes afternoon work a comfortable experience, the traditional long lunch break is in the early stages of becoming an endangered species. In a growing number of Latin American business and government offices, 9:00 A.M. to 6:00 P.M. shifts with a one-hour lunch break have become the norm. In the process, leisurely siestas are being subordinated to speedy Big Macs.

18. Alan Clendenning (2003), "A Long, Strange Trip for VW Van," *Sun-Sentinel*, September 11, p. 3D.

19. Doreen Hemlock (1999), "Familiarity Breeds Success," *Sun-Sentinel*, September 20, pp. 16–17.

20. "Los detergents de cinco paises se venden en el mercado ecuatoriano." (2004), *El Comercio* (Quito), January 22, p. B1.

21. "El sector es uno de los grandes en la publicidad." (2004), *El Comercio* (Quito), January 22, p. B1.

22. "U.S. Products Rank High Among Latin Americans." (1998), San Diego: Market Development, Inc.

23. Candace Siegle (1994), "Sewing It Up," *World Trade*, pp. 122, 124.

Part III
THE ART OF MAKING AND KEEPING THE DEAL

From concept to application. Chapters 3 and 4 in Part II set in place cornerstone concepts of history and culture that underpin why and how business is done differently in Latin America. In Part III, Chapters 5 and 6 build on those same historical and cultural foundations, applying their concepts and tools to the dual tasks of making productive business deals happen in Latin America and of preventing them from falling apart. Chapter 5 explains how to get your hands on the ball; how to run with it is the subject of Chapter 6.

Chapter 5

Negotiating and Selling Tips

THE NEGOTIATING GAME

It is a fact: Research confirms that the way we behave as bargainers has a potent effect on the outcome of negotiations. Indeed, negotiation outcomes tend to be either much better or much worse than what hypothetical outcomes would have been if based purely on the economic merits of the deal under negotiation.[1] So, no matter how exceptional your company considers its offering package, it will not automatically get the result it believes it deserves. It will get only what you are able to negotiate for it. It follows that an investment in learning how to gain an edge at the negotiating table can pay off. While literature dedicated to the art of bargaining could fill libraries, this chapter includes only those concepts that have concrete value and are directly applicable to Latin America.

Playing the Away Game

Do you trust your instincts? If you are playing on your home turf, you should. Your good instincts surely have played a major role in getting you where you are today. The longer you have been in business or practiced your profession in a given place, the more skilled you have become in sizing up the people, market, and business possibilities of that place. Your ability to make more right than wrong decisions is a measure of your familiarity with your customary operating environment. It is the same reason why a ball team's home-field playing record is usually better than its away-from-home performance. Naturally, the tables are turned when it becomes the home team's turn to be the visiting team, and it finds itself at a disadvantage playing on the opponent's home field. As a negotiator traveling to Latin America to play that away game, you have the disadvantage of having to compete on unfamiliar terrain that is sprinkled with economic and cultural land mines. You frequently notice that the Latins are playing a different game with its own ground rules, and that calls are made by referees whose eyes seem sometimes turned the wrong way.

But the record shows that in spite of their visiting-player disadvantages, U.S. negotiators are not regularly blown away by unfamiliar hazards when they travel to Latin America. Indeed, they possess at least three potential advantages that can go far to compensate for having to play in the opposition's ballpark:

1. Being on your Latin associate's home turf makes it easy to acquire firsthand knowledge of his plant and office installations, his operating environment, and his reputation among local suppliers and customers. In Latin America it is often difficult, through any means other than a personal visit, to reliably verify the difference between what is the truth about a company's situation and what you have been told is the truth.
2. That same in-country proximity gives you a convenient opportunity to size up other local firms you could deal with in case negotiations fall through with your primary target.
3. The third advantage is especially applicable if you represent a smaller U.S. company that lacks a large and imposing physical presence: The favorable impression you wish to convey as a prosperous, well-established potential business associate to appearance-sensitive Latins will not be compromised by having to reveal a lean and sparsely appointed home facility.

Imperfect Markets

The differences in the rules under which the business game is played stem from the fact that Latin American markets are imperfect, relative to freer markets, like the United States. The term simply means that the way these markets behave is at odds with the way they should behave under ideal conditions. Imperfect markets are fertile ground for nurturing dubious behavior, such as fabrication of facts or intentions during negotiations.[2] For most executives, imperfect markets qualify as a low-priority learning need. But as a cross-cultural negotiator playing with high-stakes bargaining chips, there are two specifics you should know about them:

1. If prepared, you can turn the defects inherent in imperfect markets to your advantage.
2. If unprepared, you can fall on your face as those defects pull the rug out from under your feet.

Two potent advantages can keep you on your feet as you take steps to exploit those defects:

1. Knowing the pivotal role played by cultural differences in negotiations.
2. Knowing how to use those differences to control negotiation outcomes.

Used in tandem, these two tools create a competitive asset called cultural literacy. The following sections explain how to become culturally literate with only modest effort, and how to use cultural literacy at the bargaining table as a chip that can substitute for cash.

Getting to *Sí*: Styles, Strategies, and Stages

It is the single most elemental fact of business life: Everything you want is controlled by someone else. And making yours what is theirs is the fundamental motive underlying business everywhere, including Latin America. But before any transaction takes place, decisions must be made about the terms of exchange. Some terms are straightforward and simple (e.g., the dark-alley ultimatum: Your money or your life). Other exchanges are more complex and, as a consequence, are preceded by more lengthy, but not necessarily more civil, negotiations.

If you have witnessed the high-pitched, back-and-forth haggling that takes place in Latin America's bustling *plazas de mercado* (open-air markets), you know that bargaining for the best deal can be a lively challenge. The ubiquity of spirited haggling in Latin America means that Latins are more experienced bargainers than Anglos. Does this mean that Anglos are doomed to finish in second place when trying to strike a deal with Latins? No. To the contrary, experience shows that U.S. executives regularly negotiate productive deals in Latin America. It is safe to say that executives who score the most negotiating points are those who know how to hit home run deals in negotiating's three sweet spot power zones: styles, strategies, and stages.

STYLES: HOW CULTURE AFFECTS NEGOTIATING STYLES IN LATIN AMERICA

Anthropologists know that distinctive personality patterns exist for people who share a common culture. In the process of becoming socialized into a particular culture, people acquire the attitudes, values, and beliefs of that culture. Culture conditions the way individuals view the world about them, react to situations, and relate to other individuals. Differences in cultural behaviors dictate that productive international negotiating is not simply a matter of understanding what happens between negotiators at the bargaining table. Rather, the outcome you achieve depends on your ability to read and react to culturally driven behavior that controls what is happening inside the heads of Latin Americans, and shapes their unique negotiating styles.

Culture as a Bridge to Productive Business Deals

The success of any transaction hinges on management's ability to negotiate productively and extract a favorable quid pro quo for their company. When transactions span national borders, the relationship between negotiators as cultural strangers provides such rich soil for misunderstanding and suspicion that cultural gaffes are cited as the largest reason for U.S. companies' sales failures in international markets.[3] Accordingly, it is no mystery why experienced international executives assign high values to cultural factors in the negotiating equation. By doing the same, you can become the "pro" between the quid and the quo, thus availing yourself of two powerful negotiating advantages in Latin America:

1. Being able to avoid costly surprises and to prepare for what Latins will do next by anticipating their culturally informed responses to your proposals, and
2. Presenting yourself in the most favorable light by showing Latins that you deserve respect because you (a) appreciate their personal values, and (b) behave in a predictable and trustworthy manner.

Although these are potent advantages for winning at the negotiating table in any culture, they are especially powerful bell ringers when dealing with those Latins whose behavior is more traditional. That is why you should know when and why you may encounter negotiating behaviors in Latin America that follow traditional patterns.

All Latins Do not Dance to the Same Beat

The unique personality traits associated with a given national culture do not portray all members of that culture. Everyday experience tells us that all individuals raised in the same country do not behave identically. When we describe a personality pattern associated with a certain national culture, therefore, we are referring to a predisposition of people from that country to behave in a particular way.

It is normal for individual behaviors to vary in any population. Such variation in Latin America is increasing at a brisk pace, however, because of the region's rapid insertion into the global mainstream. The SAL (Sector, Age, Locale) indicator can help you estimate whether the cultural profile of a Latin American is likely to be traditional or modern, depending on how that individual's experience has been conditioned by these three predictors of negotiating style. Latins who fit into one or more of the categories listed below are more predisposed to depart from the traditional personality profile, and to be aligned with modern (United States-like) styles of negotiating behavior:

> Sector: Belonging to the modern service, manufacturing, or nontraditional agricultural export sector, rather than a sector marked by undifferentiated products or sold primarily in the domestic market
>
> Age: Born after 1970 (i.e., having reached a professionally impressionable age during or after the definitive economic and political reforms initiated during the late 1980s and early 1990s)
>
> Locale: Raised in a mainstream urban center, rather than in a rural or provincial setting

As the Western Hemisphere becomes more globally integrated, the intensity of the SAL factors grows. In time, we may expect Latin American and Anglo American negotiating styles to converge, transcending the old divide between traditional and modern negotiating behavior. For the immediate future, however, tradition will prevail in Latin America. For that reason, the negotiating practices described as Latin American portray practices typical of traditional cultural behavior.

Seven Guideposts to Negotiating Success

The cutting edge of globalization is driven by negotiations between buyers and sellers from different cultural backgrounds. Although the field of cross-cultural negotiating attracts plenty of commentary, much of it is of limited practical value, consisting of cultural stereotyping or self-seving anecdotes. The missing advice that U.S. executives could profitably apply in Latin America is a tightly organized body of practical information that describes in specific terms how negotiating styles in Latin America and the United States differ.

This section fills that void. By orienting the seven business-culture guideposts described in Chapter 4 toward the specific task of negotiating, the process removes U.S.-Latin negotiating behavior from the realm of mysterious art form and brings it into the realm of predictable behavior and controllable outcomes.

1. Hierarchy. Ranking high on the hierarchy scale, Latins tend to concentrate decision making at the top. As the goal of the Latin executive is to hold onto power, delegating decision making makes little sense because it is tantamount to giving power away.[4] Consequently, all but the most routine matters are decided at the top. The top executive's distance from the negotiating process can cause his own whims and preconceptions to color his decisions. Because lower-level Latin negotiators seldom attempt to second-guess their superiors, they will get approval before taking any action, even on trivial issues. The back-and-forth exchanges entailed in seeking approval delay the negotiation proceedings, and can exasperate U.S. negotiators that place less emphasis on position and personal power.

What are the practical implications of differences in hierarchical attitudes between Anglo and Latin negotiators? There are two key ways in which being alert to the gap could boost your negotiating performance:

1. By knowing who is the Latin team's decision maker, you can tailor your approach to and focus your appeals on the top man. You also save the lost time and motion that can drag negotiations out forever. Keep in mind that middle-management members of the Latin team, who can consume an inordinate amount of your attention, have no authority to make key decisions. They are at the table to play one or more roles: They are there (a) for ceremonial purposes, to aggrandize the top man's status, (b) to get information and be prepared to implement any decision made by the top man, or (c) to provide the leader with technical expertise.
2. If the third reason, providing technical expertise, seems to explain why subalterns are present on the Latin team, it is always advantageous to have them on your side. Your best interests will be served by pairing up your team's experts with their Latin counterparts to

ensure that the latter fully understand the technical aspects of your offering. If those inter-team pairings can extend beyond discussing technical matters, and form personal trust bonds, all the better. Efforts at inter-team social integration can go a long way to strengthen rapport and open communication channels between the technical levels of both organizations. These attempts may fail to bear fruit because of cultural differences. The Latin technicians often are more socially polished and educated in the arts than are their U.S. counterparts. Hence, the Latins may view their opposites as technically competent, but culturally narrow. Conversely, Anglo technicians may perceive their Latin opposites as defensive on technical matters, autocratic in their behavior toward subordinates, and socially aloof.

TIPS to help you deal with a hierarchy-conscious Latin negotiator:

- Negotiate with the decision maker only. If humanly possible, do not deal with subordinates; their code of behavior makes them avoid any decision they can get their superior to make. Moreover, they have neither the big-picture knowledge nor the authority to fashion the creative trade-offs demanded by a win-win negotiating strategy.
- Latins hold sellers[5] and smaller companies in lower esteem than buyers and large companies. If your smaller company is selling, it is doubly important that it be represented by a high-ranking executive. The extra clout will at least partially offset its perceived lower status, and help gain access to the Latin firm's decision maker. If you are selling, take pains to be especially deferential.
- Latins' concern with status makes it important that the head of your team has a position title (e.g., Director or Vice President) and a professional title (e.g., Dr. or Engineer) at least equivalent to the Latins' team head. Whatever the circumstance, always make the Latin feel he is drinking upstream from the rest of the herd.
- Hierarchy breeds paralysis of the tongue at lower levels. Subordinates will agree with the head of the Latin team because he is the boss, not necessarily because he is right. Foreseeing the implications of this relationship may let you allow the head of the Latin team to get into water over his head. If that happens, you can play the role of lifesaver, thus creating valuable personal equity at little cost. Consider your rescue of him as a personal "receivable" that you can call due later.

- In all cases, helping the buyer save face helps you save the order.
- Show deference by an adept choice of gifts. Many Latin executives have a penchant for wall displays of paraphernalia attesting to their stature. Prized memorabilia include framed letters, pictures, or prestigious-looking certificates.
- Astute Latins are aware of a cultural tendency of egalitarian Anglos to champion the underdog. That tendency can be used by Latins to gain advantage, playing "the position of the weaker partner in negotiation, of the side that needs special consideration for being disadvantaged, even to flatter the stronger [U.S.] partner's capacity to provide extra help."[6]

2. *Structure-Need.* The different needs of Latins and Anglos for structure underlie the way risk affects each as negotiators. High structure-need Latins are risk averse and are more motivated to preserve what they already have, rather than risk a loss. Lower structure-need Anglos are ready to risk a loss if there is a prospect of high profit.

On the surface, the Latin propensity for structure seems at odds with a parallel tendency toward fatalism. For example, Latins commonly avoid buying high-cost local insurance, believing that attempting to insure against the dictates of fate is a futile act, hence an unnecessary expense. Therefore, your Latin associate's business assets, such as buildings, inventories, or truck fleet, would not be covered if lost to casualty. If an uninsured loss crippled Latin operations, it could injure your own firm's revenues. Hence, it is in your negotiating interest to have your Latin associate acquire insurance coverage. A two-stage approach to present this appeal in a compelling way would be (1) to offset your Latin partner's customary fatalism by appealing to his culturally determined low-risk preference, and (2) once you have made him a believer in risk management, help him find an international underwriter who will charge lower policy premiums than a local carrier.

TIPS to help you understand and deal with a high structure-need Latin negotiator:

- He will prefer to preserve the security of his company than to "bet the farm" on a potentially high-return but moderately risky venture.
- He will resist risking the possibility of a short-term loss, even if taken to achieve a high long-term payoff.

- He is looking for quick-payback deals in markets of untested or limited size, so he will find high unit profit more appealing than high-volume sales.
- He will want a tightly defined agreement, accommodating all conceivable contingencies in his favor.
- He will ask for pie-in-the-sky terms and boilerplate protection in written agreements, especially in clauses dealing with exclusivity, seller financing, shared expenses in market development (e.g., training, cooperative advertising, promotional giveaways), warranty returns, after-sales service, and technical support.
- He may be slow to settle his accounts payable if you concede the open-account or consignment-sale terms he requests.
- If you refuse to invoice in local currency, he may attempt to negotiate an adjustment in the dollar-denominated invoice amount he owes, based on adverse movement in the local exchange rate.

3. *Social Orientation.* Social orientation describes a cultural preference toward either individualism or collectivism. The high propensity of Latins to be group oriented, rather than finding social identity within themselves as Anglos are prone to do, inclines Latins toward placing a high priority on cultivating long-term relations. As a result, U.S. negotiators who have formed a bond with Latins often discover that the relationship that has evolved is one of a close personal nature between two individuals, rather than a detached business association between two companies. Therefore, if the U.S. negotiator is replaced, the personal relationship may have to be reestablished before negotiations can advance. The easy interchangeability of negotiators in the United States is less common in Latin America.

Social orientation also affects the choice of who sits at the bargaining table. Negotiators from group-oriented Latin cultures are often chosen for their family or social ties. These criteria contrast with proven competency as the basis for choosing team members in the United States.

TIPS to help you deal with a *low individualist (high collectivist)* Latin negotiator:

- Without an introduction from an individual within a Latin's circle of contacts, U.S. executives may not be taken seriously. Nonetheless, opportunities to penetrate in-group barriers are abundant, and extend even to telephone behavior: If you have a name to drop, do not hesitate to drop it early during a telephone contact. If you do not have a name to drop, get one. During initial telephone calls to the Latin firm, an alert U.S. caller will get, recall, and use the name of whomever answers in order to establish relational connections in later calls.

- Frame your negotiating proposition in terms that are important to a Latin's group culture. If the company is a family business, your appeal should press the hot buttons of the family's pride, reputation, and traditional values.
- Always portray yourself as a long-term player. For example, greet your opposite by saying, "I am happy to be here with you today because, for many years, my company has wanted to work closely with another high-quality company to establish a long-term position in your market."
- Relative to individualist Anglos, group-oriented Latins are more interested in the interpersonal dimension of the negotiation, and less focused on the cold, factual content of the deal. Therefore, the assertive sales or negotiating approach some Anglos use in the United States will not be warmly received by Latins who seek to build long-term relationships based on trust between friendly partners. It is in your best interest to be low key, and not appear constantly on the prowl for the last drop of short-term profit. If you do not shoot for the basket every time you have the ball, the Latins will view you as a cooperative player, rather than a predator.
- In contrast to U.S. executives who make decisions impersonally on the basis of cost-benefit factors, group-oriented Latin negotiators are very conscious of saving face. If you disagree with a Latin's position, be subtle about expressing any criticism. Giving face (by using titles, praising any success, or recognizing expertise) builds your negotiating advantage. But if you slam the door in a Latin's face, he will make it swing back to break your nose.
- Leaders of family firms in Latin America often are also the guardians of their family's traditions. They will not respond well if they perceive a U.S. negotiator's proposal as a threat to their customary way of doing things or as compromising privacy or disturbing stability within the family-owned firm.

4. Rule Orientation. Universalism underpins the Anglo sense of fairness, and parallels the U.S. common-law principle that all men should be treated "in common." That mind-set collides with Latin particularism, the attitude that a particular situation is outside the scope of any rule and must be judged with discretion. Latins refuse to be stamped with rank-and-file uniformity, and dispute rules imposed by others, especially outsiders. Differences between universalism and particularism become especially relevant in stage six of the negotiating process, follow through, discussed later in this chapter.

TIPS to help you deal with a *particularist* Latin negotiator:

- In addition to remembering and repeating names when you meet Latins, try to find some common ground in an effort to share and enjoy a mutual interest.
- Do not be surprised if Latins request highly personalized customer-service attention.
- Remember, where rule of law is subordinate to rule of men, the trust you establish with Latins will be worth more than their signatures to ensure compliance with the contract.
- When proposing an offer or conceding a position, make it appear that you are extending a special favor or advantage not normally available to others.
- Expect at least subconscious resistance to the implied assumption that your systems, standards, and best practices are transferable to the Latin American operating environment. They may not.

5. Communication. As discussed in Chapter 4, it is customary for Anglos to be verbally explicit and for Latins to use many nonverbal cues to exchange ideas. Communication differences lead many U.S. managers to view negotiations as exercises in problem solving. They approach the current deal as a matter that should be conducted with as much expedience and as little ceremony as possible. When the deal is done, they put it behind them, and move on. Anglos are prone to see speed and efficiency in the conduct of business as a natural, normal, and desirable condition.

TIPS to help you deal with a *high-context* Latin negotiator:

- Do not expect Latins to be held hostage to the tyranny of practicality. For Latins, negotiating calls for a level of rhetoric and imagery suitable to the import of the occasion. They gain little joy from an unceremoniously initiated, coldly conducted, and abruptly finalized negotiation.

- Your congenial demeanor, education, and pedigree are among the signs Latins will note in assessing whether there exists enough interpersonal traction to move the business relationship forward and into the future. Without the expectation of a continuing personal association, Latins will seldom be predisposed to make any significant negotiating concession.

6. *Time and Space.* A timely rule to remember: Mañana only means not today. For Anglos, time waits for no man. Once a moment has passed, it is lost forever. Our monochronic view of time leads us to a single-focus approach to negotiating. We concentrate on doing one thing at a time, following plans, and meeting deadlines. Polychronic Latins are adept at dividing their attention to synchronize their schedules with multiple time demands. While negotiating with you, a busy Latin executive may also be conferring with his plant manager, signing a purchase order, instructing his driver to pick up a customer's blueprint, and scheduling a tennis game with an old school chum. His just-in-time agenda is not a discourtesy. It is the way he is culturally programmed to respond to simultaneous demands. When those demands exceed the time available to satisfy them, he will reschedule his agenda of meetings and deadlines. Latins understand that postponing an event to mañana merely means that it will not happen today. Only non-Latins believe that rescheduling for mañana means it will happen tomorrow.

TIPS to help you deal with a *polychronic* or *multifocused* Latin negotiator:

- Take time to smell the roses: To Anglos, time is scarce, it must not be wasted on economically nonproductive pursuits. To Latins, time is also scarce and should be used to enhance the quality of life and personal relationships. Adjust your pace and expectations to respond to another cultural rhythm.
- Lifestyle orientation predisposes Latins toward negotiating goals centered on quality-of-life issues, while Anglos focus more on enhancing business performance and gaining market power.
- Be tactful, but do not allow effusive rhetoric to trump factual reality at the negotiating table. The eloquence, emotion, and conviction with which a position is expressed is more important to some Latins than the facts that support that position.
- Dress to impress. High-context Latins tend to associate quality in dress with personal power. By projecting an image of authority and success, you increase your negotiating advantage.

- Be prepared to play the waiting game, especially if you are to meet with a government official: You will join others being served strong coffee in a waiting room that varies in size according to the rank of the official. Even if you are kept at bay for hours, avoid showing any irritation when you finally gain access to the official's office. For all you know, you may have been bumped ahead, not farther back, in the waiting line. Two tips to avoid waiting-room aggravation: Always (1) carry something to read or keep a work folder with you, and (2) put your watch away.

Arm's-length negotiating? Not here. Offices that seem like public-meeting halls, embracing when meeting and leaving, and jostling in lines can exact a psychological toll on Anglo visitors to Latin America. Although both Anglos and Latins know intuitively what is the right distance to keep between people, that distance is less for Latins than for Anglos. As guests in Latin America, Anglos should adapt to the host culture's custom and be prepared to negotiate at hand's length.

TIPS to help you deal with a *close personal-space* Latin:

- When a Latin moves in to be physically close to you, do not back away. Over time, you will learn to act unfazed as the space between you disappears.
- For Anglo women, following the Latin custom of maintaining close personal space straddles a thin line between being socially congenial and sexually available. Female executives can maintain proximity without inviting intimacy by facing their bodies at least 60 degrees away from their conversational partner, placing most of their weight on the leg closest to him (to lean slightly away), directing their hand gestures toward a point located at a distance on the line bisecting the angle between the two, and making only occasional, brief eye contact.

7. Formality. Mind your manners. As appearances are important indicators of social status in Latin America, U.S. negotiators should pay attention to the images they project. Dressing appropriately, staying in quality hotels, not chewing gum or slouching, and not being seen carrying their own luggage (or any item larger than a briefcase or laptop computer) may seem like unnecessary affectations in the United States, but they are important behavioral details in Latin America. For your first meeting, dress conservatively. Subsequently, you will probably want to follow the example set by your Latin associates. Formal business dress is expected in the large cities and more temperate mountain regions of Latin

America. Even in some of the smaller provincial cities of tropical Latin America, the dress code for business meetings is formal, and negotiators are expected to appear in suits or sport coats with stylish ties. The guayabera is a most practical and welcome exception to the formal dress code. It is popularly accepted as a substitute for the coat and tie in much of Central America, Cuba, and the coastal areas of Brazil, the Dominican Republic, Ecuador, and Mexico.

TIPS to help you deal with *high-formality* Latin negotiators:

- Commensurate with their perceived high positions, U.S. executives should learn to become comfortable when being deferred to, while at the same time formally respecting the personal dignity of lower-level managers, secretaries, workers, and drivers. This is a delicate balancing act that informal and egalitarian Anglos sometimes find unnatural.
- Do not gloss over or attempt to redirect Latins' comments about history, tradition, social position, or family past. They are reference points that, although they may appear to Anglos as extraneous to the mainstream of the negotiation, Latins use consciously to subtly communicate an important point or subconsciously to judge the suitability of business partners.
- Business protocol requires you to always use formal titles, even in the heat of negotiating, and never address Latins by their first names until invited to do so.
- Be especially deferential to the oldest Latin at the table. In addition to the respect that age commands in a formal culture, the senior member of the negotiating team should have your esteem because he is likely to be the key decision maker.

Table 5.1 lays out the differences between U.S. and Latin American styles of negotiation.

STRATEGIES: NEGOTIATING WITH A TAILWIND

International negotiating is no longer reserved for Fortune 500 power brokers or silver-tongued diplomats. It is a staple of today's global marketplace and is simply a plan to get you where you want to go at the least cost. It divides conveniently into two clear-cut approaches. One is to confront your Latin negotiating opposite as a headwind that must be overcome.

Table 5.1
Summing Up Differences between U.S. and Latin American Negotiating Styles

Negotiation Variable	U.S. Tendency	Latin American Tendency
Basis of trust	Legal contract, then experience	Friendship, then legal contract
Role of personal involvement	Avoid involvement and conflict of interest	Personal involvement is major component of decision making
Negotiator selection criteria	Technical expertise, function in organization	Family or social ties, title in organization
Role of face-saving in making decisions	Slight. Decisions are based on cost-benefit analysis	Great. Preserving personal dignity is paramount
Decision-making process	Systematically organized	Spontaneous, impulsive
Negotiation agenda	Fast paced	Slow paced
Interpretation of *mañana*	Tomorrow	Not today
Extent, type of pre-negotiation preparation	Medium-high. Financial and technical analysis	Slight. Limited to awareness of company or brand name
Focus of negotiating goal	Cost-benefit ratio	Best bargain
Negotiation perspective	Win-win	Win-lose
Time perspective for deal under negotiation	Medium-term	Short-term
Time perspective for business relationship	Medium-term	Long-term

Table 5.1 (*continued*)

Negotiation Variable	U.S. Tendency	Latin American Tendency
Adherence to agenda and deadlines	Strict	Casual
View of opposite party	Neutral	Friend, social equal
Emotional sensitivity	Not highly valued	Highly valued
Emotional display	Impersonal	Passionate
Loyalty to employer	Low	High (may be family)
Risk tolerance	Medium-high, if justified	Low
Opening bid	Reasonable	Extreme
Type of arguments used to defend position	Concrete, rational	Vague, emotional
Power tactics	Real power, legal enforcement	Threat of withdrawal or stronger consequences
Taking a settlement position	Making a final offer	Reopening previously closed issues
Form of final agreement	Formal legal contract	Word of honor supplemented by brief written agreement

The other is to work in harmony with her, using her own desire to move forward as a tailwind assist to speed both of you to where you want to go.

Win-Lose versus Win-Win

Negotiations everywhere perform two purposes:

1. They bring people together who have interests in common.
2. They bring people together who have interests in conflict.

Stated succinctly, "[W]ithout common interests, there is nothing to negotiate for, and without conflict there is nothing to negotiate about."[7]

The instinct of competitive bargainers is to dominate. Viewing negotiation as an irreconcilable conflict, they use a take-no-prisoners approach, leaving few crumbs on the table for the other side to take home. This is a win-lose perspective and is at odds with the win-win approach of cooperative negotiators that focus on each side's common interests.

Win-lose strategy is also called zero-sum, because if one party is to win a larger piece of the pie, the other must give up a slice of equal size. It is a strategy influenced by commodity traders who once dominated Latin America's international trade. It is also used by unskilled U.S. negotiators that fall into the trap of status games and power plays. In either case, zero-sum bargainers see price as the main chip on the table and, as in a poker game, see nothing to be gained from cooperation among players. Indeed, as players scheme to win the pot, it is in their best interests to use bluffing, deception, intimidation, and aggression against their adversaries. At some point in their lives, these types of predatory bargainers were sold the lie that negotiating is something you do *to* others for your own benefit, rather than something you do *with* others for mutual benefit.

Headwind resistance common to win-lose approaches can be transformed into tailwind cooperation with win-win negotiating. Win-win strategies are also called positive-sum because their aim is to increase the size of the pie, so that both sides get a satisfactory slice. They rely on both parties cooperating honestly to see, among the possible negotiable tradeoffs, what the real and nonconflicting interests are that could be combined to create an acceptable package for both. If the buyer's priority is quick delivery for immediate use on a project, and the seller's priority is to have a working unit in the market to use as a demonstrator, there is a basis for agreement that may not require much haggling on price. Win-win negotiating is more like a bridge game, where each side achieves its goals by helping the other side move toward its own goals. Skilled win-win negotiators distinguish between stated positions and true needs. They understand that by looking beyond differences in positions and focusing on meeting the needs underlying those positions, each side can be a winner. To convince Latins to choose you over your competitors, get into the habit of uncovering their highest-priority needs.

Given the absence of cultural traditions that discourage bludgeoning into submission a low-power opponent or an outsider, traditional hierarchy-conscious, group-oriented Latins tend to approach negotiations from a win-lose perspective. If the Latin you are dealing with has these traditional values, and if you wish to achieve the productive outcome that a win-win strategy can produce, you must earn the trust that will give you in-group membership. It is toward the win-win model that experienced negotiators, nurtured in nontradition-bound, high-trust, and egalitarian social environments such as the United States, tend to gravitate.[8,9] The new generation of Latin negotiators also know instinctively that "we" is stronger than "me," and that they can gather more mangos when both sides shake the tree.

Alternatives to Price

Positive-sum negotiating gets win-win results because, in the process of arriving at a final agreement, the parties make trade-offs from among a wider range of possible concessions than price alone could provide. These trade-offs give you a chance to win a high-value concession in exchange for one that costs you less than it is worth to the other side. The way in which you make concessions may be of greater consequence than their economic value. Sizable concessions have been won at small cost in Latin America by U.S. negotiators who know how to make a small counter-concession look like a gold mine to the other party. To appear a winner can be important to a proud Latin, especially if he is in the presence of subordinates. It could provide him with the face-saving image he needs to put a positive spin on having lost valuable ground.

The counter-concessions that are least costly tend to be those that are not directly tied to revenue. Trades dealing with warranties, seller-arranged financing, minimum stocking requirements, packaging, exclusivity, advertising materials and samples, technical support, prospect lists, and the like can be nonprice bases for you to make relatively low-cost concessions in exchange for ones of higher value.

Smaller U.S. exporters commonly misperceive that they must negotiate on price because their size precludes them from having nonprice advantages of value to an international buyer. What they fail to grasp is that, for many Latin American buyers, dealing with a smaller U.S. firm can be desirable. For large U.S. firms, a smaller Latin American customer is often a nuisance account, one that represents the same overhead costs to service as a large buyer but does not have the latter's buying clout to merit giving it priority attention. Smaller U.S. firms, however, can give red-carpet treatment to that same Latin American customer because the latter's account can represent a large portion of the former's total sales. Smaller U.S. firms can accept small orders, adjust production runs, accommodate last-minute changes in shipping arrangements, and—important for Latin firms—be available for technical support or hand-holding whenever needed.

By turning a perceived size-weakness into a genuine strength, smaller U.S. companies can gain enough nonprice advantages in Latin America to enable them to hold firm on price.

Weighing When to Use the Two Approaches

Even if the advantage is all yours and you could drive the other party to the wall, you should not do so. A "take it or leave it, it's not negotiable" approach may work once, but it is not a formula for long-term profit. By squeezing the last drop out of the deal for yourself, you motivate the other side not to perform as agreed. Your Latin counterpart will have little incentive to do more than comply with the absolute minimum terms of the contract. He may not even perform at all. If so, your ability to force performance or seek damages through legal recourse may be slim. Moreover, the Latin will not be anxious to do business with you again and will do whatever is within his power to smear your name in the local business community. Remember, the best alternative to poor negotiating is good negotiating—not *no* negotiating. Avoid sitting at the bargaining table with a catcher's mitt in both hands. If your game plan is to win over the long term, or even in more than one single transaction, leave one hand free to throw something back. A sick sheep will follow anyone. Once it has recovered, though, it will look for a strong leader that values its long-term health.

Win-Win

When should you use a win-win negotiating strategy and when should you use a win-lose bargaining strategy? Win-win negotiating can deliver more profit over the long term. But it comes with a disadvantage. It may take more of your time to persuade and educate your Latin counterpart to play a role that is in sync with the free-flowing and honest positions that are the mark of win-win negotiators. Making the effort to get Latins on board for win-win negotiating can repay your time when any one of the following conditions are present:

- The foreseeable business at stake is long-term and sizable.
- You require a high degree of commitment by the Latin to make that sizable business potential a reality.
- It is important to the Latin to do business with you.
- The trust level between the parties is high, and the meeting mood is positive.

- The Latin's negotiating position is strong.
- You and your Latin associate find the search for trade-off options to be not just good business, but an intellectually satisfying game, akin to the greater scope for creativity that chess offers over checkers.

Win-Lose

If the requisite conditions for cooperation are absent, having a productive win-win negotiating session is not a likely prospect. But, if you still want the deal to happen, do not resign yourself to folding your hand. A better option is to mount a win-lose strategy. Be aware in advance that the mood in the zero-sum negotiating game you are about to play will be one of competitive haggling with an adversary, rather than cooperative problem solving with a partner. You and your opponent have mutually exclusive goals, and these goals are probably directly related to price issues. The following suggestions will help you make the most out of a no-holds-barred bargaining battle with a tough, hard-nosed opponent.

TIPS to help you deal with a hardball Latin negotiator:

- If this is to be a one-time deal, there is little reason to be "Mr. Nice Guy." You can be intimidating and tough, especially if your opponent uses similarly confrontational tactics. The occasional pushy Latin you encounter may be taken by surprise and subdued by what he had presumed to be a gringo pushover, but soon saw as someone who unexpectedly slammed his fist on the table, cried, screamed, or threw papers into the air.
- Beware of the extreme "first pencil" quote. If you are buying, this will be an extravagant offer designed to test your reaction, while simultaneously creating bargaining space for the buyer to raise his own bid and still make a good profit. If you are accustomed to negotiating rationally, you probably assume that the final price would be at the approximate midway point between the buyer's first bid and the seller's first asking price. If you are given a ridiculous initial price, react in one of three ways: (1) show shocked disbelief, then respond with an equally extreme offer in the opposite direction; (2) use silence, simply sitting, not saying a word; or (3) begin to gather your things together and stand up. Before walking out, however, make certain that you have considered the consequences of a scrubbed deal and have backup options available. The sight of you heading for the door will always get your opponent's attention, but it may not always motivate him to bring you back to the table with a more attractive counteroffer.

- Hard-bargaining Latins want you to surrender, not settle with a compromise. They may use their force of personality to intimidate and issue ultimatums. In this scenario, your worst enemies are confusion and lack of information. To take them out of their game, insist they use objective claims supported by fact.
- Always separate fact from faith. If your Latin opposite makes an undocumented claim that affects how you value the transaction, do not accept it as truth until you can substantiate it. If you need time to verify it, do not hesitate to delay the negotiation. If requesting a delay evokes anger, hysterics, or a guilt trip for impugning the Latin's honesty, your doubts are probably valid. Feel free to walk away.
- Information is your best ally. Guard it closely. As a buyer, do not disclose what you think is a fair price. A tough Latin opponent will not budge from that point. As a seller, do not disclose your cost. Your opposite will pressure you to sell at that level. Similarly, use information to find chinks in the Latin's armor. Piece together bits of information to estimate the Latin's likely target and resistance points.
- Just before reaching final agreement, try to extract additional small concessions from your opposite. The eager anticipation of being close to a finalized deal may drive an anxious negotiator to cave in on a demand if he believes that not conceding would kill the deal. Small nibbles can add up to a big bite.
- Beware the booby-trapped negotiating environment. Office temperatures that are too warm are not uncommon in midsize companies in the tropics. Steamy settings can impair your ability to think clearly. So too can endless small but potent servings of espresso. While that tasty coffee is a common companion of discussions in Latin America, too many of those demitasse servings can jangle your nerves and distort your judgment. Also abundantly present in out-of-office negotiating sessions is alcohol. Avoid drinking until after the deal is completed, feigning a medical condition if necessary.

STAGES: UNDERSTANDING THE PATTERN OF NEGOTIATING IN LATIN AMERICA

Formal studies of how real negotiations take place confirm that the process conforms to a predictable pattern. As if following an unwritten law, the negotiation process divides itself into clear and predictable stages. The take-away value of knowing about the stages pattern is the edge it gives you in knowing what kind of behavior to anticipate from the other side at each stage. While it is useful to view the negotiating process as being divided into stages, the term may be misleading. Negotiating stages are not neatly sequential, and discussions do not always follow a linear logic in Latin America. A new stage may begin while the earlier stage is still going strong, and issues raised in an earlier stage may still be present during a subsequent one.

Researchers differ on the number of negotiating stages, finding three, four, and five distinct stages.[10, 11, 12, 13] When these varied academic research results are viewed in a present-time, real-life context by negotiating veterans of Latin America, yet another pattern emerges. The negotiating pattern described below is the way successful deal making among smaller U.S. and Latin American firms really happens today. The practical advantage of this realistic model is the heads-up framework it provides so that you can plan and prepare your own negotiating strategies and tactics. Using the six-stage negotiating model that follows will help you to define goals, estimate costs, allocate time, and assign staff responsibilities to your Latin America negotiations. As a management tool, it will allow you to cost-effectively line up and aim your deal-making artillery at the most productive targets.

Stage 1: Preparation

A man surprised is half-beaten

—Thomas Fuller

Preparing and planning are as important as are cultural literacy and business sense for negotiating success in Latin America. Time taken to prepare is an investment, not an expense. Researchers confirm that planning is never wasted and found that negotiators who spent two or more times the average in planning doubled their success rate, while reducing the time spent negotiating by more than two-thirds.[14] Planning dividends are especially large in Latin America, where you can routinely expect the unexpected to happen.

Do your homework

There is no substitute for good intelligence. Research the target firm and team. Know its competitive position, both locally and internationally. Learn the business and industry environment in which it operates. Know the advantages or problems that could result if it did business with you. Find out if it is known for being ethical.

While the benefit of going into a negotiation with good information can be priceless, it does not have to be costly. Banks, chambers of commerce, industry associations, trade show contacts, commercial officers at U.S. embassies, country desk officers in the U.S. International Trade Administration, freight forwarders, and even Latin American MBA students at your local university can give you first-rate intelligence at very little cost. At the very least, some weeks before departing the United States, make it part of your daily routine to read the local Latin American newspapers in order to become familiar with the operating environment and issues that will be on the minds of the people with whom you will be talking. Being up to date on local conditions before you arrive is inexpensive and easy: Almost all major, and many secondary newspapers (including English language) in Latin America have same-day availability on the Internet.

Having taken care to be current on business-related issues, be certain you will not be blind-sided by logistical concerns. When planning travel arrangements, make it a point to factor in enough time for settling in and jet-lag recovery. Your appointment schedule should be less compressed than if you were traveling for business in the United States. Having to cope with the unavailability of people in their offices during the midday siesta break and on Friday afternoons, meeting delays and cancellations, and conflicts with national holidays and religious celebrations is an inevitable part of doing business in Latin America.

The Power of Partnership

Whether he is a prospective distributor, licensee, or supplier, the Latin with whom you are going to negotiate should be viewed as a potential partner or strategic ally. It is a good bet that he will also be measuring you for that role. It is surprising how many seemingly routine business transactions begun by smaller U.S. firms in Latin America have evolved into close-knit partnerships with their Latin associates. For the smaller firm, especially, there is truth in the old adage that there is safety in numbers. Such firms know that fifty percent of a profitable business with a reliable partner is worth more than one hundred percent of a failure. Robert Heckman, CEO of U.S. Filter, said it this way: "If you don't have trustworthy [Latin American] partners, you can get into trouble; only idiots try to figure it out themselves."[15] To make cash flow happen as soon, as much, and as long as possible, prepare for each negotiating situation as a potential long-term relationship, rather than as a one-time deal. It is no coincidence that researchers confirm that superior negotiators comment twice as much about long-term issues than do negotiators of average performance.[16]

Vision without Action Is a Daydream, Action without Vision Is a Nightmare

Before beginning the negotiation, know what you hope to achieve at its end. First, you must write down your desired results, then use them as a blueprint to plan your negotiating strategy. The process is the opposite of rushing into the negotiation, assuming that desirable outcomes will somehow become self-evident.

Step back: Take a wide-angle look at your game plan and their game plan. Weak negotiators make up their goals as they proceed. Being in control of negotiating outcomes requires you to specify your objectives. Picture your objectives as the end points of a scale of possible price outcomes. At one extreme is your firm's target, a price that is acceptably profitable, and that research suggests you could reasonably expect to bring home. At the opposite end is your company's resistance point, the minimum price your company would accept. Make a sworn oath to yourself that any offer that falls short of your resistance point constitutes a no-deal condition, and a proposal from which you must be emotionally prepared to walk away.

Your next step is to estimate the same target and resistance points of your Latin opposite. By estimating what the other side expects to get out of the deal, you will have a clear idea in advance of where your goals are likely to overlap with the other side's and where they could be in conflict. Keeping those limits firmly in mind puts you in position to control an outcome that makes it possible for both parties to win. By having estimated in advance the true cost of the concessions you may be asked to make, and knowing the value of what you can expect to receive in exchange, you will be prepared to defend yourself against any surprise assault, and can position yourself to respond with a well-informed counteroffer.

By superimposing one scale over the other, as shown in Figure 5.1, you gain a big-picture view of how negotiations are likely to proceed before they begin. That overview will also enable you to adjust your approach by sensing when the Latins are taking a hard position and when they are bluffing. To play this poker hand, you must have a clear idea of the value to the Latins of what you can afford to give away, as well as the value to you of what they may concede. Figure 5.1 shows how, by comparing the tar-

Figure 5.1
Price Negotiation Range

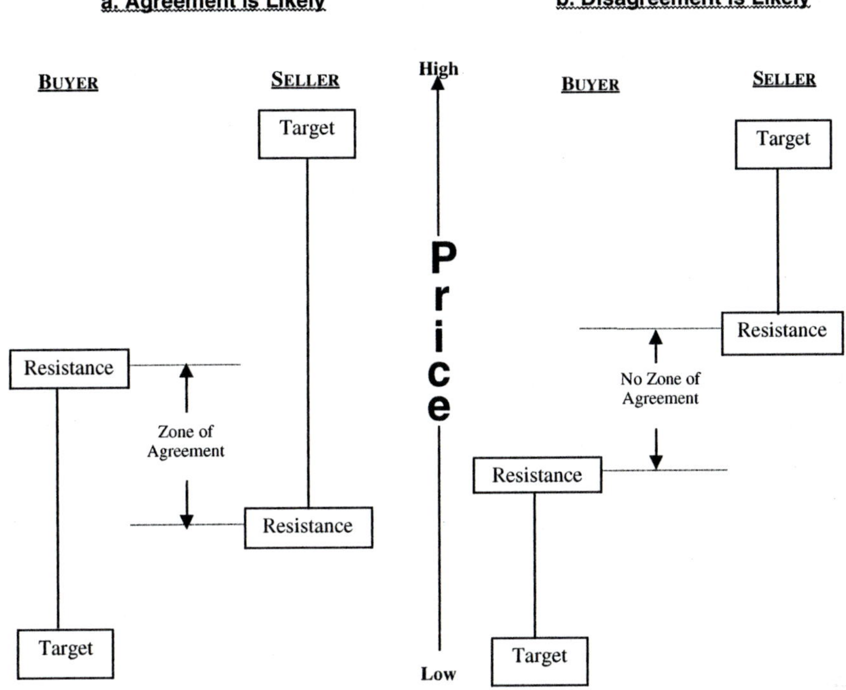

get and resistance points of buyer and seller, you can estimate whether an agreement can be reached and, if so, to what extent effective negotiating could improve your position.

Because the ranges of acceptable prices overlap in Figure 5.1a, there is room for a mutually satisfactory agreement to occur. You will know you are in an agreement zone if the response to your offer was a reasonable counteroffer. If so, with each successive counteroffer, you and your Latin opposite will be converging on a final settlement price.

Figure 5.1b poses a trying negotiating scenario. If the parties cannot move beyond price, the talks will fail because there is no zone where any price is acceptable to both parties. The talks can succeed only if nonprice factors can overcome the price impasse. To sell "beyond the wallet," a win-win approach is needed to create a range of nonprice benefits that buyer or seller values enough to close the price gap between them. For example, if you are the seller, and the Latin buyer objects to your lowest (resistance) price, you could shift the buyer's focus from purchase cost to usage cost by responding, "Yes, you could buy a [competitor's brand] product for a little less. But if it does not arrive in Villahermosa on time, or if it fails to function properly on your offshore rig, it will cost your company many times the slight difference in price you would save."

Avoid being a slave to a finger in the wind. It pays to plan the play and play the plan. Research shows that negotiators who invested more time in defining their negotiating limits and preparing their options were remarkably more successful than those who spent less time and had rigid objectives.[17] Research also confirms the advantages of having a clearly planned schedule of objectives. Successful negotiators tended to have five or more options prepared in advance, while less-successful negotiators focused on only one main objective, and were only occasionally prepared with one backup alternative.[18]

Luís Cabrera, a Mexican author, wrote, "On the field of battle, the gringos will always beat us, but we have the advantage at the negotiating table."[19] Latins' self-confidence, sense of hierarchy, and nonverbal communications practice can cause them to rely more on appearances and oratory than on solid preparation for negotiating advantage. Being prone to enter a negotiating session with only one or two vaguely defined goals (most often price, credit terms, or exclusivity) in mind, and counting on inspiration of the moment for a successful outcome, makes them shoot from the hip. As shots from the hip seldom disturb the target, Latins are left with two options: They must either wear down the other side by firing off a large number of noisy and time-consuming rounds, or save face by calling whatever they hit the target. Whether it be through expensive clothing, stylish grooming, an imposing office décor and furnishings, framed credentials and pictures, a large negotiating team, or "important" telephone-call interruptions, projecting an appearance of power is a poor substitute for the on-target results that an objective, well-aimed negotiation plan will yield.

Organizing Basis of U.S. and Latin Negotiating Teams

But if maintaining appearances can be the Achilles' heel of image-conscious Latin negotiators, obsessively individualist Anglos can fall into the Lone Ranger trap. When preparing for negotiations, ethnocentric U.S. executives may succumb to the I-can-go-it-alone attitude. Excessive self-confidence places U.S. negotiators at a serious numerical disadvantage when the negotiating pace accelerates. Experienced executives like to have at least two people with complementary skills on their negotiating team for three reasons.

First, it is advantageous to have available an extra pair of hands provided by at least one other person. Negotiating can be physically, intellectually, and emotionally exhausting. Your performance will improve if you can occasionally pass the ball off, or have a colleague handle distracting tasks like running spread-sheet scenarios, verifying information, editing a PowerPoint presentation, copying, faxing, or finding a 24-hour pharmacy to subdue the ill effects of the previous night's wining and dining.

Second, you may have left home feeling secure in your ability to handle decisions in the field on your own. After all, the Lone Ranger never had to check back with the home office, so why should you? In the heat of fast-paced negotiations, however, you may find yourself pressed to make a decision, either when you have little time or at an inopportune moment. Having a workmate on board lets you to buy time to reassess things by calling a break to confer. You may also see strong advantages in denying yourself the authority to have the final say. By claiming to have to refer final decisions back to the home office, you can extricate yourself from those situations when having to say no could risk setting back still-fragile interpersonal relationships. Finally, by sending only one representative, your company runs the risk that it will be seen by status-conscious Latins as having attached a low priority to the negotiation.

U.S. negotiating team members are usually selected for their professional competence and less often for their interpersonal or language skills. When trying to determine who will be sitting opposite them at the negotiating table, Anglos may assume that technical criteria were also applied when the Latin team members were chosen. That assumption is becoming more valid today among publicly held Latin American corporations. Nonetheless, among traditional family businesses, it is still rare to find Latin negotiating teams whose members are selected primarily on the basis of technical merit. Therefore, you will often see examples of Latins chosen to represent their employers because of family or club ties, or their *ubicación* (span of informal influence) in their firm's unseen hierarchy. While not always the sharpest technical knives in the drawer, their rhetorical and social skills are likely to be highly honed.

Latins may use an all-hands-on-deck team strategy. Their premise is that the sheer weight of their team size will put the (usually) smaller U.S. team at a psychological disadvantage. When facing legions of bodies across the table, you may find comfort in knowing that few of those bodies will affect decision outcomes. Most are empty suits, on stage only for show.

The U.S. penchant for participative management clashes with Latin traditions of one-person decision making. In Stage 1, it is important, but not always easy, to spot the decision maker on the Latin team. The member holding the greatest personal authority will be the Latins' kingpin. It would be a mistake for a U.S. negotiator to assume that the Latin team's power center necessarily resides in the member displaying the highest position authority (i.e., the most impressive job title) or the highest expert authority (i.e., the most technical skill). You will weaken your position by being unaware of the Latin team's pecking order and by not identifying the key Latin decision maker at an early moment. You could lose time and stature by misdirecting your attention to someone who has no final authority to buy or sell, and by offending the power figure by not showing him (seldom her) the respect that he feels he is owed. Sometimes the key decision maker is easily recognized by the presence of a deferential underling that screens calls, carries documents, or acts as a gopher for the main man. At other times, appearances may be deceiving, and the top man may be neither the one who seems to be orchestrating the meeting nor the one sporting the Rolex watch and the Giorgio Armani suit, but the rumpled-looking chap sitting on the sidelines who has not spoken at all. When dealing with family firms, elders having the same family name as the firm's are likely candidates for the top-dog role.

Be smart when organizing your team. If you decide to send a group, cost and psychological factors argue to keep it small. A large negotiating group not only inflates travel, lodging, and meal expenses, it may also intensify the colossus image linked to the United States. Take care to match the status of your team leader with the Latin team leader. As it is common for the Latin team to be headed by a senior officer, make sure that an executive of equal or higher rank is at the helm on your team. While your team head should be technically strong, it is also essential that he be a relationship engineer. After ensuring that members having the requisite technical skills are on board, make an effort to roughly match the ages, professional status, and personal characteristics of your team members with their Latin counterparts. Having professional and personal parity makes it easier for Anglo and Latin team members to interact productively during the critical relationship-building stage.

Regardless of your team's size, each of its members should play a defined role (e.g., marketing, engineering, financial, legal) and be responsive to the team leader whose purpose it is to coordinate these roles and provide policy guidance. Prior to leaving home, the team should meet to discuss objectives, strategies, fallback plans, competitors, and responsibilities, and to be briefed on the economy and culture of the target country and firm. A good plan can be a powerful organizing tool. But, by itself, it gets nothing done. Only well-prepared people make plans happen.

Each member of your team should have an ample supply of business cards. These will be exchanged formally and frequently with almost every new person at every business and social meeting. The cards should be printed in English and Spanish or Portuguese on high-quality coated paper, or the parchment-like stock described in Chapter 6. Academic titles should be used to the fullest extent possible. In addition to the usual contact instructions, do not forget to print your firm's regular telephone number in place of your 800 number (unless you have international 800 service). The same 800 number precaution extends to all of your correspondence, advertising, product labeling, and literature.

Failing to prepare is preparing to fail. Every football coach knows that behind the ninety minutes of play of a Saturday afternoon game lie countless hours of pregame training and preparation. While spectators assume the team won or lost the game on the field, the coach knows that the scoreboard result was predetermined by the preparation that took place months before the kickoff. Negotiating is no different. The quality of preparation is the single most important determinant of the outcome. Regardless of how urgent it seems to seal the deal, do not let yourself go into negotiations unprepared. Trying to fix in San Luís the mess created by having failed to prepare in St. Louis is like trying to overhaul an aircraft engine while flying 500 miles per hour at 30,000 feet.

Stage 2: Building Relationships

Trust Means Business in Latin America

Where the rule of law is weak, personal trust is the only secure foundation on which a business transaction can rest. In Latin America, personal relationships take precedence over business affairs. While their legal systems are improving, Latin America's executives are convinced there is still no substitute for knowing the person with whom you are doing business.

It takes cultural literacy to build trust. Culturally literate U.S. executives know that earning Latins' trust is the competitive-advantage equivalent of night-vision goggles. Their goal is to relate so well that their Latin customers refuse to buy from anyone else. The key ingredient of trust is sincerity. Treating each of your Latin associates as unique and special puts you on the shortest road to a buying decision.

You will know you are on the right road when both you and your Latin opposite openly recognize a common goal: to reach a productive, enduring agreement. When your mutual interest in reaching an agreement has been voiced and is on the table, the stage is set to use cooperation as the basis for arriving at a win-win solution. Having built a bond of trust with Latins does not mean that they will be any less determined to protect their interests. It only means that when the inevitable hard issues appear in the road ahead, they will be approached fairly.

You never get a second chance to make a first impression. A Latin's process for deciding whether to trust you is emotional. It bypasses his intellect, and is formed during the first moments after meeting you. As you project personal integrity, warmth, and concern, you are behaving at the emotional level required to overcome the Latin's trust barriers. Until you penetrate those trust barriers, any statement you make will have to pass through a fine-mesh screen before it is believed. Once trust barriers are pierced, you will enjoy the professional cooperation and personal warmth Latins extend to their *amigos de confianza* (in-group friends).

The personal touch pays. If cold-calling is a hit-and-miss approach to sales in the impersonal United States, it is always a miss in relationship-oriented Latin America. The balance of your personal-power account with a Latin is the sum of all the personal ties you have in common. A referral from a friend, an old classmate, or a colleague respected by your Latin opposite can be a good first deposit in your power account. More than one builds your balance. Good references raise your account value still more. If no personal acquaintance is available to introduce you, references from your local chamber of commerce or your bank (preferably one that is a correspondent with a prominent bank in the Latin's country) can help move you toward *de confianza* status.

In Latin America, industry associations and chambers of commerce (especially, the local affiliate of the U.S. Chamber of Commerce) are substantial organizations with influential members. They serve members' needs to make business contacts, influence government policy, and exchange informal information on topics such as supplier performance, customer payment behavior, and the honesty of public officials. Membership in these organizations opens doors by making you more credible, and also supplies pivotal information you will need if you intend to do more than sporadic business in a country. Trying to compete without being a member of these networks will dilute your ability to achieve your firm's full business potential.

Obey the negotiating speed limit in Latin America. Old Latin America hands know that time and deals are lost by U.S. executives who, ironically, are in a hurry to get down to the numbers, and not waste time on small talk. Speeding to the business agenda is prevalent in the United States, where it is considered normal to follow Vince Lombardi's advice on competing: "Winning isn't everything. It's the only thing." But rushing through the relationship-building stage makes U.S. executives commit the negotiating equivalent of drawing so fast that they shoot themselves in the foot. Their linear logic compels them to view the negotiation process as a means to establish a relationship between two companies in the shortest period possible.

Latins, on the other hand, view negotiations as a first step to test if the two parties can relate as individuals. For Latins, the time taken to build personal rapport is essential because, in its absence, no advance can be made toward a productive agreement. That is the reason why, in Latin America, it is usually pleasure before business. It is also the reason why you must allow time in your travel schedule for warming-up exercises: Local tours, ceremonies, social functions, and small-talk sessions are the cornerstones in building a foundation of personal trust. As a rule, the more important the deal, the more time that will be spent building relationships.

International business and negotiating are not for short-term players. The surest way to bring negotiations to a quick end is to agree to whatever proposal is in front of you. It gets you home sooner, but you will not have much to bring back with you. Investing the time to negotiate *al paso tropical* (at tropical speed) pays off in two ways. The first is the personal trust you convey by not appearing to be impatient to just sell a bill of goods before rushing off to the next deal. The other is to have time available for fact-finding.

Negotiating in a rush can make you miss crucial information. For example, if Latins seem to go off on a long, seemingly pointless conversational tangent, do not interrupt. They may be making an important point using deductive-reasoning logic. You will know this is happening when they first describe the form they would like the relationship between the parties to assume in the future. Then they address the specific transaction being negotiated, couching it in the context of a longer-term relationship. This is a logical approach, albeit one to which many inductive-thinking Anglos are not accustomed. Listen carefully. As with a rehearsed cough at the beginning of a short speech, the prologue centers attention on oratory, allowing Latins to be creative and exercise their personal flair. The best information is likely to come at the very end. On one occasion, a U.S. executive was in the departure lounge of an airport with the head of the Latin firm with whom he had spent three days of leisurely recreation and wide-ranging conversation. During that period, there had been only rare references to business. Only after the boarding call was made and the executives were saying their final good-byes did the Latin tell the Anglo that he looked forward to doing business with him, and that the Anglo would soon receive a purchase order. Returning to his office the next day, the U.S. executive found a faxed purchase order from the Latin's firm requesting, at list price, more units than he had expected to sell.

Two Different Teams from Too Different Cultures

The different criteria by which Anglo and Latin negotiators are selected can become an obstacle to building rapport between them. Because Anglo negotiators are chosen for their professional skills and Latins for their social position or family background, those different criteria can interfere with developing relaxed personal relationships. U.S. team members may feel that the Latins are more concerned with appearances than technical substance. The Latins, for their part, may view their U.S. opposites as parochial, limited in aesthetic awareness, and obsessively focused on narrow technical matters.

Compounding the possible social asymmetry between the U.S. and Latin negotiating teams can be cultural differences. Low-context members of the U.S. team may perceive their Latin counterparts as ambiguous, sneaky, or nondisclosing. For their part, high-context Latins may view Anglos as redundant, too obvious,[20] or *antipáticos* (unsociable). Small differences in communications context between Anglos and Latins can cause big misunderstandings. For example, it is normal for Anglos, while walking side by side with Latins, to converse by only occasionally turning their heads toward the latter. As Latins are accustomed to maintaining visual contact while conversing, they may abruptly stop, turning to directly face their companion. If an Anglo fails to fall into this type of stop-and-go pattern of walking and talking, Latins may be unsure whether the Anglo understood or, worse, if he was seriously interested in the topic.

To help bridge the social gap between U.S. and Latin negotiating teams, some U.S. companies have purposely included U.S. Hispanics as negotiators. Such attempts may be initiated by well-meaning U.S. managers who assume that U.S. Hispanics and Latin Americans will hit it off because they share a common language. The results of these initiatives are seldom neutral. In the best of cases, the U.S. Hispanics have been technically competent, well-educated, well-spoken in Spanish, and at ease in an urbane social setting. At the opposite end of the spectrum are many cases where, although the U.S. Hispanics were well qualified technically, their working-class origins placed them at a social and linguistic disadvantage with the upper-middle class Latins with whom they interacted. U.S. executives who are culturally adaptable and make efforts to overcome the language barrier, even if their Spanish or Portuguese is weak, will be well received. "But there's far less acceptance . . . for a U.S. Latino who travels to Latin America for business with poor language skills and limited cultural understanding."[21]

The visible hand rule: U.S. visitors should be aware of the role assigned to hands in Latin American society. They are always seen on top of tables, never in pockets, and are used to reinforce spoken words with vigorous, expressive gestures. Handshaking is always done when meeting and leaving. You should shake hands with everyone in the group, holding eye contact with that person before moving on to the next. While their grip is softer than the vice-hold used by Anglos, Latins frequently use both hands to emphasize personal warmth, and shake hands considerably longer than the customary two to four seconds allocated to the ritual in the United States.

In addition, a hand may be used as a potent communicator of confidence and trust by laying it on the shoulder or grasping the upper side of the lower arm. Obviously, the simpatico Anglo should not draw away from similar gestures made by Latins when used to signal nonsexual personal regard.

Feeding rules: Meals are considered more of a social ritual than a physiological imperative in Latin American business circles. While the business lunch atmosphere may seem relaxed and casual, the event is governed by its own set of rules. The first rule relates to suitable conversational topics. Although the event is a business lunch, you should not bring up any business matters. If business becomes a topic, it should be initiated by the Latins. Preferred topics are sports (if you know the local soccer team statistics, you will be revered as a God), travel (especially to European destinations), ages and interests of your respective children, local historic and cultural attractions, literature and philosophy, and current events. Being aware of protocol, you will always address Latins with their professional titles, never referring to them by first name until invited to do so.

Finally, remember that lunches are the largest meal in Latin America and last at least two hours. Dinners and elaborate cocktail receptions are socially intensive fetes, often lasting well past midnight. Therefore, you will be facing large amounts of alcohol during business-meal rituals. Even if the conversation does not touch on business, it is wise to control your alcoholic consumption if you wish to stay poised that evening and be at your best the next day. If a bout with liquor is unavoidably in the wind, two suggestions can prevent you from being blown away: (1) never drink more than you can lift, and (2) ingest a half-cup of vegetable oil prior to meeting with the *compañeros*. It will coat your stomach walls, diluting the effects of the alcohol. (Do not despair if you overlooked the vegetable oil when packing: The salad oil served at your table will do nicely, just find an appropriately surreptitious moment to consume it without raising eyebrows.)

Image management: Adding to trust barriers imposed by social distance is a long history of U.S. economic, military, and cultural dominance. Moreover, Latins see themselves stereotyped in U.S. TV and movies as unreliable, uneducated, lazy, or violent. Adding fuel to this smoldering resentment is a knee-jerk habit of some Anglos to view themselves as models of progress in matters relating to business, economic development, technology, and democracy. This perception of superiority compels some Anglos to prescribe rules of behavior for Latins. It requires a subtle sensitivity to say, "This approach worked for us when we had a similar problem," rather than, "Your idea is all wrong. The right way is the way we do it in Cincinnati." A warm showing of personal and professional respect defuses the potential for emotional face-offs. Smart U.S. executives know they are visitors in Latin America and display the social grace and modesty suitable to appreciative guests.

Stage 3: Information Exchange

This stage represents the outset of formal business negotiations. It is customary for the senior member of each team to inaugurate the first session with a broad, upbeat statement about the purpose of the meeting (the U.S. side will take care not to attempt to break the ice by telling a joke at this ceremonially serious moment) and a commitment to proceed in good faith to accomplish that purpose. If the initial mood of the meeting is to be one of win-lose bargaining, the remarks will be made between bared teeth, and aggressive demands will be voiced. On the other hand, if the Latin team is inclined toward win-win negotiating, that cooperative intention will be signaled by expressions of interest in discussing what each side can bring to the table.

Opening Moves

Following the initial general statements, your team should provide information on your firm's profile (e.g., sales, assets, number of employees, key customers), the professional and academic backgrounds of its negotiators, its competitive position, and specific data regarding its product and quality control, distribution channels, pricing, and sales support. Unless you have good reason to believe otherwise, assume that the Latin team has no knowledge of the background information. For that reason, you should describe in simple and direct terms what you hope to achieve in the negotiations, and explain why your goal is logical. This is the opportunity for the opposite side to gain a wide-angle view of your expectations and contributions, as well as your best offers and nonnegotiable positions. As the opening statements you make will set the stage for the rest of the negotiations, you must be well prepared, and careful in phrasing your position. As many Latins will have special needs for the non-physical components of your offerings, such as technical support, installation, training, financing, warranty, return policy, and the like, the presentation of your position should place the greatest emphasis on the competitive advantages of your overall value package, not just your core product.

In all cases, but particularly when dealing across language frontiers, take pains to be certain that your points are understood. Divide your discussion into bite-size pieces, pause to give Latins enough time to chew and digest each thought. Recapitulate often, repeating key points covered earlier. Encourage Latins to respond verbally to your thoughts or to rephrase them in their own words for you to verify.

During this stage, you should ask questions to fill in information you missed collecting in the preparation stage. A bonus to asking questions is that the deductive mind-set of Latins may predispose them to go beyond superficial or fragmentary answers, giving you big-picture insights into previously unseen patterns of market structure, business policy, or competitor behavior.

Authority Limits

This stage also provides an opportunity to establish if your Latin counterpart has authority to negotiate the final agreement. If not, you should learn exactly what are her negotiating limits. You may learn, for example, that she has authority to approve purchases of up to $1 million. If your deal is likely to close at $2 million, and if you have heard through the grapevine that her boss is a tough dealmaker, do not despair. You now know that your negotiating goal is to structure two deals at $1 million each.

Easy Transition: Common Personal Interests to Common Business Interests

You created common personal bonds with Latins in the earlier stages. Now is the time to capitalize on them by advancing naturally from those shared personal interests, taking a short step to present the negotiation process as a joint search for shared business interests. A simple means to accelerate that process with Latins is liberal use of the word *we*. Whereas using *I* and *you* calls attention to the space that separates you, reference to *we* points out the bridge that joins you. For example, if the Latin says, "I have too much capital tied up in slow-moving inventory," you say, "That's an issue *we* need to solve. *Let's* see if *we* could apply to *our* situation here in Lima what worked in Phoenix." Your taking part ownership of the Latin's problem makes him feel that he is no longer alone and can rely on your help to find a solution.

That commitment to a joint search for shared business interests is the psychological bedrock upon which win-win negotiating strategies are built. A routine reality of the win-win process is discovering that the parties' goals are not congruent. As differences surface during the question-and-answer sessions used to define each side's position, they should be addressed by focusing objectively on issues, rather than emotionally on personalities. Researchers find that negotiators who take more time to establish a collaborative feeling with their opposites are more successful than those who take less time and who frequently become bogged down in confrontational disagreements.[22] By maintaining a collaborative mood, you minimize the potential for conflicts that may arise later in the negotiations.

U.S. negotiators tend to take firm stands and state positions frankly during the information exchange stage. Research shows that, by contrast, Latins often resort to evasive responses, indirect answers, a change in topic, or lengthy commentary of little substance when they begin to feel uncomfortable with an issue or the way the negotiation is proceeding.[23] Backing off temporarily from the business at hand may help to reestablish a comfort level at which a productive information exchange can take place.

Active Listening versus Hearing

Because of cultural differences, Anglos may perceive Latins to be suspicious and oblique. The reality is distinct. Latins are testing the waters for strategic comfort, before diving into discussing the particulars of a specific transaction. From their side of the table, Latins may see U.S. negotiators as being pushy and having too narrow a view of the potential significance of this early contact between the companies. Thus, the U.S. side should avoid over-defending its position. It may paint itself into a tight corner from which it will be difficult to escape to pursue more desirable objectives that might emerge later.

Even when you disagree with the Latins, it will pay you to convince them that you understand their viewpoint. Ignorance of their limits (e.g., cost structure), language barriers, or emotion impedes clear communication. Therefore, when differences arise in how an issue is perceived, make those differences explicit, taking time to discuss them with the other side. To be aware of those differences, you must cultivate the habit of observing and listening, rather than merely seeing and hearing. Letting the Latins know that they have been heard and understood is the cheapest negotiating advantage you can gain. One benefit of active listening is the added knowledge and rapport you can use to gain concessions later. Another benefit is that Latins will be more attentive when it is your turn to explain your position if they feel you made the effort to understand theirs. Developing a habit of taking notes will help you be an active listener, and will also encourage Latins to keep the discussion on track and make their points in a clear and focused manner.

Muscle-Building Exercises

It is important during the information exchange stage to get a clear fix on your relative negotiating power. Knowing how important it is to the Latins to do business with you will be useful later on. If you are a seller, for example, find out early about your competition. Ask, "What other suppliers are you considering?" If the response does not seem plausible, it probably is not. If it does seem plausible, use it as an opening to put the spotlight on the comparative strengths of your offering and your firm.

Another way to measure the strength of your negotiating power is to ask, "What is your target date for delivery?" The response to this question will give you an insight into the Latin's sense of urgency. If the buyer requires the product immediately, then you have gained the triple advantage of knowing that (1) you are not dealing with a shopper but a serious buyer, (2) price may not loom as the most critical factor in the Latin's buying decision, and (3) you should emphasize your ability to be time competitive in the persuasion stage.

Gathering useful information is only one advantage gained from asking questions. Asking questions can be a powerful psychological tool. As the one who asks the questions, the negotiator is in a stronger position to control the negotiating process, thereby achieving better results.[24]

To further sharpen your negotiating edge, it is advantageous if the Latins believe you have options. This stage is an opportune time to create that belief. By implying you have other deals available, you gain the leverage to ask for concessions later on. Any credible efforts you make to reinforce the impression that you have alternatives will help strengthen your position. The more subtle you are in communicating those other options, the more credible and simpatico you will appear to relationship-sensitive Latins. One practiced U.S. executive improved his position during a negotiating session by "inadvertently" exposing the letterhead of the major competitor of his Latin opposite as he removed working files from his briefcase. Without having to appear boorish by directly asserting he had contact with the competitor, he won strategic ground in the subsequent negotiations.

Image works in favor of U.S. companies in Latin America. Latins tend to view U.S. firms as having unlimited access to capital, managerial skills, technology, and markets. Playing plausibly to that image can enhance the negotiating clout available to a smaller U.S. firm that would be considered an industry lightweight back home.

Stage 4: Persuasion

By this stage, you have established which are the likely points of agreement and which are points that still need to be resolved. Your goal is to persuade the Latins to resolve the points of conflict in a way that gives you what you need and also delivers what they need. If the Latins are now on board with a win-win approach, that is their goal as well. By demonstrating to them how your proposal meets their real needs, you will have advanced far along the road to a successful outcome.

The most direct route to a successful outcome lies in making it easy for the Latins to make a decision in your favor. Helping them see that it serves their interests to agree to your proposal is the key to persuasion. The surest way to bring them into agreement is to make them think it was their idea.

When reasonably approached, Latins are responsive to this tactic, falling comfortably into the cooperative dialog that underlies win-win negotiating. You can strengthen this cooperative mood by making some low-cost concessions to encourage reciprocity. If you must refuse a concession request or reject an offer, a careful explanation of your reasons for having to do so will soften the blow. Your tone should be assertive, neither pleading nor aggressive, placing you in the middle ground between being soft and being tough.

Your middle-ground position is bolstered by being able to present a strong, factually supported proposal. By comparing your product against that of your competitors, you will be able to point out why it is advantageous for the Latins to buy from you. As you make those comparisons, take care not to openly denigrate your competition. By impugning a competitor, you also point a finger at the prospective buyer for having chosen a rival as a supplier. Therefore, never directly tell a Latin something that he can tell you. The goal here is to ask the Latin questions that will make him expose your competitor's weaknesses. Your presentation of comparative benefits accomplishes three important goals in the persuasion stage. First, by communicating your own expertise, you present yourself as a knowledgeable expert who must be taken seriously. Second, you show yourself as a source of technical support to a field representative. Third, you model an effective sales presentation that Latin resellers can use to sell to their own customers.

Always act to reinforce that cooperation-building, middle-ground manner. If the Latin is buying, and offers an unrealistically low price, avoid responding in a challenging manner: "That is unacceptable. We thought you were a serious buyer." Rather, answer in an even tone: "Our costs for that unit are much higher, and I know that headquarters will ask why I would ever consider that price. Can you help me defend it? What market or cost factors support it?" Arguing creates a gulf. Questions create a bridge. Imply that the two of you are jointly determining a fair price based on objective, factual evidence. Use questions to invite fact-supported positions. But do not yield to the conditioned buying response that impels some Latins raised in an open-air market environment to ask for a lower price, regardless of the amount initially quoted.

Neither should you be deterred by emotional arguments. Latins often rely more heavily on rhetoric and drama than on logic and fact when attempting to persuade.[25] Research shows, for example, that Brazilians use the word *no* nine times more frequently in negotiating discussions than do U.S. negotiators.[26] Although Anglos are culturally prone to treat emotional outbursts by Latins as antagonism or frustration, such conduct is common in cultures that emphasize passionate expression and energetic elocution to communicate. That is why it is counterproductive to display resentment when responding to a Latin's emotionally intense behavior.

Nonetheless, the culturally ingrained and emotional manner of some Latins can become a significant factor in the persuasion stage. The factual evidence you present to support your proposal may be ignored by the Latins. Their impatience with empirical data stems as much from a distrust of documentation as from considering it an obstacle to reaching an accord on general principles.[27] In such cases, it can be effective to remark, "Many of our customers asked the same questions initially. Now, they are our company's strongest ally." Then support your statement with testimonial letters or other evidence of satisfied customers.

It would be naïve to assume that all your negotiations with Latins will be without pressures. Negotiations can become downright confrontational. If there are destined to be some hardball exchanges, the gloves are most likely to come off during the persuasion stage. When the mood turns confrontational, the exchanges may temporarily or irreversibly regress from win-win negotiating to win-lose haggling. If the process is to be turned away from fruitless altercation and exasperating shouting matches, and redirected back toward productive agreement, it is essential to understand the core reason for the change in negotiating climate. Experienced negotiators can turn a degenerating process around by being able to discriminate whether the mood swing can be explained by real business-related differences or by interpersonal differences attributable to unfamiliar cultural behaviors or negotiating tactics. Do differences appear to be real (i.e., not fabricated to create a tactical advantage), and are they business-related? If so, it is a signal to call for a time-out to reevaluate both parties' positions. Can other offers or counteroffers be made that could salvage the deal?

When resolving business-related differences, never lose sight of the role that politeness can play in bridging the cultural gap. The direct manner of many U.S. negotiators may appear rude, triggering animosity in Latins that use diplomatic, indirect approaches to reconcile differences. To avoid friction, let Latins know you appreciate their point of view. Substituting *but* with *and* can be helpful. In that Latins have a trained ear for verbal camouflage, when they hear the word *but* they tend to discount whatever precedes it. Thus, rather than risk hard-earned rapport by saying, "You may think that price is important, *but* you're not taking into account . . ." say, "I understand your concern for price, *and* know that another important consideration for you is . . ."

If the fading spirit of cooperative problem solving is less the result of real business differences and more attributable to personalities, it is a sign that the trust you believed was well established earlier is now unraveling. The negotiation table is not the place to patch up the torn fabric of frayed relationships. More time, a change of scenery, and light distractions are needed. It is time to call for a break, and schedule a round of golf or a social event after both parties have had a cooling-off period. Before doing so, reiterate your commitment to reaching a mutually satisfactory agreement, and your belief in the good faith in which both sides are negotiating to achieve that goal. When you resume negotiations, avoid the temptation to make any significant "Monday morning concession." Instead, let the Latins make any first move to smooth ruffled feathers by conceding their formerly rigid position.

Listening with Your Eyes

There is more to communicating in Latin America than meets the ear. Many Anglos would be surprised to learn that face-to-face negotiations with Latins are conducted in three languages: speech, silence, and body language. Of the three, U.S. executives depend most on speech to explicitly transmit their messages. Being more implicit, Latins rely more on silence and body language to convey meaning. Overlooking those nonverbal messages can undermine an otherwise strong negotiating strategy, dooming U.S. executives to the tactical equivalent of entering the bargaining arena blindfolded. By relying less on their mouth and ears, and more on their eyes, U.S. negotiators will move the ball farther into the Latins' end zone.

Silence. Experienced negotiators know that when the customer is talking, the sale is moving forward. But, there are frequent occasions in cross-cultural negotiations when silence prevails, and you should understand its significance and how to react to it.

The significance of silence in negotiations is different in Latin America than in Asia. A silent response by Japanese or Chinese negotiators to an offer indicates that the other side's proposal is being respectfully weighed. The Asian axiom, "He who knows does not speak, he who speaks does not know,"[28] expresses the wisdom of meditating silently before responding. But when Latins respond to a proposal with silence, they likely are driven by different motives. One reason is that polite Latins simply wish to maintain social harmony and use silence to avoid seeming rude by openly disagreeing with you. You must break the impasse in such cases, because you need to understand what lies behind their opposition. To grasp their position, reframe the discussion. Express your proposal in other terms, then ask the Latins if they understand it, or which of its elements they would like you to further explain. This approach solves two problems: (1) it allows the Latins to avoid appearing rude by having to say no to you, and (2) it forces to the surface the information you need to identify and address the real sticking points.

Some Anglos react awkwardly to silence, seeing it as an impasse that must be broken by a new proposal or concession. Hence, silence can become a tactical tool of culturally savvy Latins to make U.S. negotiators uneasy, pressuring them into taking a softer position or revealing sensitive information. Indeed, Latins may intuitively sense that "silence [is] deafening" to Anglos whose low-context cultural orientation makes them feel a responsibility to keep the conversation in motion.[29] Skillful Latin negotiators also use silence to unhinge Anglos who see time as money and view silence as an unwanted expense. The Spanish saying, "Uno es esclavo de lo que dice y rey de lo que calla" (One is slave to what he says and king of what he withholds) mirrors the culturally ingrained regard Latins have for the value of silence.

Whatever the Latins' purpose for using silence, do not be shaken off balance. Use the rephrasing and questioning technique described above to get the ball back under your control, and rolling again. But avoid making any loosely considered attempt to reengage the discussion. You not only risk giving the Latins a psychological advantage, but may reveal damaging information, learning that it is easier to let the cat out of the bag than to put it back in. Instead of digging down deeper when you are in a hole created by your own culturally based responses, turn what you sense are manipulative intervals of silence to your own advantage. Excuse yourself to use the restroom, check your e-mail, or—if you believe the Latins are using silence as a power play, and you know your position is strong—ask the secretary to call for a taxi to your hotel.

Body Language. Your body language makes it difficult to hide your true feelings or tell a lie. In Latin America's high-context communication culture, a mood, a change in posture, a tone, a gesture, a look, a movement, can convey more than words or silence. It is estimated that as much as 93 percent of face-to-face communication is nonverbal.[30]

High-context Latins are masters of the art of body language. They constantly signal their meanings at a level that operates below the conscious threshold of many Anglos. Be attentive to your instincts, they are working full-time to transmit important messages to you, and they are probably right. Take the time, and have the patience to listen with your eyes to what the Latins are saying nonverbally with their bodies. Be alert to nuances that silently signal whether you are going down the right or the wrong path. If something intuitively seems wrong, it probably is wrong. Fix any misunderstandings before they become a problem. But always act relaxed and in control while doing so. If you see the Latins getting tired, call for a break. When you resume, ask, "Would you like me to go over that last detail again?" Repeating points made earlier is especially useful if talks are being conducted in English. When communication is nonverbal, those who use only their ears to spot red flags are blind to hazards on the road ahead.

Anger

Although anger is only one letter short of danger, it is a common tool for blunt-spoken negotiators to use when trying to hammer out a deal. Beware of using this tactic with Latins, who react adversely to emotional outbursts by non-Latins. Displaying ire to Latins is a cultural variation on Russian roulette. You can get away with it now and then, but eventually, the hammer will fall on a loaded chamber. When that happens, the least of your problems will be having to explain to the home office why you are returning with an unsigned agreement that the prospective buyer flung in your face. Having you and your company blacklisted forever in a Latin country by an insulted and influential member of its business community is a real risk you take by allowing yourself the momentary satisfaction of venting your anger.

Executives experienced in Latin America know that when the negotiating atmosphere becomes emotionally charged, they have two options: They can either control their own emotions or be controlled by them. So, before becoming unhinged when you feel exasperated, consider whether you are being the master or the prisoner of your emotions. It will help you decide which battles to pick. Ask yourself, "Will this matter one year from now? One month? One week? Tomorrow?" And when you make a mistake, make amends immediately. It is easier to eat crow while it is still warm.

Anger is also a two-way street. And, fairly or not, the cultural rules of dealing with incoming anger from Latins are not the same as the rules that control your outgoing anger. In addition to having the same dreams, fears, and hopes you have, Latins are an emotionally spontaneous people who sometimes blow off steam. You can gain the upper hand when that happens by responding to their outbursts with restraint. How to respond is a judgment call and depends on the legitimacy of their outrage and their need to make or save face. Three options are to (1) encourage Latins to continue to vent until they deplete their venom, (2) ignore their outbursts, pretending that nothing untoward happened, and continue on a different discussion track, and (3) cool heated emotions through humor.

The last option, humor, is a risky tactic to deflect anger. But it can also be the most effective because Latins have a deep-seated appreciation for wittiness. An incident that occurred not long ago serves as an example: It was well past midnight, and the U.S. and Latin teams, having been negotiating since midmorning, had moved the talks to a restaurant. The U.S. team wanted to include a dispute-resolution clause in the agreement and suggested applying U.S. law in a U.S. state court. The leader of the Latin team who, I belatedly recognized as having had many-too-many drinks, asserted that I (as our team's interpreter and spokesman) had offended the dignity and honor of his nation's justice system. After lengthily berating Anglo arrogance and my own shameful complicity with U.S. economic and cultural imperialism, he paused long enough to pour himself another drink. In an even tone and with a straight face, I took advantage of the brief interlude, asking him, "You've been talking to my mother-in-law, haven't you?" In an instant, he burst into an uproarious belly laugh, the tension dissipated among all present, and he stood to give me an energetic *abrazo*. Without a word passing between us, we both knew that he had been testing my ability to relate as a human being, and not as a calculating machine, in the event that a dispute should ever arise between the firms. We said our goodnights, agreeing to meet for lunch. When we met again at the same restaurant, some twelve hours later, he greeted me with an already-signed memorandum of agreement. At that moment, I realized that my light-hearted response had allowed our team to pass his test.

Stage 5: Concessions and Agreement

Negotiation's fundamental truth is not complicated: Agreement is reached when each side believes its own interests will be served. Engaging that simple fundamental truth, however, requires you to obey negotiation's equally uncomplicated fundamental law: Once you have granted a concession, you cannot take it back. Because of this, always link your concession to the condition that the other side make a counterconcession. Recalling that if is the middle word in the *life* of a successful negotiator, make your proposals conditional. Say, for example, "I will agree to 60-day payment terms *if* you will agree to order a full container." Knowing how to trade off a concession of low value for one of high value is the mark of a skilled negotiator. But, regardless of how satisfied you are with the concession you won, it is essential to make the other side feel satisfied. To make the Latins believe they have fared well, make them work hard for any concession you grant. Then commend their prowess in having won it.

Time-conscious U.S. negotiators tend to be in a rush to make concessions, seemingly overlooking the fact that any position that can be conceded in the morning can also be conceded that afternoon, or next month. Surrendering a position in small increments is an effective way to convince Latins that they worked to earn a concession they won from you. If you are given a $10 offer after making a high first-pencil quotation of $20, do not accept it at once, even if the $10 offer meets your target price. Counter at $15, and let the Latins draw you down to $12.50. Your stubborn descent down the price slope makes the Latins feel that they bought at a fair price at the same time that it allowed you to win a 25% premium above your target price. Unless you retreat in small increments, it will appear to Latins that you would have been willing to sell for even less.

Whenever you make a concession, avoid creating the impression that your concession establishes a precedent for future negotiations. By magnifying the significance of any concession you make, and setting a deadline to take advantage of it, you remain in control and fortify the perception that your offer is a one-time opportunity. Most often, you will want to concede on nonprice issues before giving in on price. But, when you inevitably find yourself under pressure to concede on price, avoid appearing desperate or yielding to real or artificial urgencies, such as time demands. Never lower your price until you have answered these questions:

- How will this price affect profit?
- What is the value to you of any nonprofit advantage (e.g., market access, prestige, visibility) for getting this business?
- Can you add value rather than subtracting price?
- Will your buyer commit to a larger order?
- Will selling at a cut-rate price establish an irreversible and undesirable precedent?
- How important is it to the customer to do business with you?
- What is this client's potential to be an ongoing source of profitable business? Aggravation?
- What are the likely consequences if you do not lower your price?

If discounting your price appears unavoidable, consider doing it in the form of future discounts. A cumulative discount-pricing policy can be attractive to price-sensitive Latin buyers, providing them with an opportunity to save as they continue to purchase from you in higher volume. By crediting a portion of current invoice amounts to future purchases, you (a) create a price barrier that makes it difficult for competitors to lure away your Latin customer, (b) capture a larger share of your Latin customer's purchase total, and (c) postpone the cash flow consequences of the discount.

The Roles of Personal Pride, Saving Face, and Negotiating Etiquette

The agreement that is finally consummated is the end product of a series of concessions. The simplicity of that truth masks how critical it is to be culturally adept about how those concessions are made. Making cultural literacy and negotiating strategy interact to your advantage can earn you sizable concessions.

Pride is a decisive factor in the behavior of many Latin males. Maintaining an appearance of personal dignity and honor extends to all aspects of their lives. Negotiating is no exception. Male Latin negotiators are acutely aware that their personal images are on the line and will be affected by how others perceive their results. The negotiators will be careful not to let a concession appear as a weakness. Pride can become an obstacle to reaching an agreement in that it is difficult for the negotiators to give up ground. Therefore, you should make any concession appear to be a wisely deliberated decision. Being respectful, coaxing egos, and doling out ample amounts of "ear candy" opens the door to unlimited business opportunities. Implying in any way that you won or apologizing for your gains opens the door to the street.

The tendency of Latin males to avoid yielding turf is so ingrained that it is even reflected in their language. While compromise is a routine assumption in U.S. win-win negotiating mind-set, the word connotes a different meaning in Spanish. A *compromiso* is an obligation and often even implies a commitment made under duress, rather than a voluntary move toward conciliation. In the absence of a face-saving motive for doing so, Latins often resist making concessions. Here is where your skill in strategic negotiating comes into play: By knowing how to develop and use a win-win negotiating strategy to provide Latins with a face-saving motive, you gain a potent advantage. Knowing how to deal with the issue of price is a key tool in that skill set.

Dealing with the Pricing Issue

Some U.S. executives see price as the negotiation's centerpiece, an issue that should be addressed at the first possible moment. This is a mistake in Latin America. Playing the price card too soon can upset the negotiating process, clouding it with a win-lose bargaining mentality. That mentality can undermine the powerful psychological and strategic advantages you gain by approaching your Latin opposite from a win-win perspective. As pricing is usually the most emotionally sensitive factor under negotiation, all nonprice issues should be discussed and agreed upon, at least in principle, before tackling the pricing issue.

Whenever you let price take center stage, the spotlight goes off the nonprice benefits that justify your price, and you risk relegating your product's star attractions to bit-part roles. Your aim is to avoid discussing price until you have had a chance to present your offering's unique benefits. Only then are you in a position to negotiate the best possible price. Price concessions made at an inopportune moment or under pressure are grave errors. In the heat of the moment, what may have appeared to be a minor price concession can negate months or years of cost-cutting efforts, and exact a serious toll on profits over the long run.

Postponing the price issue is good negotiating strategy anywhere. It is an especially effective practice in Latin America, where it is considered socially boorish to rush business. Your Latin associate will not be shy about letting you know when it is time to discuss price. However, when the time comes for the price card to be played, you must know which of your leads could be trumped.

Like all good negotiators, Latin buyers will try to make you be the first to name a price. They will do this for two reasons. First, they get a benchmark estimate of how low you will go. Second, by rejecting your first offer, they retain a price lure, using it to hook you on other concessions. Being the first to name a price virtually assures you will commit one or the other of the two greatest errors a seller can make: (1) quoting a price that is too low, or (2) quoting a price that is too high. If you name a high price, it could be so far above what the buyer had in mind that she will walk away. If your price is too low, you will be stuck with having to accept less than the amount the buyer was willing to pay. Moreover, a lower-than-anticipated price may arouse the buyer's suspicions—"Is there something wrong with this seller's product?"

Many experienced exporters quote an inflated initial price. Believing that when they ask for less, they get less, this technique gives them latitude to make price concessions later. This approach entails taking a gamble, and if the game goes against you, you will have to be fast on your feet to avoid losing your wager. The gamble you take is twofold: (1) your credibility as a trustworthy, long-term business partner is at stake, and (2) the focus of negotiating may become price-oriented, thus weakening your ability to arouse the buyer's interests in the desirable nonprice features of your offering package.

Nonetheless, gambling on a high first-price quote may be worthwhile. Researchers support that practice, showing that more profitable outcomes tend to be achieved by beginning with extreme price positions.[31, 32] One approach to asking for a high price (if you are the seller) or a low price (if you are the buyer), without risking the cooperative mood that you have created, is to quote a range of possible prices. You explain that the specific final price would be contingent on other variables such as product features, order size, payment terms, field support, or after-sale service. In this way, you can turn the focus of the negotiating discussion back to nonprice topics if you feel you need more time to demonstrate the value of the product's nonprice features. Another escape mechanism is to use qualifiers such as "we estimate" or "approximately." These are signals that the price door could be open to negotiation.

Beware of invoice adjustments. Consider a not-uncommon concession-stage scenario: Over the course of several meetings with you, your Latinoland prospect has repeatedly complained about corrupt Latino officials. He has been particularly vehement about denouncing Latinoland's income-tax officials for extortionate practices. As you have been favorably impressed with the professionalism and integrity he has shown so far in dealing with customers, other suppliers, or employees, you tend to believe his claims and sympathize with his plight. Over a leisurely lunch, he asks you to help alleviate his predicament by over-invoicing shipments to him, crediting the difference between the real price and the inflated price to an accommodation account in his name in a Swiss bank. By overstating the invoice amount, your prospective representative's reported income would be understated by a like amount, and his liability to Latinoland fiscal authorities would be correspondingly reduced.

Be cautious about agreeing to this price-related concession. Like early signs of an ingrown toenail, it seems nonthreatening and can be easily prevented. But, if allowed to grow, it can become a painful experience. In addition to the possible legal penalties (see Chapter 3), the practice of adjusting invoices could complicate your relations with other company representatives, compromise your own accounting and tax-reporting practices, and undermine employee morale and organizational ethics.

Common Oversights

Agreements should always be written. It is common in Latin America to disregard unwritten agreements made out of passion or politeness. To ensure written agreements are prepared correctly, you or a teammate should volunteer to take notes on what was agreed to verbally. Those notes will be used to distill the more casual statements made at the negotiating table into the formally worded clauses contained in the final document. As the one who takes notes, you gain the advantage of tinting the content of the formal agreement to match your own color scheme. Also, by controlling the meeting notes, you can ensure that no important loose ends are left untied. Here are some contingencies that are often left hanging in the rush to bring deals to a close.

Exclusivity. If you are appointing a distributor, he will want reassurance that his investment in money, effort, time, and reputation to build a market for your product will pay off. Thus, it is natural for him to ask for exclusivity in representing you. That exclusivity can be defined by geography, market segment, function, or time, and is often subject to meeting a sales performance standard. Of those four types of exclusivity, you need to be especially cautious about conceding any of the first three: geography, market segment, or function. Latin America's national legal systems can impose harsh penalties for firing a distributor, making it impossible for your firm to ever again do business in a country. Only representation contracts specifying an expiration date have a chance in court and even these have been successfully contested by fired distributors.

Choice of Agent. As distributor agreements can create painful severance liabilities, consider using an agent as your legal representative in the target country. Interposing an agent between your company and the distributor could make your exit problems less sticky should you later wish to change distributors or abandon the market. Certainly, competent counsel should be consulted to assess the legal feasibility of this option.

Foreign Sales Corporation (FSC). Selling directly to your Latin buyer may cause you to forfeit a U.S. income-tax exemption of up to 15 percent of your export profits. Be sure to include in any sales agreement a provision allowing you to sell through an FSC under the same terms negotiated for the direct-sale transaction. Having said that, it is important also to say that the World Trade Organization has ruled the FSC illegal twice since

1998.[33] Therefore, in 2004, the United States was under heavy pressure from the European Union to eliminate the FSC. As that effort will almost certainly prevail, be certain to include in your agreement any legal provision that Congress may enact to replace the FSC.

Lawyers

Lawyers can be a key tool in the process of structuring an agreement. Be certain that you are in control of that tool. You can lose control of the negotiation if you let attorneys muddy the waters you have been careful to keep friendly and clear. Moreover, the off-putting presence of lawyers in a negotiation with a government agency, for example, may prevent you from anticipating and avoiding *el león por debajo de la alfombra* (the lion beneath the rug—the public official who must be paid off).

Knowing When to Fold and When to Close

In the heat of the often-intense exercise of give and take, negotiators can lose sight of the fact that the process they are going through is a means to an end, not the end itself. The end of negotiating is to reach an agreement that is better than the result you would have had without it. That result is called your BATNA (Best Alternative to a Negotiated Agreement).[34] By setting your BATNA in advance and sticking to it, you gain a decisive psychological advantage: your readiness to break off negotiations that do not exceed your no-deal resistance point. That readiness enables you to present your proposal forcefully, signaling to your Latin opposite that the line you have drawn is both firm and fair and that you will not step over it.

The Fold. Most possible business relationships probably should not happen. In the heat of negotiating, it is easy to overlook that sales alone do not equate to business success. Sustainable profits and cash flow do. Trying to force an agreement by making unwarranted concessions or pushing the other side too hard presages a deal that, sooner or later, will fail. Rather than refusing to accept defeat, skilled negotiators recognize when it is wise to walk away from formal talks and amiably agree to not agree. Finishing negotiations without signing an agreement, but on simpatico terms, lets you retain the personal rapport and trust you have built and leaves the door open to collaborate on a future project whenever the circumstances of either party change. By making a strategic withdrawal, you transform the certainty of imminent failure into the possibility of future success.

The Close. On the other hand, if and when the gap separating the parties closes, they may come to believe that entering into a formal relationship could be fruitful. A common error of U.S. negotiators in Latin America is to try to force a close prematurely, before the Latins are comfortable with personal relations and the deal's long-term business prospects. As timing is important, you should be alert for these nearing-the-finish-line signals to let you know when your Latin associate is getting close to putting the hook in his own lip:

- The gap between your positions is closing.
- Your arguments are being met with fewer and weaker counterarguments.
- Concessions are becoming smaller and taking longer.
- The Latin prospect makes references to final arrangements.
- The Latin is leaning forward at the conference table and is asking more information questions.
- The Latin asks you to identify who in your organization would handle his account and resolve any controversies that arise.
- You are introduced to one or more of the Latin company's key stakeholders (e.g., division vice presidents, account managers, other suppliers, directors, or major stockholders).
- The Latin mentions the possibility of traveling to the United States to visit your company's facilities.
- The Latin extends a social invitation, particularly one involving spouses.
- The Latin asks if you could help arrange U.S.-origin financing.
- Agreement is reached on a timetable defining dates on which key events (e.g., financing approval, delivery, training) will be performed.

While both parties are still nodding "yes" after the final terms of the agreement have been hammered out and the formal contract is being prepared, do not have that document delivered for signing. This is not a Fed-Ex moment. It is an occasion for a formal signing ceremony (yes, even if it means taking another trip back!), followed by a celebration. The investment required to top off the formal negotiation stage appropriately will be repaid by the time and money you are likely to save in the postcontract, follow-through stage.

Stage 6: Follow-Through

A deal is a deal

—U.S. adage

A contract is only a pause in negotiations

—Mexican adage

Successful negotiation is a cycle. It has no beginning or end. Although the formal stage of your negotiation ended with the signing ceremonies, the business stage of your Latin connection has just begun. Researchers believe that between 30 percent and 60 percent of international joint ventures fail after being formed.[35, 36] The propensity for international accords to unravel underscores that this last stage controls whether the agreement you just signed is going to be a profitable, ongoing association or a found-and-lost opportunity. After the ink has dried on the contract and the echoes of the celebration toasts have faded away, the Anglos and Latins who negotiated it may view their new agreement quite differently.

Low-context Anglos consider a signed agreement as the final act of the negotiation, a document defining the rights and responsibilities of the parties under all circumstances and sacrosanct under the force of law. That view contrasts with high-context Latins who find little joy in a cold, written contract. In fact, Latins regard the entire formal negotiating process not as a self-contained and completed event, but rather as an initial means to test if there exists a basis for personal trust. The Latins view the contract more as a first rendering rather than as the final blueprint of a future business relationship. The contract constitutes the first concrete step in what is hoped will become a lasting business and personal relationship. As such, the document represents an intention to behave according to the performance norms specified for as long as the bonds of personal trust are intact and for as long as acting in accordance with those norms produces the anticipated business result.

By contrast, Anglos leave a conference room secure in the belief that the agreement is legally enforceable and that no special additional effort need be expended to sustain the personal bonds formed during negotiations. If the Latins had been driven to the wall or coerced into signing a dry-bone agreement during the negotiations, they will have little incentive to honor it. Indeed, even if the agreement was fair to both parties when it was signed, Latins may be motivated to walk away from it if conditions change. This does not mean that Latins act in bad faith when they sign contracts. Rather, it reflects the higher uncertainty that marks Latin American business environments. Political and economic circumstances regularly shift in Latin America, making the assumptions that underpinned an original agreement change over time. Shifting conditions can turn a dream profit into a nightmare loss. A purchase contract for construction equipment, for example, may have seemed a routine agreement at the time it was signed. But, if that contract specifies periodic fixed payments in dollars, and the peso later weakens against the dollar, Latin customers will suffer losses they had not anticipated. Under such conditions, Latins may (reasonably) expect the U.S. vendor to unlock them from their obligations, sharing in the loss imposed by an adverse exchange rate. Underlying that expectation is the Latin's assumption that the personal ties linking the two parties prevail over any contractual obligation, and that they will work together in good faith to absorb losses arising from an exchange rate fluctuation that neither could foresee.

If, under such circumstances, Anglos sue for nonperformance, they may be thwarted, finding that relying on the legal system to seek satisfaction for breach of contract is less effective and more costly than they expected, regardless of whether charges are brought in the United States or Latin America.[37] Anglos' dependence on formal documents, rather than on informal personal ties can jeopardize a potentially productive business relationship. Indeed, such a reliance may set in motion the very forces of distrust that will provoke Latins to renege on the agreement, thus transforming what was originally an attractive win-win business pact into an ugly lose-lose legal imbroglio.

Loyal Customers Are a Gift, Not a Given

Familiarity breeds content in Latin America. Without it, done deals routinely become undone deals. The viability of Latin American business ties goes beyond the terms of written agreements, and is rooted in the circumstances existing when the agreement was signed: the business conditions, the intentions of the parties, and the personal relationship that prevailed. If any of those three circumstances change, so will the commitment to abide by the original terms of the agreement. Having firm personal ties makes it relatively painless to amend an agreement if, as, and when business conditions or intentions change. Adding value to business and personal relationships establishes you as someone with whom Latins will want to do repeat business and send referrals to. Consider some postnegotiating actions to keep you at the top of the Latin's mind after you return home:

TIPS to keep new-buyer enthusiasm at a high level:

- Within twenty-four hours of returning home, send your associate a letter thanking him for his hospitality and time. The immediacy of your message will be appreciated. Also appreciated will be your commending some aspect of his personality or behavior. If you met a member of his family, comment on what a pleasure it was. Most important, mention that you look forward to a long professional and warm personal relationship.
- Again, after returning home, send a gift that is compatible with your associate's interests. Include with the gift a note written in pen. Nothing expresses more individualized attention than ink on a personal thank-you card. Don't scrimp on this gift. It should be tasteful and have "wall appeal," something that he will be proud to display on his wall or desk. Its constant visibility will remind him of you when it is time to reorder or refer a business friend.
- Go the extra mile. Latins are not surprised when promises are treated as a momentary intention, not an enduring commitment. By promising small and delivering big, you build a level of credibility with your Latin associates that can make you an exceptional business partner.
- Establish a file of your Latin partner's key personal dates. Send cards or gifts on the occasion of his *onomástico* (personal Saint's Day) or birthday, his daughter's *quinceañera* (fifteenth birthday, an important coming-out event), his wedding anniversary, and his country's independence day.
- Call often. Although letters, faxes, and e-mails may serve you well for matters of routine account management, nothing (short of a country visit) transmits personal regard as well as a friendly phone chat.
- Send your Latin associate a copy of your company newsletter, trade magazine, or local newspaper that reports on the new agreement, and mentions his name and his company's name prominently.
- Issue an invitation to visit your facilities in the U.S. Remember to ask him to schedule an extra day or two for golf, fishing, or local sightseeing as your guest.

Notes

1. J. Z. Rubin and B. R. Brown (1975), *The Social Psychology of Bargaining and Negotiation*, New York: Academic Press.

2. D. R. Beeman and T. W. Sharkey (1987), "The Use and Abuse of Corporate Politics," *Business Horizons*, vol. 30, no. 2, pp. 26–30.

3. John Pfeiffer (1988), "How Not to Lose the Trade Wars by Cultural Gaffes," *Smithsonian*, vol. 18, no. 10, pp. 145–156.

4. Glen Caudill Dealy (1977), *The Public Man—An Interpretation of Latin American and Other Catholic Countries,* Amherst: University of Massachusetts Press.

5. Nancy J. Adler, John L. Graham, and Theodore Schwartz Gehrke (1987), "Business Negotiations in Canada, Mexico, and the United States," *Journal of Business Research*, vol. 15, no. 5, pp. 19–38.

6. Glen Fisher (1980), *International Negotiation: A Cross-Cultural Perspective,* Yarmouth, ME: Intercultural Press, p. 41.

7. Robert T. Moran and William G. Stripp (1991), *Dynamics of Successful International Business Negotiations*, Houston: Gulf, p. 84.

8. Barbara Perdue and John Summers (1991), "Purchasing Agents' Use of Negotiation Strategies," *Journal of Marketing Research*, vol. 18, no. 2, pp. 175–189.

9. John L. Graham, Alma T. Mintu, and Waymond Rogers (1994), "Explorations of Negotiating Behaviors in Ten Foreign Cultures Using a Model Developed in the United States," *Management Science*, vol. 40, no. 1, pp. 72–95.

10. John L. Graham and Ray Herberger, Jr. (1983), "Negotiators Abroad—Don't Shoot from the Hip," *Harvard Business Review*, vol. 62, July–August, pp. 160–168.

11. Joanna M. Banthin and Leigh Stelzer (1990), "Ethical Dilemmas in Transacting Business Across Cultures," in *Global Business Management in the 1990s*, Fariborz Ghadar, Phillip D. Grub, Robert T. Moran, and Marshall Geer, eds., New York: Beecham Publishing, pp. 9–16.

12. Nancy J. Adler, John L. Graham, and Theodore Schwarz Gehrke (1987), "Business Negotiations in Canada, Mexico, and the United States," *Journal of Business Research*, vol. 15, no. 5, pp. 21–42.

13. Helen Deresky (2000), "Managing Across Borders and Cultures," Upper Saddle River, NJ: Prentice-Hall.

14. Robert Gulbro and Paul Herbig (1996), "Negotiating Successfully in Cross-Cultural Situations," *Industrial Marketing Management*, vol. 25, pp. 235–241.

15. *Wall Street Journal*, October 28, 1994, in Helen Deresky (2000), *Managing Across Borders and Cultures*, Upper Saddle River, NJ: Prentice-Hall, p. 79.

16. L. W. McCarthy (1985), "The Rule of Power and Principle in 'Getting to Yes,'" *Negotiation Journal*, vol. 3, no. 1, pp. 59–66.

17. Gulbro and Herbig (1996), pp. 235–241.

18. Robert T. Moran, Philip R. Harris, and William G. Stipp (1993), *Developing the Global Organization*, Houston: Gulf Publishing.

19. "Marcada Por Conflictos, la Relación México-EU Vive Su Mejor Momento." (2001). *El Universal* (Mexico), February 17, p. A15 (author's translation).

20. P. A. Anderson (1988), "Explaining Differences in Non-Verbal Communication," in *Intercultural Communication: A Reader*, eds. L. A. Samovar and R. E. Porter, Belmont, CA: Wadsworth.

21. Doreen Hemlock (1999), "Familiarity Breeds Success," *Sun-Sentinel*, September 20, pp. 16–17.

22. Moran, Harris, and Stripp (1993).

23. John L. Graham (1985), "The Influence of Culture on the Process of Business Negotiations, and Exploratory Study," *Journal of International Business Studies* 16, no. 1, pp. 81–96.

24. Graham and Herberger, Jr. (1983), pp. 160–168.

25. D.W. Hendon, R. A. Hendon, and P. Herbig (1996), *Cross-Cultural Business Negotiations*, Westport, CT: Quorum Books.

26. J. L. Graham (1983), "Brazilian, Japanese, and American Business Negotiations," *Journal of International Business Studies*, vol. 14, Spring, pp. 47–61.

27. Pierre Casse (1982), *Training for the Multicultural Manager: A Practical and Cross-Cultural Approach to the Management of People*, Washington, DC: Society for Intercultural Education, Training, and Research.

28. Martin S. Gannon (2001), *Understanding Global Cultures, 2nd ed.*, Thousand Oaks, CA: Sage Publications.

29. Linda Beamer and Iris Varner (2001), *Intercultural Communication in the Global Workplace, 2nd ed.*, New York: McGraw-Hill/Irwin, pp. 183, 262.

30. R. L. Daft (1989), *Organizational Theory and Design, 3rd ed.*, St. Paul, MN: West Publishing.

31. S. S. Komorita and Alan E. Ellis (1989), "Level of Aspiration in Coalition Bargaining," *Journal of Personality and Social Psychology*, vol. 54, no. 8, pp. 421–431.

32. D. R., Weingart, L. L. Thompson, M. H. Bazerman, and J. S. Carol (1990), "Tactical Behaviors and Negotiation Outcomes," *International Journal of Conflict Management*, vol. 1, no. 1, pp. 7–31.

33. "A taxing dispute" (2003), *CFO*, August, pp. 29–30.

34. Roger Fisher and William Ury (1982), *Getting to Yes*, Boston: Houghton-Mifflin.

35. John H. Dunning (1995), *Multinational Enterprise and the Global Economy*, New York: Addison-Wesley.

36. J. Michael Geringer (1991), "Strategic Determinants of Partner Selection in International Joint Ventures," *Journal of International Business Studies* vol. 22, no. 1, pp. 41–62.

37. E. Buscaglia, Jr., M. Dakolias, and W. Ratliff (1995), *Judicial Reform in Latin America: A Framework for National Development*, Stanford, CA: Hoover Institution.

Chapter 6

How to Avoid Letting Your Good Latin American Deal Go South

Chapter 5 described the key negotiating and selling skills you will need to become a good horse trader in Latin America. But it is not enough to know how to trade horses. To stay in the money, you also must know how to care for and ride them. This chapter describes tactics to keep personal relationships healthy and business operations productive long after you have closed on your new Latin America business deal.

TAKING CARE OF RELATIONSHIPS

Hunters and Farmers: Would You Buy Again from You?

It cannot be overstated: Profit is in the repurchase. To make repurchases happen, you must be spotlessly trustworthy to your customers. Trust means business in Latin America. Trust brings customers back to buy from you again and again. In today's Latin American markets, the strongest defense against competition is not to win the largest number of new customers, but to gain the loyalty of the most profitable customers.

Never underestimate the profitability of creating a customer for life. Managers who think that winning a new customer in the Latin American market is a one-time event, like shooting a lion on safari, should think again. And they should think differently the second time. Winning a good Latin customer is not like bagging a trophy animal. It is like planting a field. It will take longer and require more effort than shooting a lion, but if you steadily cultivate the field, it will yield continuing returns. Its yield will depend on your adeptness in managing the new personal relationships and the operating issues that arise when your Latin American venture has been transformed from a momentary negotiating exercise to a 24/7/52-week ongoing reality.

Communications Command

The most obvious difference between doing business in the United States and in Latin America is language. Despite the prominence of the language difference, many business visitors to Latin America do not exploit its potential. That is a mistake. Your ability to communicate in Spanish or Portuguese lets you compete against others on another basis in addition to your product offering. Being able to converse in the language of your Latin associate is always a competitive advantage. But the advantage of being proficient in Spanish or Portuguese is especially applicable if either your firm or the Latin firm is not a multinational giant. Smaller companies everywhere, but especially in the United States, tend to lack the multilingual managers commonly found on the payrolls of the Fortune 500.

As business takes you to Latin America more frequently during the postnegotiation phase, you will expand your circle of contacts. As that circle grows, you will find yourself well positioned to acquire more business if you speak Spanish or Portuguese. If there is a language barrier, you can expect not only to miss new opportunities, but to spend costly time trying to untangle the effects of old opportunities gone wrong because of avoidable misunderstandings.

Language Tips for the Wise . . . and Language Traps for the Unwary

Many U.S. executives fail to appreciate the implications of not speaking at least a few Spanish or Portuguese phrases. They assume that as English is the language of international business, their Latin associates should already have learned to speak it. Their assumption that communication should be exclusively in English conveys an attitude of indifference toward the language and culture of their hosts. Moreover, it forces U.S. executives to rely on the linguistic competence and goodwill of their Latin associates, or to mix primarily with other expatriates. As a result, their English-only radius of contacts limits them to connect with Latins at a superficial level, consigning them to the personal-interaction equivalent of making love without touching.

Make Spanish or Portuguese easy. If one could swallow an instant-language pill, and immediately be able to converse in Spanish or Portuguese, language choke points would no longer restrain the ability of countless U.S. executives to achieve their full business potential in Latin America. But, although science has not yet developed an easy cure for monolinguals, learning the rudiments of Spanish or Portuguese does not have to be a sweating-palms experience. It is a benevolent act of inter-American commerce that Spanish and Portuguese are among the easiest foreign languages for English speakers to learn.

Being able to hear the rhythm of the language, and to learn and pronounce correctly 200 to 300 words will give you a surprising ability to communicate within your expanding community of Latin contacts. By learning as few as three words a day, within three months you will be comfortable interacting with a growing circle of Latins. Your core vocabulary will enable you to learn on your own. Your solo excursion into Spanish or Portuguese conversational space will trace much the same route you used to learn English, not by following a phrase book or dictionary, but through context, probing, and interaction with others. As you explore the new language, you will earn real admiration and respect from Latins for your effort, and you will become familiar with the local scene from a new perspective. Your new language ability will open doors on new worlds of business and social possibilities, and you will discover that you are no longer a tourist. As you step outside of the safety of living on cultural autopilot, you will also discover that doing business in Latin America is no longer a job. It is a lifestyle.

As the instant-language pill is not yet an available option, how else can you put your second-language desire on fast-forward? For most busy executives, enrolling in a traditional university language course is not the most time-efficient solution. Better alternatives are available through commercial language schools, compact-disc programs, and the Internet. Of those three alternatives, commercial language schools may be the most expensive, but could prove to be the most cost-effective if you purchase their services through a contract that guarantees you will reach a defined performance level by a given date. While the quality of CD language products varies widely, this medium offers the flexibility of being able to study during periods that would otherwise be unproductive. For example, if you were to listen to a CD during daily thirty-minute commutes to and from your office, in two months you would exceed the classroom equivalent of a one-semester university course. Online language instruction has also become a viable option. One site, www.studyspanish.com, makes it easy to learn basic vocabulary and grammar, while increasing your pronunciation and listening skills with audio plug-ins.

Make English easy. Until your Spanish or Portuguese skills are well advanced, you may find it impractical to rely on the services of professional interpreters for every conversation. That means your discussions will likely be conducted in English, and the Latins will have to bear the brunt of making communication happen. Unless the Latin who plays the role of interpreter is highly proficient in English, misunderstandings are inevitable in a language that permits one to park in a driveway but drive on a parkway, to send trucks by ship but ship by truck, to watch a house burn down as it burns up, or to take an identical risk with a fat chance and a slim chance.

If interpreting the English language can be difficult, interpreting English jargon can be impossible. To ease the task of Latins who serve as interpreters, avoid using language that:

1. Requires understanding U.S. sports jargon, like:

   slam dunk
   huddle time
   get on the ball
   step up to the plate
   play for all the marbles

2. Requires understanding homonyms, like:

   if he would get the lead out, he could lead
   he was not close enough to close the door
   the present is the best time to present the present
   the tourist deserted his dessert in the desert

Such examples suggest why Latins would prefer to strike a deal with Germans or Japanese whose English is limited but understandable, rather than with Anglos whose speech sounds like cryptic code.

It is helpful to cite examples to clarify the concepts you are explaining. When doing so, avoid the temptation to be witty. The cultural and linguistic context of humor complicates communication. Moreover, Latins are not always amused by what some Anglos consider good humor. Active listening helps ensure that the message you are sending is the same message they are receiving. So when discussing key points, frequently ask Latins to repeat in their own words what they understood you to mean.

One final precaution will help avoid misunderstandings: Express all technical standards in metric units. The United States is the last outpost among the world's advanced nations to defend English-system measures. As a result, U.S. executives often fail to appreciate that those standards are unknown or are considered archaic in Latin America. All references to physical (linear, area, volume) and temperature measures should be converted to metric units in your spoken and written correspondence, advertising, product labeling, and literature. Imagine how thwarted you would feel if the tables were turned and, as a prospective buyer for a fleet of delivery vehicles, you were given the following standards:

> *Vehicle fuel consumption of 8.6 kilometers per liter at 80 kilometers per hour with tire inflation of 2.82 kilos per centimeter^2 @ 24° C* (= 20 miles/gallon at 50 mph with tire inflation of 40 lbs/in^2 @ 75° F)

Failing to make some effort to communicate in Spanish or Portuguese is a social misdemeanor, but failing to communicate product and performance standards in metric units can be a capital crime. The financial and human capital you have invested may be sent to death row for your fatal business offense.

Be cautious about second languages. Interpreters are like toll collectors. They charge to make a bridge between two parties that are separated by a language gap. Anglo and Latin businessmen with second-language pretensions can fall into the trap of thinking that they will avoid repeated toll charges if each builds one-half of the bridge. This misguided belief leads each to attempt to communicate in the language of the other. The usual result is two half-bridges that will never meet because they were based on faulty designs, inferior materials, or were built at different locations. The inevitable communication dead-ends underscore the fact that whomever relies on half a bridge is either going nowhere or is heading for a fall.

The prestige value conferred by a second-language ability can create status obstacles that make it difficult for Anglos and Latins to interact smoothly. The education and lifestyles of Latin executives often make them more able to communicate in English than Anglos can in Spanish or Portuguese. Hence, Latins frequently prevail in playing the role of interpreter, and talks are held in English. With less frequency, U.S. executives will take the lead, attempting to conduct conversations in Spanish or

Portuguese. In either case, the assumption implied by the executive who takes on the role of interpreter is, "My second language is better than your second language." The potential for that implied claim to offend is real, and is often at odds with the claimant's true second-language ability. If U.S. or Latin executives attempt to use a language beyond their ability, it will come as no surprise when frustration, misunderstandings, and perceived condescension combine to undermine the optimism, cooperation, and rapport that marked the celebration of the negotiation agreement. When things go wrong, it will be easy for each party to blame the other, recalling, "I clearly told him that . . ."

Avoid losing your brand equity in translation. Assume you have made the right preparations to achieve success in your new Latin American venture. But it is the market that has the last word in whether your business will really succeed. Beware of second-rate translations that can make that last word sound like sales crashing. If linguistically and culturally inappropriate choices of text in your ad copy, information materials, brochures, and other marketing messages are not corrected by your translator, costly results can ensue. Assigning a high-profile translation to an employee simply because he or she has a Hispanic surname can throw sand in the gears of your new venture. Consider, for example, the profit-robbing effect of the following product-launch misfires that should have been caught by competent translators:

- Ford Motor Company marketed a subcompact car in Mexico as the *Cometa*, a direct translation of the Comet that its Mercury brand was selling successfully in the United States. Aimed at affluent urban housewives as an economical vehicle in which to do errands and ferry kids back and forth, the launch failed to meet sales targets in the key Mexico City market. Research revealed the culprit responsible for the sales failure: *Cometa* is slang in Mexico City for the flashy, brightly sequined nighttime streetwalkers with whom few high-society aspirants wished to be associated.
- To fulfill a large export order to Mexico, General Electric's Locomotive Division needed to translate its operating manual into Spanish. GE attempted to cut costs by contracting the job to a Chilean firm at three cents per word, instead of the twenty-five cents per word it customarily paid for translations in the United States. The anticipated savings proved to be a false economy when it was discovered that the Chilean translator had little familiarity with the technical terminology used for operating and maintaining locomotives. As a result, the

job had to be redone at a much higher cost than GE would have had to pay the "expensive" U.S. company to get the locomotive translation moving on the "write" track the first time.

- The soft drink Fresca was withdrawn from several Latin American markets when slow sales prompted management to engage researchers to identify the problem. The researchers informed management that the name labeled on the bottle with the suggestively elongated neck was a slang word for lesbian.
- Now-defunct Braniff Airlines suffered a translation gaffe when it tried to promote luxury passenger service on its South American routes. Having reupholstered its first-class seats in leather, the carrier promoted its upgraded seats with a Spanish translation of the "Fly in leather" slogan that had been successful in the United States. As competitors and customers enjoyed a good laugh, the Braniff executives were embarrassed to learn that their translated slogan meant "Fly in the nude."
- A publicity campaign mounted in Mexico by U.S. dairy farmers turned sour when its translated slogan failed to produce an upturn in market demand. Its catchphrase, "Got milk?" connoted an unintended meaning when translated to Spanish. Mexicans interpreted the question to mean, "Are you lactating?"
- Attempting to promote its product in Latin America, a U.S. swimsuit manufacturer's ad claimed that a beachgoer could spend all day wearing its product in the sun, and the fabric would not fade. The advertising message and expense were largely wasted on Latins who prefer not to spend much time outside of the shade, because the hot tropical sun is uncomfortable.
- An advertising campaign for pens failed to write many orders in Latin America. Intending to convey that users of the leakproof product would not be embarrassed by clothing stains, the ad translation instead assured that customers could avoid pen-induced pregnancies.

Don't Call Him Phil

Picture this scene: You and your Chilean agent are representing your firm at a trade show in Santiago. You are momentarily alone while your agent has returned to his office on an urgent matter. An affable visitor stops at your booth and shows a lively interest in your product. Explaining that he has a previously scheduled appointment to attend, he leaves a business card and promises to return in thirty minutes to discuss making a trial order. Examining his card, you note that your Chilean prospect is the director general of a prominent firm that your agent has mentioned as a high-priority sales target. You also note from the card that the new prospect's name is printed as, Ing. Felipe Arévalo Gómez.

Question: When he returns, how do you address him? Three rules govern this common situation. The first rule is to use the correct professional title. Latins venerate education and work hard to earn the privilege of acquiring professional titles through academic study. In this case, the appropriate title is *Ingeniero,* indicating that the prospect has completed a university program in engineering.

The second rule of address is uncomplicated: Avoid calling Latins by their first (given) name until invited to do so. Using a Latin's first name without prior permission is considered a rude intrusion upon one's personal dignity. If you are operating in a tropical climate, social conventions tend to be more relaxed, and chances are that you will soon be invited to refer to your new Latin acquaintance by his first name. Where the climate is cooler in mountainous or in higher-latitude locations, so is the social atmosphere. In Santiago, Buenos Aires, and Quito, you may find it will take longer before your Latin counterpart invites you to call him Felipe.

The final rule is sometimes confusing to Anglos: When two surnames (last names) are used, you should only use the first when speaking to Latins. In this case, the engineer's paternal surname is Arévalo, and his mother's maiden name is Gómez. It is no mystery that, as a male-dominated society, Latins expect only their father's surname to be used when being addressed directly. The mother's family surname is included in third-person references to identify the Latin's lineage, thus distinguishing him from others bearing the same patronymic.

In the time it took you to absorb the preceding information, the Latin prospect has returned to your booth. Your opening line is scripted according to the accepted formula: Smiling broadly and warmly grasping his hand, you greet him, saying, "Buenas tardes, Ingeniero Arévalo, what a privilege to see you again!"

TAKING CARE OF BUSINESS

Know the Customers and Competitors of Your Customer

There is no such thing as an average Latin American market. Each country and each region is unique. Still, there are rules that are common to all markets. As Latin American markets become more open and competitive, three rules will guide the practices of business winners:

1. Know thy customer
2. Know thy customer's customer
3. Know thy competitor

You Have to Eat Your Own Dog Food

There is no substitute for understanding the way your customers view your product. And, if your customers are resellers, your competitive edge will be at its sharpest when you know the reasons that drive their customers to buy your product, instead of choosing a competitor's brand. There is no better way to understand marketing's frontline than to spend time in the marketplace. The time you invest in the trenches will pay dividends. Making direct contact with final consumers, wandering through retail aisles, or accompanying your distributor's sales people on their rounds, brings you closest to where the real profit potential lies. The best market wisdom is the market.

Equally important are the gains you can make by transferring hard-won marketing and management lessons you learned in the United States to your Latin American representative. As the modernizing effects of globalization spread throughout Latin America, it is common for Latin marketers to suffer some of the same headaches your company experienced and solved in the United States, perhaps during the Asian onslaught of the 1970s and 1980s. Your expertise can make your representative see you more as a unique source of business solutions and less as a replaceable vendor who is only as good as his last deal. As your value to him as a mentor grows, his loyalty as a customer will increase, as will his order volume. In the process, of course, your representative becomes an ally that will work hard to promote your product in his market.

Much of your U.S. marketing experience is transferable to Latin America. But assuming that all of it applies can be fatal. It could be a mistake to infer from the simple fact that because a few customers in Latinoland have bought your product, others will respond in a similar fashion to the same buying propositions that you promote to your U.S. customers. To assume that, in all but the most obvious ways, the Latinoland market behaves like your U.S. market will nullify much of the value of your considerable potential to guide your new representative by passing on the benefit of your U.S. business experience.

Know Customers or No Customers

The best way to understand your Latinoland representative's market is to understand it the same way he does, at the street level, the sales call, and the desk level of market analysis. Only by gaining a full appreciation of who the buyers are and their purchasing habits, will you be able to separate facts from assumptions. Listening to the Latinoland market will enable you to understand, relative to your U.S. experience, what is different about its buying propositions, and what is similar. Wise executives know what they do not know. This wisdom can prevent you from offering X when Latin buyers want Y.

As you accumulate experience in the region, you will find sharp differences in buying motives from one country to the other. That low energy-usage product that sold so well in Ecuador, for example, may flop in Argentina. Why the difference? Electrical energy costs in Ecuador are almost five times the kilowatt/hour rate in Argentina.[1] Whereas you could count on lower operating costs as a strong motive for buyers to choose your brand in Guayaquil, you will have to find a different feature to move the product in Buenos Aires.

If your representative handles consumer goods, you may learn that the merchandise orders she fills vary widely depending on her customer's location. She knows that the tastes of buyers in mountainous locations (*serranos*) tend to be conservative, whereas buyers living on the coast (*costeños*) lean toward bright colors, light and informal clothing, loud-volume audio speakers, and spicy flavors. You may learn that in traditional sectors of macho Latin America, most buying decisions are still dominated by the male leader of the household (see Table 4.2). Perhaps you will also find out that the best way to reach either the *serrano* or the *costeño* consumer is through advertising by means of hand-delivered flyers (*volantes*) and by local radio and TV spots, rather than by newspaper ads. Whereas *volantes* and radio spots are relatively inexpensive and can be tailored to reach a local market, most newspapers are directed toward a national audience and most of the readers exposed to their costly ads are not viable prospects for geographically limited offerings. Although experience with coupons as a promotional tool has been disappointing,[2] smart retailers have scored sales by linking a customer's purchase to a chance to participate in a raffle or contest, thus taking advantage of Latins' zest for gambling. By being close to the market, you may also learn that consumer credit is a potent sales tool. Without the ability to buy on credit, the most attractive market segment for consumer goods in Latin America—the middle-class household—could slip away from your representative's reach. Credit enables the rapidly expanding middle class to access the much larger purchasing power that is based on buyers' future income, rather than on their current cash flow.

Trade Show Know-How

Trade shows can be a cost-effective way for you and your representative to help roll out the product in your new Latinoland market. But cost-effective does not mean free. After adding up the salaries, transportation costs, and lodging of the expert employees you brought to answer customer questions; free gifts or samples; direct mail promotions; and booth materials, it will not be surprising to learn that the charge for exhibit space amounts to no more than 10 to 15 percent of your total participation costs.[3] Latin American trade shows differ from the U.S. variety in some important respects. Assuming the show's calendar and industry theme are right for you, your plans to exhibit should take into consideration the following points:

- Customary booth visits in the United States are short-lived, information-gathering affairs. Latin visitors tend to stay longer, spending more time on social preliminaries. To encourage productive visits, your booth (*estante*) should provide hospitality. As a good host, you should have coffee, soda beverages, and light snacks available inside, near the back of your booth, to offer to serious visitors.
- Your promotional material and product literature should be available in Spanish or Portuguese. A stack of inexpensive, single-sheet text-only materials should be available at the front of the booth, within easy reach of students and casual passers-by who, although voracious devourers of printed materials, are seldom interested in buying. Such visitors can tie you up in endless, seldom-productive conversation.
- Tastefully display some copies of your expensive, four-color glossy translated materials on a visible angled surface out of easy reach, toward the back or side of the booth. As you give these to serious visitors, replenish them from boxes located out of view, behind the booth's curtain. By appearing to have only limited copies left, you can avoid sacrificing premium literature to the tire-kicking crowd.
- Have some imprinted gifts on hand for distribution to serious visitors. Perennially popular items are baseball caps, T-shirts, pens, in-

sulated beer-can sleeves, and key holders. Keep them removed from the sight of the crowds in the aisle.

- Your and your representative's ample supply of high-quality business cards should be printed in Spanish or Portuguese. An impressive card stock often used in Latin America is a thin, slightly translucent, parchment-like plastic paper.
- Take turns manning the booth with your representative. In that way, each of you can take a break without running the risk that an important prospect will be received by less-prepared staff.
- During busy periods, manning a booth can be demanding. To be able to follow up on leads, do not wait until after the show to wade through an ocean of business cards, trying to recall who was interested in what. Instead, immediately after talking to a visitor, and before greeting the next visitor, use a pocket recorder to rapidly summarize the key points of the conversation you just had. By reviewing your tapes during more leisurely moments at the show, or at the end of each day, you will be in a better position to take the right follow-up actions before a prospect's interest cools.
- Make sure that exhibition workers are on your side. Offering to buy lunch or tipping will reduce damage, pilfering, and delays.
- If you are displaying large or heavy products, such as machinery or construction equipment, consider selling them at a discount after the show has finished. Not only will you have put demonstration products in the local market, but the freight, insurance, and handling costs you will avoid by not having to ship them back may amount to less than the price discount you will grant the on-site buyer.

Do's and Taboos of Signing Up and Motivating Representatives in Latin America

Finding a Representative Who Will Work for You

Too many epitaphs have been written about the demise of what was conceived as a lively Latin business project, either because the wrong representative was signed up or because the right representative was signed up in the wrong way. The representative you appoint becomes both the legal face and the market image of your firm's new venture in Latinoland. That dual role affects your firm's chances of surviving long enough to achieve its potential in any Latin American venture. Yet, despite exposing themselves to serious legal and business threats, some U.S. firms approach the decision to appoint a country representative by throwing the dice rather than making a strategic choice. They would be better served by having no representative, rather than by gambling on one who could ruin them forever in a potentially important market.

A key step in the process of strategic choice is to decide which legal form you should use to appoint your representative. Representatives come in two basic varieties: distributors and agents. Distributors ow[illegible] goods they have bought from your firm. They employ a sales fo[illegible] vertise to promote the sale of those goods; maintain stocks [illegible]nt parts; perform installations, repairs, and maintenance; [illegible]nties; and handle returns. An agent, on the other hand, serves as [illegible]al representative of your company, and may engage in some promotional efforts, but usually lacks the detailed knowledge, capital, and organizational capability to market your firm's product effectively. Despite having less clout as a marketing force, some smaller firms new to the Latin American market prefer to use agents as representatives because, relative to distributors, agents generally:

- are easier to acquire.
- make it easier to avoid costly legal penalties if they have to be fired.
- are subject to control over how the product is presented and priced.
- charge lower commissions or fees.
- provide a legal and physical beachhead from which to conduct low-risk reconnaissance before launching a frontal attack on the market.
- can pull strings at high levels within the government to smooth regulatory wrinkles and get approvals.
- can be your best means to approach or attract a powerful distributor.

For legal reasons, some U.S. firms have found it beneficial to set up a two-tier representative system in Latin America. This approach entails contracting with an agent who is legally responsible for all in-country company operations. If distributors are later appointed by that agent, their legal relationship with, and possible claims against the company are buffered by the agent. A downside to two-tier distributor appointments is that distributors may not feel very secure. As a consequence, they may be reluctant to carry large inventories, dedicate sales people to your line, or invest in a service capability. For that reason, two-tier appointments are often made for a probationary period to test if a candidate is right.

Beware of smooth talkers. Latin America has its full share of local-born and expatriate influence peddlers who are looking for up-front money or an exclusive representation contract in exchange for a promise to move your firm's product. These parasites tend to surface and attach themselves to you at trade shows, in hotel lobbies and bars, and as airline seat partners. Although they may be quick to show how high they can jump, it is what they do when they come down that counts. Just as a good first act[illegible] not save a bad play, neither can the glib initial claims of self-proclai[illegible]' marketing wizards save you from high-loss market failures. Th[illegible] business judgment you use in the United States will prevent yo[illegible]sing one of the goats in a flock of sheep.

Another s[illegible]rd to observe on the road toward finding a suitable representative for your firm's product is to be cautious about following the advice of some Latin American consulting firms. Staffed by experts with academic credentials, these firms can be more oriented toward intellectualizing at a relaxed pace over economic analysis issues than to grinding out concrete solutions to urgent business problems. Colin Powell described them well when he commented: "Experts often possess more data than judgment. Elites can become so inbred that they produce hemophiliacs who bleed to death as soon as they are nicked by the real world."[4] There is no substitute for a distributor who is reliable, well positioned in the market, and committed to serving you.

How do you find Señor Right? Choosing a representative can be the most important decision a newcomer to Latin America makes. Yet, many otherwise prudent U.S. executives will bet their firm's future in Latinoland on the first good story they hear. When opportunists come out of the blue and are allowed to describe their awe-inspiring feats, without comparison or verification, they can look like golden opportunities. To avoid losing their wagers on a potentially lucrative market opportunity by naming Señor Wrong as their Latinoland representative, U.S. executives should place their bets on quality information to find a representative that is right for their firm.

Fortunately, quality information is available. Sources like Dun & Bradstreet publish trade directories listing data on Latin American representatives classified by country and by product. In most countries, the local affiliate of the U.S. international chamber of commerce is an excellent source for information on potential representatives. The U.S. Department of Commerce provides an array of cost-effective services to help U.S. exporters find suitable representatives. By signing up for USDOC's International Company Profiles service, for example, your company can take advantage of the expertise of commercial specialists working for the U.S. embassy located in your target market. Within thirty to forty-five days, you will receive a custom-tailored ICP giving you up-to-date information on potential representatives, including bank and trade references, principals, key officers, and managers, product lines, number of employees, financial data, sales volume, reputation, and market outlook.[5]

A good representative is one who has good customers and good product lines. Do your due diligence: Visit top retailers or users of your type of product. Ask them what their service expectations [illegible]upplier, and from what vendor(s) they prefer to buy. As La[illegible]e forthright about their opinions of other Latins, chances a[illegible] soon begin to hear the same names being repeated for the same re[illegible]ns. Those reasons should form the core of your marketing strategy, and the roll call of buyers' preferred suppliers should form your candidate pool of high-potential sales reps.[6]

When you approach these prime candidates about becoming your representative, do not be discouraged if they are somewhat cool and have little time to talk. Top-performing representatives are busy selling products to customers. They are probably distributors who stock products, and have clean, efficient facilities that also offer good installation, maintenance, and repair services. They have their hands full handling the quality lines they currently represent. If, among those lines, a direct competitor is represented, be prepared to explain why your firm and brand would be better choices.

The one- and two-man shops that will be eager to come on board with you, but that you may want to avoid, are probably commission agents with no investment in inventory, and no product service capability. These "line collectors" will be easily available to talk to, because they spend most of their time selling promises upstream to sew up exclusive representation contracts. Then, having cast scores of mostly low-brand-name-recognition product lines in the water, their game is to simply wait for the phone to announce a bite, and reel in a commission from you for every downstream customer who falls into their boat. In general, you should be wary of representatives who do not have large local accounts or local subsidiaries of multinational firms as active customers.

Hand in Hand or Arm's Length?

The special roles played by personal trust, geographic distance, and the transfer of experience argue strongly for smaller U.S. exporters to maintain closer rep relationships in Latin America than in the United States. These closer relationships are of two separate, but mutually reinforcing interactions: mentoring and partnering.

In your role as a mentor, your new representative expects that you will transfer as much product and marketing expertise as possible to help him perform competitively. It follows that you will provide him and/or his technical and sales employees with training and materials on topics such as product standards and function, competitive profiling, selling propositions, adv[illegible]epair, installation, maintenance, and ordering procedures. As [illegible]nglo, your presence on sales calls could help persuade Latin prosp[illegible]our firm is committed to the market. When on such sales calls, inc[illegible]tally, you may be pleasantly surprised to notice that closing rates in Latin America are higher than you are accustomed to in the United States.

You also may be in a position to coach your representative on management practices that will help him stay competitive as he copes with the more exacting performance requirements of a globalized operating environment. As discussed in Chapters 3 and 4, many of Latin America's family-owned, smaller businesses are still using management practices more suitable to yesterday's protected markets than to today's open markets. The most egregious of those obsolete practices is to micromanage nonfamily employees. If you see signs that your representative is taking on water because of outdated autocratic management methods, your tactful questioning and gentle coaching may prevent his (and your) business from sinking under the wave of modern management practices that is sweeping across Latin America. To help him keep his head above water, try to bring him around to seeing that the people who make up his organization *are* his organization.

If, on the other hand, your representative seems the type who routinely peruses the *Harvard Business Review*, attends management seminars, and is regularly ringing up new customer accounts, you may wish to borrow *his* management techniques. At the least, you should tie him down as a long-term partner.

Should you take on a partner? As a rule, the smaller the U.S. firm, the less advisable it is to attempt to go it alone in Latin America. Too many Lone Rangers have learned too late that having a piece of something always beats owning all of nothing. Others have learned that the modest beachhead they built yesterday with strong Latin American allies has become today's fortress of profitability. These allies are likely to be strong because, like you, they can be street fighters or diplomats in the market and, unlike you, they know the local streets.

In theory, you and your representative cast your lots together because each saw the other as the best player available to be on his team. Again, in theory, these interlocking dependencies made each of you a member of the same team, sharing the same goal of winning. In practice, however, too many supplier-representative relationships fail to score because they are playing a two-team game against one-team competitors. Rather than keeping their eyes on the playing field, they are distracted by discord over pricing, credit terms, market development costs, cooperative advertising, and product returns. These matters can become real [illegible]s when the arm's-length relationship that exists between suppli[illegible]presentative makes the issues appear to be zero-sum outcomes. [illegible]ever one side gains, the other side loses.

Having an equity foot in each other's camp minimizes unproductive disagreements because the game strategy shifts from minimizing individual loss to maximizing mutual gain. Through means like gross-profit-sharing accords or cross-ownership of shares, each side has a stake in advancing the other's financial performance. Latin firms can find it appealing to diversify by having an interest in a U.S. company. Such arrangements can provide forward-motion traction to a supplier-representative relationship formerly stalled by friction.

Getting Paid: The Three *In*'s of International Payments

Can utopia for Latin American traders be described in a few words? For U.S. exporters who used to face payment risks on their shipments to Latin America, an ideal state was having their settlement "*In*sured, *In* Gold, *In* Zurich." While those payment terms were seldom realistic in times past, modern markets and tax treaties now make them the stuff of fantasy. Nevertheless, today's exporters to Latin America can rely on receiving secure payments through updated versions of the protection once wishfully sought through the three *In*'s.

It is a dilemma that has plagued international trade since early exporters watched the sails of outbound merchant vessels slowly disappear with their goods over the Mediterranean horizon 3,000 years ago: Buyers want products in hand before releasing payment; sellers want payments in hand before releasing products. Reconciling those conflicting positions involves various ways of interposing third parties between buyers and sellers.

During the quarter century following World War II, Latin America was a relaxed hunting ground for U.S. exporters. It was a period when there were few competitive local producers and only a modest presence of European and Asian rivals. Sales were in dollars, payments were upfront or by letters of credit, and the ability to sell was determined by nominally competitive levels of price, quality, and delivery. For the last quarter century, these happy seller's market conditions have been eroding. In today's rapidly modernizing Latin American markets, more demanding buyers have added a critical fourth factor to the traditional price-quality-delivery buying formula: the seller's willingness and ability to grant credit and to either invoice in pesos (or other local currency) or share in the risk of fluctuating exchange rates.

If, to remain competitive, U.S. exporters extend increasingly longer terms of direct credit, their cash flow will become increasingly tight. By extending direct credit, exporters assume the usually misguided role of acting as bankers for their customers, exposing themselves to nonpayment risk. For many smaller exporters, a default by a single customer could stretch their liquidity to the breaking point. As it is easier to avoid bad debts than to collect them, it will pay exporters to verify customers' creditworthiness through easily available sources:

- World Traders Data Reports (WTDRs) are maintained by the commercial offices of U.S. embassies in Latin America. Though not available on all companies, this $100 service can provide you with information about your customer's payment reputation and reliability.
- International departments of regional and national U.S. banks can find out about your customer's credit standing through their own subsidiaries or correspondent relationships in Latin America.
- Trade Data Reports provides financial evaluations of Latin American firms.
- Dun & Bradstreet maintains foreign credit reports.

At the other end of the payment spectrum, Latin buyers may pay CIA (cash in advance) or by letter of credit. (If confirmed and irrevocable, a letter of credit gives the seller comfort, knowing she will be paid if she provides the required documentation.) In either case, buyers face the costs of having working capital tied up and/or of incurring interest charges and processing fees. These are costs to buyers that, to remain competitive, U.S. exporters may have to offset through rebates or price concessions.

Just as credit terms exact a cost in cash flow and fees that must be absorbed by the U.S. exporter or the Latin importer, so too do the costs arising from changes in the peso-dollar exchange rate. As in the case of credit cost, the policy chosen to cover exchange rate risk can weaken or strengthen a U.S. exporter's competitive position. If the exporter invoices in dollars, the Latin buyer will suffer a loss if the local currency depreciates. Latin buyers are naturally hesitant to pay invoices denominated in dollars when they are reselling in pesos. Directly or indirectly, they will look to the U.S. exporter to help absorb the exchange risk either by paying for the cost of hedging or by conceding on price or credit terms. Alternatively, if the U.S. exporter accepts payment in pesos, he will suffer a revenue shortfall if that currency declines in dollar value between the invoice and collection dates.

One solution to the growing need for sellers to Latin America to be competitive on both credit terms and exchange risk is to use export factoring. This tool, which has been common in Europe for some time and is now beginning to be used in Latin America, enables U.S. exporters to sell in pesos on open account terms without having to assume credit and exchange risks. Not only does it enable buyers to save on letter of credit and documentary collection fees, it also frees up their working capital, making more credit available to them for additional purchases. The U.S. exporter sells some or all of its accounts receivable at a discount in exchange for immediate cash in hand. Factoring fees are not trivial: They range from 2 to 7 percent a month, and they are paid as long as the receivable is outstanding.[7] A variation on the basic factoring model is advance factoring, and is similar to the "red clause" used in letter of credit financing. It allows the exporter to receive in advance up to 90 percent of the order amount, thus providing the means to pay for the materials and the labor needed to prepare the export order.

Getting It There: The Limitations of Good Intentions as Road Paving

Just as you should not test the depth of a river with both feet, neither should you trust shipping your goods without being certain that you will be on a firm footing. The primary factors affecting secure and timely delivery of your product to Latin America are cargo insurance and logistics. Subsequently, communications, customs, and intellectual property rights come into play as factors that also affect your firm's ability to manage the physical movement of its product in the local market. The sections below deal with important practical considerations relevant to shipping your goods to Latin American markets.

Cargo Insurance

As banks will not lend money against uninsured goods in transit, protecting your goods is basic to your risk management and trade financing strategies. Cargo coverage protects your maritime or air shipment (airfreight is covered under an all-risk attachment to the marine policy form) from its departure point to its final destination. Ocean cargo coverage ends at the port of arrival. If your shipment then has to be transported over land to reach its final destination, it will require inland marine insurance.

Know Your Coverage. It is imperative that the terms of your sales contract match the terms of your insurance coverage. A CIF ([invoice] cost, insurance, and freight) contract, for example, requires the seller to arrange and pay for the transport of goods from its U.S. warehouse to the buyer's Latin American warehouse. The seller is also responsible for arranging and paying the premium for warehouse-to-warehouse insurance. In contrast, a FOB (free on board) sales contract only obligates the seller to arrange and pay for the transportation and insurance required to move the goods to the port and be loaded onto the ship. As the goods pass over the vessel's railing, the responsibility for their protection passes to the buyer. Clearly, any misunderstanding of the sales and policy assignment terms between buyer and seller could lead to the shipment being either over insured (by virtue of both the buyer and the seller each paying an insurance premium) or being completely unprotected. Take time to learn the standard international commercial terms (INCOTERMS). Not having to explain how your uninsured merchandise became an FOT (fell off truck) shipment will repay your effort.

Know Your Risk. Parts of Latin America are considered especially susceptible to loss by risk underwriters. In Mexico, for example,

> The perils are obviously theft, hijack[ing] and especially traffic accidents which result in breakage, missing merchandise . . . in many cases the thieves do not even know what they are stealing. If they cannot sell the goods, they sometimes call the producer or insurer directly, claiming to have found the merchandise roadside . . . most thefts are inside jobs. We therefore recommend that clients investigate all employees prior to hire, and also that they reduce the number of people who know what merchandise will be sent and where. Give instructions at the last minute, so the chance of outsiders finding out details is less. Also send an empty truck occasionally as a decoy.[8]

The proliferation of cargo theft in places like Brazil, Colombia, and Mexico is forcing carriers to use an array of measures to protect shipments. To stem losses, truckers are using Global Positioning System (GPS) tracking, sending armed escorts, reducing load sizes, intermingling high-value goods with low-value shipments, using double packaging (an unmarked outer package for protective purposes enroute and an inner display package for customer destination), and stacking at-rest containers end to end. But despite taking such precautions, losses are mounting, and when shippers are able to find a willing insurance carrier, the premium cost is high.

Physical security is only one component of protection against cargo theft. The most costly injuries may not be inflicted from sharklike attacks mounted by predators on the outside, but by your own employees in the United States or by those of your representative in Latin America. Tight administrative security is essential to guard against inventory nibbling by insiders. Putting a logistics auditing system in place is the first step in letting employees know that the company knows where its inventory is going. But establishing a paper trail is only a first step; the solution lies in rooting out dishonest employees. Honest employees will be sympathetic to antitheft actions if they are made to understand that such actions are necessary to maintain the firm's and the employee's financial well-being and friendly working environment. Inviting in a security expert to conduct the investigation can be a good measure. This objective outside presence can help minimize what could otherwise be an emotionally upsetting experience of questioning long-standing and often high-level employees with whom you have developed personal as well as professional relationships. Finally, if it becomes necessary to fire an employee for theft, do not underestimate the need to support your action with an airtight case. Most Latin American labor codes give strong benefit of the doubt to employees let go for indiscretions, imposing severance penalties if cause cannot be irrefutably established.

Protecting against cargo theft that takes place only in Latin America is not the only theft precaution that U.S. shippers to Latin America should take. Conservative FBI estimates place cargo theft at \$8 to 12 billion per year in the United States. South Florida, the largest jumping-off point for southbound U.S. merchandise, is one of the most notorious locations for stolen Latin American shipments. As a direct result, policy premiums for cargo moving through south Florida have approximately doubled in five years, presently averaging about 0.4 percent of shipment value. Policy deductibles of \$20,000 are common for easily salable goods such as cellular telephones, computer parts, and electronics.[9]

Experienced exporters have learned it is better to be safe than sorry. Hearing the news that your shipping container was last seen disappearing down a jungle trail leading to an armed guerilla camp is always an unpleasant lesson in risk management. If the value of its contents, however, has been covered by an all-risk policy, you also will have learned that the premium was a small price to pay for being able to sleep soundly that night.

Supply Chain Management

Logistics costs are not insignificant. They represent between 10 and 30 percent of the total landed cost of an international order.[10,11] Moreover, the act of physically filling Latin American customer orders can produce outsized operating headaches, creating dissatisfied customers and absorbing countless hours of management time. It can be an educational exercise by which unhappy shippers learn hard lessons from easy math. Consider this example: If your company successfully executes fulfillment activities at the 90-percent level, the good news is that its chances of satisfactorily performing any single one of ten scheduled events is nine in ten. The bad news is that the same law of probability decrees that the odds of getting all ten independent events right is only slightly better than one in three. There is worse news: If you are relying on a Latin company to provide logistics services, and that company's single-event execution success rate is only 80 percent, the chances of it coordinating all ten events correctly falls to less than one in ten. Under those conditions, you rarely get what you expect, only what you inspect: Make it a point to conduct field checks to ensure your product is reaching the point of sale. It will not sell if it is not on the shelf.

Be smart about customer service levels. In times past, low customer service levels were not a critical business concern in Latin America's production-oriented economies. The goal was to minimize logistics costs. System flaws were routine. Globalization raised the bar on the willingness of Latin Americans to tolerate second-rate customer fulfillment. As an increasingly fundamental determinant of competitiveness and profitability in Latin America, the logistics function is swiftly shifting from a goal of minimizing costs to one of maximizing value. U.S. firms that can adapt and help their Latin American partners adapt to a changing logistics world will win strong competitive positions in the region's markets. Many old-line competitors will miss the boat simply because tradition restricts them to seeing only the easily measurable cost of logistics, blinding them to the larger value-added potential to profit through greater customer satisfaction. Such firms are Latin America's dinosaurs, menaced by extinction and unaware that globalization and modern logistics have shifted value toward the consumer, making downstream marketing more profitable than product manufacturing.[12]

But maintaining high customer service levels is not a cost-free option. Because speedy delivery and flexible order response can be pricey promises to fulfill, it can be a costly mistake to provide them to your Latin customers who do not need or value them. For that reason, you should clearly establish what constitutes an acceptable service level to your customer. If your policy is to deliver in five days to a customer who is willing to receive merchandise in thirty days, the higher cost you incur can prevent you from being more competitive on price or other features your customer values more highly. If speedy deliveries are not needed to compete, then making them is a wasteful luxury.

If five-day or sooner delivery is required to be time competitive, however, airfreight is the likely alternative for most Latin American destinations. The direct transportation costs of Latin American airfreight may average some twenty times higher than ocean freight. In lightly industrialized, mainly agricultural areas, it may be even higher because the lack of back-haul freight means southbound shippers are charged rates that pay for empty return flights to the United States.[13] Still, airfreight may be the only option for some Latin American destinations accessible from ports that may not be visited by your carrier's vessel for weeks or months. Moreover, airfreight often involves savings that result in a lower door-to-door expense than you might imagine, especially for high-density (weight-to-volume) and high-value (price-to-weight) merchandise. In addition to making the product immediately available for use or resale, these benefits can help offset the higher transportation costs of air shipment: less inventory dwell time; reduced insurance premiums for theft, pilferage, and damage; lower protective packaging costs; lower shipping minimums; and less internal transportation costs at destination. In addition, if you have airfreight destined for multiple consignees in a single country, it may be more economical to consolidate those small-package deliveries. By sending them as a bulk-palletized shipment to a central in-country distribution point, you may save by paying for airfreight charged on a per-pound, instead of a per-package, basis.

Keep your cash-to-cash cycle short. In addition to matching service levels to customers' expectations, a central goal of your logistics strategy should be to shorten your cash-to-cash cycle. By reducing dwell time costs (i.e., the cost of keeping a productive asset, say inventory or delivery vehicles, idle), you gain the ability to remove cash from operations without lowering either productivity or customer service levels. At a 15 percent annual cost of working capital, for example, a shipper will save about $82 for every day saved in transit time for a container carrying goods worth $200,000. In Latin America's high capital-cost environment, free cash spin gives you one more competitive lever to pull. A cost-saving tool used by Toyota Motor Sales U.S.A. to reduce inventory dwell time was to schedule its Mexican shipments weekly or daily, rather than monthly. The increased delivery frequencies lowered inventory levels by 8 percent.[14]

Sales forecasting is another tool that has a powerful potential to minimize dwell time. It is also a tool that historically has not been well developed in Latin America. However, it is coming into its own today as modern information and communications technology bring the region closer to being able to implement inventory postponement strategies. The goal of postponement is to avoid ordering inventory until the sale is made, thus minimizing the possibility of building up a supply of dead stock when large changes in local buying patterns occur. Given the order-to-delivery reality of the region's slow-paced transportation and customs processing environment, this is not always easy. For example, the delay involved in delivering an order to a Latin customer's facility could exceed by six times the time required to make the U.S. pickup and fly the shipment to the customer's airport. Still, a response-based production and inventory-ordering posture is realistically attainable if based on forecast sales, rather than on booked orders. By planning collaboratively, U.S. shippers and Latin distributors can reduce inventory overstocking and redundancy, raising the certainty that whatever will be produced or ordered will be sold. As if living a procrastinator's dream, U.S. sellers and Latin buyers can share the rewards of increased cash flow by not doing today whatever can be postponed until tomorrow.

Know the limits of internal transportation. The bad news: The obituary for the death of distance has not yet been written for Latin America. The good news: The transportation problems that abound in Latin America provide ample chances for you to raise your firm's profit flag over the region by finding creative ways to solve them. The challenge is not trivial: Internal air service is expensive and unpredictable. Nonstandardized track gauges and/or lackluster management make rail a dismal prospect almost everywhere except in limited areas of Argentina, Brazil, and Mexico. Few of the region's major markets are directly accessible by boat or are served by ports that have modern and efficient container-handling capabilities.

By default, the backbone of Latin America's transportation system is truck-borne freight and bus-borne passenger traffic. It is an ailing backbone, however, sorely in need of attention to relieve the aches and pains it has accumulated over the years. Despite years of public investment in building and maintaining highway infrastructure, many markets are still not served reliably by truck delivery. While land routes between major population centers almost everywhere in Latin America vary between adequate and excellent, access to smaller rural markets is often restricted by mountain roads that are temporarily blocked by rock slides or that remain choked with snow for much of the year. Secondary highways become regularly impassable when they are flooded for weeks at a time or when bridges wash out. Even in major cities that enjoy good highway access, local delivery is impeded by frenzied traffic conditions resulting from a rapidly exploding population squeezed into the chaotic confines of narrow streets left over from the colonial era.

Newcomers may be tempted to believe that the same colonial-era legacy explains the region's elderly truck fleet. The difference in the average age of trucks in the United States and in Latin America is explained by the relative cost of labor and capital in the two locations. Putting a new truck on the road is a capital-intensive decision, and is taken more often in the United States where capital is comparatively cheap. Continuing to maintain and repair an old truck is a labor-intensive option that is routinely taken in Latin America where labor is less expensive than capital. The ingenuity displayed by Latin mechanics to keep their aging relics rolling is unmatched by their counterparts in the United States. Many Latin American fleet managers truly deserve the title of curator.

Adding to the physical challenges of shipping goods are crime rates that, as mentioned earlier, prompt the use of armed highway escorts and, for at least a decade, have made security the number-one criterion used by customers to select public warehouses.[15,16] Recently, there have been signs that alert shippers can take steps to improve cargo security. Logistics experts advise that tracking shipments through the Internet and performing preshipment inspections in the United States can reduce theft losses at the same time that they help to strengthen trust bonds between U.S. shippers and Latin consignees.[17]

Consider a 3PL future. If your firm's product is shipped from the United States, to be distributed directly to retailers or to multiple wholesalers or storage terminals, it risks incurring costs and customer complaints from inaccurate documentation, missed shipments, and idle trucks. One solution to reducing international and in-country transportation risks is to use reliable third-party logistics providers. Acting as consolidators, good 3PLs are specialists in solving supply chain headaches that can arise when delivering your product locally. By teaming up with a logistics partner who maintains a local management presence and physical infrastructure, you and your distributor can offer customers a competitive advantage that old-line firms will be hard-pressed to match. Although the demand for quality one-stop 3PL firms has outstripped their supply and made them a scarce commodity, finding and working with one can be key to gaining share in Latin American consumer markets.[18]

Climbing on board the 3PL trend enables you and your distributor to focus on your core competency by outsourcing to specialists those logistics requirements that are their core competency. The idea is catching on: 3PLs are projected to grow 20 percent per year in Latin America. As 3PL market penetration was only 7 percent in 1999,[19] it is clear that while a new wave of logistics outsourcing has entered the region, much of the old wave of mediocre in-house logistics performance still remains. Latin America is riding between those two waves. As with all historic turning points, those firms that are slow to ride the incoming wave of modern practices run the risk of being swept out of the market by the outgoing wave of obsolete ways.

Communication

Prior to the advent of cellular telephones, decades of neglect had produced decrepit telecommunications systems in Latin America. The existence of hopelessly obsolete and overloaded landline-based telephone systems has spurred leapfrog growth into wireless telephone technology. Cell phone use has become so ubiquitous that parallel markets have sprung up in several countries for *fraudulares*, nonfunctional plastic devices made to appear like the real thing, that citizens of modest means buy for $2 to $6 in order to enjoy the prestige of appearing to be wireless.

Competition, spawned by deregulation and privatization, is beginning to drive local telephone rates down and service quality up in Latin America. International rates, however, are still high enough to represent a material cost of doing business with the region. For example, a recent call to a prospective buyer in Mexico City from an exporter in Dallas cost thirty-nine cents per minute. If the same minute had been spent talking to a prospect in Tokyo, it would have cost sixteen cents, or ten cents to a potential buyer in Quebec.

Dealing with Customs

The cultural customs discussed in Chapter 4 can be strange and frustrating. But they pale in comparison to another type of customs: That web of arcane regulations and often venal officials that make up Latin American government agencies which control the entry of your product into its target markets.

Should the machine be lubricated? "I have an expensive doctor's appointment and can only work two hours today. I don't know if I'll be able to get to it." Variations on this theme are not uncommon from Latin American customs officials. They are thinly veiled invitations for you to speed up the official processing mechanism by providing lubrication to its otherwise immovable parts. It is said that in a world populated by Latin American customs authorities, even a camel can be passed through the eye of a needle—if it is lightly greased.

Although they are the target of ongoing reform efforts in countries like Mexico, Brazil, and Costa Rica, grease payments are still an unavoidable regular cost of doing business in much of Latin America. Whatever your ethical attitude toward a shakedown request by a customs official, you may find some comfort in knowing that routine facilitating payments are ordinarily permitted by the U.S. Foreign Corrupt Practices Act of 1977. The more relevant concern is that the increased operating pressures spawned by Latin America's more competitive business environment make it difficult to avoid complying with payoff demands. The cost of avoiding payoffs by outwaiting the mañana pace of customs processing is the failure to remain competitive because of not having product available for instant delivery to a new wave of time-sensitive customers.

The good news is that Latin American customs organizations are beginning to adopt some of the rapidly evolving improvements in logistics technology. One major result of this welcome trend is that electronic processing of customs paperwork is becoming common practice in the region. The bad news is that the speed of moving goods through the system, although improved, is still a slow process. This is because the fast-paced pull of modern processing is tethered to a short leash of tradition. The system's choke point is the dogged determination of many of Latin America's customs agencies to stay linked to the familiar and lucrative practices of the past by parallel-processing the mountainous accumulations of documents by hand. When a customs official pauses before lowering his right hand to impress your document with the mandatory hand stamp, the delay provides him with an occasion to extend his left hand, palm open, in your direction.

Ambiguous and complex product standards, classification codes, and duty schedules give customs a wide range of discretion in interpreting under what conditions your product will be admitted for import to your target market. Local product standards may impede or even lock out your product's admittance. Examples: Venezuela has imposed some 300 product standards that are applied more rigorously to imported goods than to goods produced domestically. Colombia is enforcing country-of-origin certification requirements that rely on a largely unfeasible Colombian certified-testing process. Brazil has revived formerly disregarded measures to ensure that imports meet domestic standards of safety and quality. Argentina has changed the criteria for approval of electrical products, requiring imports to pass the certification process of a national standards body.

Latin America's varied structure of tariffs can also be frustrating. For example, the MERCOSUR customs union (Argentina, Brazil, Paraguay, and Uruguay) maintains common external duties on some 85 percent of all goods. These common rates range from 0 to 23 percent, averaging about 14 percent. Each member country imposes its own tariffs on the remaining 15 percent of goods.[20]

To mitigate the effects of exasperatingly slow clearance procedures, you may wish to hold contingency inventories ex-customs and close to the customer. While holding dead inventory always costs money, it could still be a cost-effective practice, especially if your firm is faced with profit-eroding contractual consequences of time penalties imposed for late delivery or installation. Even if time penalties are not a factor, a warehouse presence sends a visible and reassuring signal to customers that your firm is committed to the market for the long term. Another option to reduce the pain of customs bottlenecks is to break down shipments by priority. If and when it is possible, send time-critical components early, to be followed later by less-vital shipments.[21]

The ATA Carnet

ATA Carnets act for some goods like passports act for people. ATA is an acronym formed from the French and English words *Admission Temporaraire*/Temporary Admission. While most imports enter a country permanently, some merchandise enters only temporarily. You can avoid having to pay duty if you are carrying demonstrator samples, promotional materials, trade-show gear (like a sound system or projection equipment), tools and measurement devices, or any item that will leave the country when you do. Without a Carnet, customs may delay your entry or charge you unnecessary duty on items that are duty-exempt or are being admitted into the country only on a temporary basis. The U.S. Council for International Business (see http://www.uscib.org/) has been designated by the U.S. Customs Service as the issuing and guaranteeing organization of ATA Carnets.[22]

Is Your Product Ready for Prime Time? Intellectual Property Rights

Piracy and counterfeiting of branded consumer goods "costs U.S. companies as much as $250 billion a year" and are rife in Latin America.[23] Popular targets are computer software programs, music, videos, clothing, and luxury items such as watches and liquors. "Brand borrowing" has become so much of a concern to legitimate producers that Levi Strauss de Mexico bought ads in major Mexican dailies to thank the attorney general's office for seizing several hundred thousand of its labels that had been counterfeited.[24] A casual stroll through street markets in Buenos Aires, Rio de Janeiro, Lima, Caracas, Bogotá, Guatemala City, or Guadalajara will expose you to hawkers harassing you to buy merchandise brazenly branded as Microsoft Windows 2000 for $5, Chivas Regal scotch for $8, Gucci purses for $24, Viagra for $1, Hermes scarves for $3, Tommy Hilfiger shirts for $6, or Rolex watches for $30.

The infringement or loss of your company's key copyrights, trademarks, or patents could cripple its new Latin American venture. The commercial codes of many countries of the region either have inadequate laws to protect intellectual property or fail to enforce what statutes are on the books. The loss of intellectual property is inevitably costly in terms of time, money, market reputation, and lost momentum. Numerous, and especially smaller U.S. firms have learned the hard way that not taking steps at the earliest moment to protect their intellectual property can push the fast-rewind button on the costly, time-consuming preparations they have taken to create a profitable business. Unlike in the United States, where first usage can establish the right to use a trademark, in most of Latin America protection belongs to the first company to register a trademark. Happily, in the Andean community (Bolivia, Colombia, Ecuador, Peru, and Venezuela), cancellation of a registered trademark may be requested if it has not been used for three years.[25]

SUMMING UP

Only within the last two decades has Latin America begun to throw off its historical burden of self-contained economics, self-serving politicians, and self-important bureaucrats. This is a Revolution with a capital R because the forces it is unleashing are fundamentally altering economic, political, and social institutions throughout the Americas. As a half-billion Latin consumers enter the global economic mainstream, the region's markets are undergoing deep changes, and winners and losers are being created daily. To be on the winning side and in a position to exploit its opportunities, Latin American firms are anxious to find U.S. allies as trade or joint venture partners. As so many of those opportunities are responsive to competencies that are superbly present in smaller businesses, the ongoing economic shifts in Latin America pose uncommon profit potential for those smaller U.S. firms committed to developing their possibilities.

This book has been written to prepare you for those possibilities by explaining the fundamentals of doing business in the new Latin America. It is my hope that it will be your faithful guide as you capitalize on what may prove to be the greatest profit opportunity for smaller U.S. businesses at the beginning of the new millennium.

Notes

1. "Cinco ejes para atenuar el costo en la baja de tarifas." (2004), *El Comercio* (Quito), February 2, p. B5.
2. "World Business Roundup: The Americas." (1998), *Export Today*, May, pp. 8–9.
3. Sherrie Zhan (1999), "Trade Shows Mean Big Business," *World Trade*, September, p. 86.
4. Oren Harari (2002), "Behind Open Doors," *Modern Maturity*, vol. 45 (July–August), pp. 40–43.
5. U.S. Department of Commerce (2003), *The Commercial Service.* Retrieved October 21, 2003, from http://www.ita.doc.gov/uscs.
6. Thomas H. Becker (1991), "Taboos and How-To's about Earning an Honest Peso," *Management Review*, vol. 80, no. 6, pp. 17–21.
7. Mark E. Battersby (2001), "Tame the Ebb and Flow," *Small Business Computing*, February 2001, p. 25.
8. Robert C. Meder (2000), "Insuring Goods Internationally," *World Trade*, vol. 13, issue 4 (April), pp. 44–46. Quotes Peter Weber of Protección Dimámica, a Mexican insurance broker.

9. Peter Zalewski (2002), "Cargo Theft," *The Herald* (Fort Lauderdale), June 16, pp. 12–14.

10. Richard T. Hise (1995), "The Implications of Time-Based Competition on International Logistics Strategies," *Business Horizons*, vol. 38, no. 5, pp. 39–45.

11. "A Moving Story." (2002), *The Economist*, December 7, pp. 65–66.

12. Richard Wise and Peter Baumgartner (1999), "The New Profit Imperative in Manufacturing," *Harvard Business Review*, September–October, pp. 133–151.

13. Shura Bary (2001), "Delivering the Goods," *World Trade*, September, pp. 42–44.

14. Anthony Coia (2002), "Keeping Mexico on the Road," *World Trade*, vol. 15, issue 8 (August), pp. 12–22.

15. Dan Sarel and Walter Zinn (1992), "Customer and Non-Customer Perceptions of Third-Party Services: Are They Similar?" *The International Journal of Logistics Management*, vol. 3, no. 1, pp. 12–22.

16. Walter Zinn (1996), "The New Logistics in Latin America: An Overview of Current Status and Opportunities," *The International Journal of Logistics Management*, vol. 7, no. 1, pp. 61–71.

17. Anthony Coia (2000), "South America Struggles to Open Its Markets: Political, Legal, and Infrastructural Issues Affect Shipping," *World Trade*, vol. 13, issue 7 (July), pp. 66–67.

18. Jaime Quintana (2000), "Be There or Beware: Logistics in Latin America Calls for Local Knowledge and Presence," *World Trade*, vol. 13, issue 2 (February), pp. 54–58.

19. Donald J. Bowersox (1999), "Trends in Global Logistics," "Supply Chains in South America: Challenges, Opportunities, and Experiences," Supply Chains in South America Conference, Miami.

20. Coia (2000), *Op. cit.*

21. Gail Dutton (2002), "What Are You Going to Do," *World Trade*, January, pp. 34–36.

22. "ATA Carnet." (2004), International Trade Data System. Retrieved July 2, 2004, from http://www.itds.treas.gov/CARNET.html.

23. Ronald Fink (2004), "Battling the Property Pirates," *CFO*, January, pp. 51–53.

24. Mary Sutter (1998), "Mexico Piracy a Concern for Manufacturers," *The Journal of Commerce*, May 26.

25. http://www.mondaq.com/article.asp?articleid=18985&email_access=on (2002), "Ecuador: Right to Use of a Trademark and Registration." *Bustamante & Bustamante*, retrieved July 2, 2004.

Appendix: Information Resources

When experienced executives set their sights on a Latin American business target, their first aim is to avoid the information trap. Knowing that too little information can be just as damaging as too much information, they aim to gain the information they need in as expedient a manner as possible. Helping to direct your aim to the most expedient targets is the purpose of this appendix.

The sections below divide the vast body of information on Latin American business topics into two broad themes: business readiness and country and cultural content. Business readiness concentrates on matters that are subject to company control and that are germane to the region as a whole. These matters include managing the process of exporting, finding markets and buyers, lining up financing and logistics, and researching customers, competitors, and suppliers. Country and cultural content focuses on economic, social, and political information that is specific to a particular Latin American country, market, or sector.

While there is inevitable overlap between those two themes, they classify subject matter in a way normally consistent with its practical need. It is hoped that by listing only a few quality sources, the reader will avoid becoming buried under a staggering mass of only marginally useful information.

When trying to piece together Latin American business deals that are happening in real time, busy executives need up-to-date information. As a rule, international business puzzles are made up of many pieces, some of which have complex shapes. These puzzles should not be made more complicated by including pieces that are hard to find or configured with obsolete information. For these reasons, information sources included here are accessible online and are believed to be frequently updated.

BUSINESS READINESS

First Steps

- www.Export.gov is the main U.S. government source of export assistance and market information. Whether you are looking for free export counseling, help with the process of exporting, trade leads, or a calendar of trade events, this should be one of your first steps to selling any product or service in Latin America.
- www.BuyUSA.gov supplements www.Export.gov by combining the power of the Internet with the network of the U.S. Department of Commerce's Commercial Service trade specialists in your state and across the world.
- www.usda.gov/MarketingAndTrade/exporting, sponsored by the U.S. Department of Agriculture, is the U.S. government Web site designed specifically for exporters of agricultural products and services. In addition to general export assistance, it is a top information source for export credit guarantee programs, export regulations, country and market reports, veterinary services exports, and statistics on bulk, intermediate, and consumer-oriented trade.
- www.fas.usda.gov/info/agexporter/agexport.html, also sponsored by the U.S. Department of Agriculture, takes you to the *AgExporter*, a monthly magazine for businesses selling farm products overseas. It offers tips on exporting, descriptions of markets with the greatest sales potential, and information on export assistance.
- www.owit.org is the site for Organization of Women in International Trade. It promotes women doing business internationally by providing networking and educational opportunities.

Finding information on U.S. firms is usually easier than researching foreign companies. But that difficulty is relative and does not make it impossible to be aware of business-critical knowledge when you deal in Latin America. The key is to understand that as information on Latin American companies is so dispersed, you may have to scout multiple sites to assemble what you need. These resources will help you navigate that landscape of scattered information:

- http://library.uncg.edu/news/nq-all.asp?dbreg=lac provides access to hundreds of Latin American newspapers, many of which can be searched for articles reporting on your target company.
- www.google.com and www.excite.com are examples of search engines you may use to find the Web site of your target company that contains press releases, product features, financial and market data, or competitive performance.
- www.wayp.com/eng/amerika3.shtml provides data for Latin American companies listed in their country's Yellow Pages telephone directory.
- http://babelfish.altavista.com is the site to use if you wish to translate into English any of the newspapers, company Web sites, or Yellow Pages material that is printed in Spanish or Portuguese.
- www.kompass.com is the Web site of Kompass, which claims to "provide product, contact and other information for 1.8 million companies worldwide, [listing] . . . more than 53,000 products & services." Some information is fee based.
- www.internationalcreditreports.com/?source=overture&OVRAW=export&OVKEY=export&OVMTC=standard and http://www.owens.com are examples of companies offering fee-based services for reporting on the creditworthiness of your customer or competitor.
- www.latpro.com is the largest job site concentrating on Latin America. It can be searched by company name to give you an indication of whether your target company is expanding and, if so, in what areas.

COUNTRY AND CULTURAL CONTENT

- www.export.gov/marketresearch.html gives registered users access to the U.S. State Department's Country Commercial Guides, Industry Sector Analyses, Marketing Insights, and Best Market reports. Updated frequently by U.S. embassies, "these reports, often more than 100 pages in length, aim to present 'a comprehensive look at countries' commercial environments,' [and cover] economic and political trends, the investment climate, marketing, trade, project financing, and business travel. Appendices include U.S. contacts, local government contacts, trade shows, law firms, consultancies, banks, and research firms in each country."

- http://tse.export.gov is the site for the U.S. Commerce Department's TradeStats Express, which provides access to the latest data for trade volume in your product between the United States and your target market.
- www.state.gov/p/wha/ci/ introduces you to *Background Notes*, publications of the U.S. Department of State that contain "facts on the [Latin American] country's land, people, history, government, political conditions, economy, and its relations with other countries and the United States."
- www.odci.gov/cia/publications/factbook/index is where you will find *The CIA World Factbook*, published by the U.S. Central Intelligence Agency. That publication is arguably the single most-used source of country-specific information in the world.
- www.loc.gov/rr/international/portals.html is the Web site of the U.S. Library of Congress. "Portals to the World," contains links to a broad range of information on Latin American countries. For some purposes, this source is more useful than the *CIA World Factbook* because its links, arranged by country, "were selected by Area Specialists and other Library staff."
- http://lanic.utexas.edu is the primary gateway for a wide array of Internet information on Latin America, and contains editorially reviewed directories for over 12,000 unique URLs.
- www.sice.oas.org is the source of trade-related information from the Organization of American States. The site features sections on antidumping, competition policy, dispute settlement, electronic commerce, intellectual property rights, trade policy developments, and investments that are specific to Latin America.
- www.aaccla.org is the site for the Association of American Chambers of Commerce in Latin America. It represents "23 American Chambers of Commerce in 21 Latin American and Caribbean nations [with a] combined membership of . . . 20,000 companies, which together manage over 80% of all US investment in the region [and having] a reputation as one of the most useful sources of practical business information."
- www.latintrade.com reports the monthly electronic edition of *Latin Trade*, the region's largest business magazine.
- www.latinfinance.com provides electronic access to *LatinFinance*, "the only magazine covering cross-border finance, business and investment in Latin America and the Caribbean."

- www.natlaw.com is the entry to the National Law Center for Inter-American Free Trade, providing "Access [to] over 10,000 laws, regulations and decrees promulgated by countries of Latin America and the Caribbean."
- www.latin-focus.com brings you to LatinFocus. Describing itself as "the leading source for Latin America economies," the site carries up-to-date news and commentary from Latin America, market analyses, economic indicators and monthly forecasts, political risk estimates, and daily exchange rates.
- www.transparency.org/surveys/index.html#cpi features Transparency International's Corruption Perception Index, a guide to what informed sources perceive to be the degree to which public corruption—a key risk factor for business—exists in countries around the world. In 2003, for example, Chile had the highest clean score in Latin America, Paraguay the lowest.
- www.fita.org/index.html is the site of the Federation of International Trade Associations. Declaring as its goal "to provide the most content-rich international trade site [and] a comprehensive global trade shop featuring goods and services needed by those involved in international trade," FITA offers users a free online subscription to its bimonthly newsletter, *Really Useful Sites.*

Index

About the Author

THOMAS H. BECKER is an economic development authority and management trainer specializing in Latin America. He has lived, operated businesses, or worked in sixteen Latin American countries and currently serves as advisor to government agencies, private businesses, universities, and NGOs. His academic background includes degrees in Latin American Studies and a Ph.D. in International Business. He has served on the Business faculty of five universities in the United States and Latin America, has written over one hundred articles and book chapters in English and Spanish, and is a former President and Managing Director of the Business Association of Latin American Studies.